OMAN: POLITICS AND DEVELOPMENT

Oman: Politics and Development

Ian Skeet

MACMILLAN

First published 1992 by
MACMILLAN ACADEMIC AND PROFESSIONAL LTD
Houndmills, Basingstoke, Hampshire RG21 2XS
and London
Companies and representatives
throughout the world

Copy-edited and typeset by Grahame & Grahame Editorial, Brighton

ISBN 0–333–56941–5

A catalogue record for this book is available
from the British Library

Printed in Hong Kong

For the people of Oman
and others who have lived and worked there

Contents

List of Tables

List of Plates

1. The Royal Hospital, Muscat: Accommodation Block, by kind permission of Wimpey Group Services Ltd.
2. The Ministry of Foreign Affairs, Muscat, by kind permission of The Fitzroy Robinson Partnership.
3. Rusayl Industrial Estate, Headquarters Building.
4. Sultan Qaboos University, Muscat, by kind permission of YRM Partnership Ltd.
5. Sultan Qaboos University, Muscat, by kind permission of YRM Partnership Ltd.
6. Sultan Qaboos University, Muscat, by kind permission of YRM Partnership Ltd.

Preface

There are few working Sultans in the world of 1990. In Oman, Sultan Qaboos bin Said, fourteenth of the Al Said dynasty,[1] has been ruler for 20 years. In 1970 he took over from his father a country that had oil exports but no other infrastructure. Today that country is liked, admired, worried over, envied and criticised by those who know it and, of course, by those who don't. Its per capita GNP is around $6000 which puts it statistically far ahead of most of the LDC world, its political voice is firmly independent, its influence, within the limitations of its size, significant. That seems a fine feat for only 20 years of work.

In this book I am going to see how a country starts from, as it were, nothing and becomes a respected member of the international community within 20 years; how a social infrastructure of health, education, communications and economic activity is created from a non-existent base. I also want to find out what tensions this process of development may have created and what problems it has posed for the future. And, surely, somewhere in this story there must be lessons that could be useful for other societies in other parts of the world.

Oman, for those who know it, is a happy place in which to live and work or to visit. Situated, coming from the West, at the far corner of the Arabian peninsula, it is surprisingly scenic, its inhabitants surprisingly different from the Arabs of imagination or the popular press. Oman is, indeed, full of surprises for the visitor. Perhaps its present state of development is surprising also for Omanis if ever they pause to consider the question. If not surprising, it should at least give those who knew it before 1970 a sense of wonder.

Perhaps it does, although I suspect that the pre-1970 era has been relegated to a near mythological past. Grandfathers may visualise it if they dredge their memories, even some fathers and mothers, but the vast majority of a population, at least half of which is under twenty, have experienced nothing except the giddy pace of development under Qaboos. They now take for granted what they see as a norm. History is only of passing interest to a few.

I am not in this book dealing with Oman's pre-1970 history, although the fact that it exists and, indeed, has a long pedigree of achievement is important as a factor in moulding the Omani character. The reason for this is that I have done it already in a previous book.[2] To that extent this is a companion volume to the first. It will, however, be a quite different type of book, primarily because the country itself has been transformed, and the story that is now being told bears no relation to what has gone before. The point is that Oman, for various reasons, preserved characteristics and attitudes that were part Victorian, part semi-medieval, up to 1970 and that in July 1970 it plunged into the twentieth century. This is the story of that plunge.

It has not been easy for me to decide how to present the story. It is in principle a slice of history, but the difficulty in producing useful and objective current history is well known. In the case of Oman there are few documents available; worse, where they are known to exist and are self-evidently in the public domain, they are still nearly impossible to obtain. It was only by chance that I was able to find a record of some of the earlier Royal Decrees which were obviously, at the time of their publication, public documents. To find, let alone gain access, to any less public a document – from a Ministry, for instance, or the Diwan – would be virtually impossible.

However, although most documents are difficult, if not impossible to come by,[3] and there has been only a very limited list of scholarly publications about Oman in books or journals, there is one source of information that is surprisingly complete. The statistics and five-year plans published both in Arabic and English by the Secretariat of the Development Council are a mine of interest and information. Anyone who wants to understand the growth and development of Oman cannot afford to be without these excellent publications. Naturally, however, they illustrate only part of the story.

The other source of information is, of course, people. I have had the good fortune to talk with very many people in Oman both officially and unofficially. They have shared much knowledge with me[4] and it is largely on the basis of what I have learned from them that I have been able to write this book. There has to be a word of warning, however. Oral evidence, as those who have used, or relied, on it will know, is both useful and dangerous. Useful for the obvious reasons, dangerous because people are often and quite unwittingly unreliable with their memories. I have checked and double checked what I can but it is not always possible to do as much as one would wish.

There is a further point. People in general, but in the Arab world more so than in the West, are extremely sensitive to criticism, perceived or real; states even more so. Oman is no exception. I have always made it clear in my interviews that what I hear is off the record and that no quotations or information will be attributable to individual persons. I believe that to be the only practical way in which one can and should operate. It does mean, however, that the historian in oneself is somewhat frustrated. Much as one would like to give specific references for this or that statement it is not possible to do so. It will be equally frustrating for the next generation of historians who will not know the basis of references, pieces of information or opinions. I can only say that any facts or discussions introduced into this book are drawn from what I have heard and are not, except where indicated, simply the expressions of my own imagination. That may be a satisfactory assurance for some, but I realise it will not be for others.

I have two other important points to make at the outset. The first is to acknowledge most warmly the help given me by countless people in Oman and by others who have known Oman but who now live outside the country. I am not listing them because I do not want it claimed by anyone that any individual person may be responsible for particular pieces of information. I do not want to embarrass anybody. In particular, however, I want to thank the Ministry of Information for supporting this project, not only for making it possible for me to visit Oman but also for arranging interviews and visits within Oman. Without this assistance I could not have written the book. I am also most grateful to those who have read the manuscript in whole or in part and have given me their comments and help.

Secondly, I want to make it clear that the book has not been commissioned. Nobody in Oman, nor anywhere else, is in any way responsible for what I have written, nor am I beholden to anybody in its writing. This includes the Ministry of Information whose generosity was given on this specific understanding. I say this in what may seem to be unnecessarily firm language because I do not want there to be any doubt about it. I have tried to be as objective as possible and this, simply because of the possible sensitivities involved, may create difficulties for some readers. I hope not. To have suppressed discussion of topics simply on the grounds that somebody might have preferred them not even to have been mentioned would not have served any useful purpose; nor, anyway, could I have done this.

Sensitivities. This is a simple word for a complex subject, a sensitive subject.

The real point at issue is the clash of cultures. Since it is a large subject – and not at all the subject of this book – I can deal with it only in very general terms. It is, however, important in the context of this book, specifically in the way in which one deals with the attitudes and behaviour of people whose outlook and traditions are quite different from those of Western cultures.

I believe that it would be unhelpful to make judgments about Oman as if it were a Western democracy – unhelpful, but also meaningless and misleading. The underlying puritanical principles of Anglo-Saxon morality are, I suspect, becoming increasingly inappropriate even in dealing with modern European society but to apply them to an Islamic autocracy can only lead to cynical and snide judgments. In order to gain a modicum of understanding and perspective about such a society it is essential to observe and make judgments from their point of view rather than ours. This I will try to do, at least by indicating where Western values are in my view unsuited as the measurement for Islamic, in this case Omani, decisions and actions. I am making this point somewhat more forcefully than might be expected because Oman has, to the ordinary observer, absorbed more of the external trappings of the West than many other states of the area. It does not follow, however, that its motivations or nature have become Westernised.

In this book I am, therefore, dealing with the development of Oman from 23 July 1970 when Sultan Qaboos took over from his father, Sultan Said bin Taimur. Part One looks at Oman as it is today. Part Two deals with the processes by which the country has reached its current state of development. Lastly Part Three looks forward and tries to determine how Oman is likely to fare as we break the bogus but beckoning barrier of the year 2000. In the Islamic world it will be, in more mundane manner, 1421.

IAN SKEET

Glossary and Abbreviations

Glossary

Beit	House
Badn	A local fishing boat
Diwan	Office of the Royal Court
Falaj	Water channel
Firqat	A company of locally recruited Dhofaris
Ghaf	A type of acacia tree
Jalalat	Majesty
Jebal	Mountain
Jiddat	Flat gravel plain
Mina	Harbour
Muhafiz	Governor
Suq	Market
Tahr	A type of mountain goat
Wali	Local mayor

Abbreviations

BATT	British Army Training Team
BBME	British Bank of the Middle East
BIOT	British Indian Ocean Territory
CAD	Civil Aid Development
CAT	Civil Aid Team
CSAF	Commander, Sultan's Armed Forces
DLF	Dhofar Liberation Front
ESF	Economic Support Funds
FMS	Foreign Military Sales
GCC	Gulf Cooperation Council

IDA	International Development Agency
IFC	International Finance Corporation
NSC	National Security Council
NDFLOAG	National Democratic Front for the Liberation of Oman and the Arab Gulf
OPEC	Organisation of Petroleum Exporting Countries
PAMAP	The Public Authority for Marketing Agricultural Produce
PDO	Petroleum Development Oman Limited
PDRY	People's Democratic Republic of Yemen
PFLO	Popular Front for the Liberation of Oman
PFLOAG	Popular Front for the Liberation of the Occupied Arab Gulf
PFLOAG	Popular Front for the Liberation of Oman and the Arab Gulf
PLA	People's Liberation Army
PLO	Palestine Liberation Organisation
RAFO	Royal Air Force of Oman
RAO	Royal Army of Oman
RDF	Rapid Deployment Force
RDJTF	Rapid Deployment Joint Task Force
RNO	Royal Navy of Oman
RO	Riyal Omani
SAF	Sultan's Armed Forces
SAS	Special Air Service
SGRF	State General Reserve Fund
SOAF	Sultan of Oman's Air Force
SON	Sultan of Oman's Navy
SSF	Sultan's Special Force
SYB	Statistical Year Book
UAE	United Arab Emirates

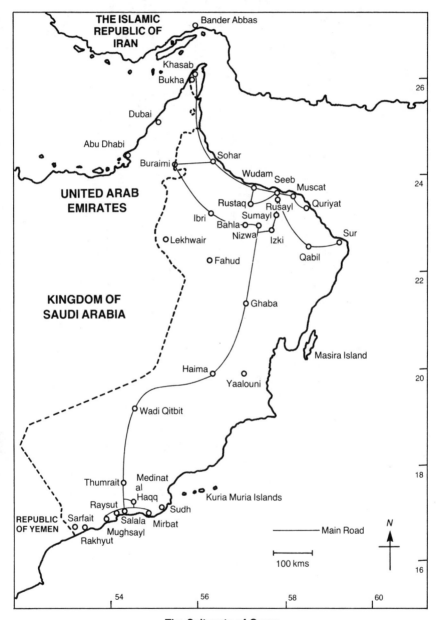

THE ISLAMIC
REPUBLIC OF
IRAN

Bander Abbas

Khasab
Bukha

Dubai

Abu Dhabi

Buraimi

Sohar

UNITED ARAB
EMIRATES

Wudam
Seeb
Muscat
Quriyat

Rustaq
Ibri
Bahla
Nizwa
Sumayl
Rusayl
Izki
Qabil
Sur

Lekhwair

KINGDOM OF
SAUDI ARABIA

Fahud

Ghaba

Masira Island

Haima

Yaalouni

Wadi Qitbit

Thumrait
Medinat
al
Haqq
Kuria Muria Islands

Raysut
Sudh
REPUBLIC
OF YEMEN
Sarfait
Salala
Mirbat
Mughsayl
Rakhyut

Main Road

N

100 kms

The Sultanate of Oman

Part One
Scenes, Oman 1990

Part One
Scenes, Oman 1990

INTRODUCTION

Oman is a country in which change has collided with permanence at unprecedented speed. Life has been transformed, rules have been uprooted, even nature has been wrenched into new shapes. Twenty years have brought Oman economic and social development and a positive place in the world but many of the old traditions and truths remain embedded in its new way of life.

Oman is still, as it always has been, an intensely visual country. It is not a country that can be comprehended simply in terms of oil production or balance of payments or social statistics, although these are what have caused the transformations. That is why this book opens with a section called *Scenes*. These are designed to give the reader a flavour of how the country feels in 1990. This is an integral part, in terms of actual achievement, of the processes of political and economic planning and decisions. To that extent it has, even though it is a wholly subjective set of impressions, a genuine historical component just as, more obviously, the rest of the book, with its analysis of how and why things happened, is an attempt to produce an objective historical record, increasingly instant as we get to 1990, of twenty years in the life of Oman.

THE CAPITAL AREA

Hot dry hills have, ever since they burst out from some ancient volcanic eruption, surrounded Muscat and crowded into Muttrah. In the 1920s a single track road was hacked along the coast between the two towns. Today double carriage highways swoop over and through, and curve elegantly round the sides of, those hills. They are edged by splashes of green grass and by the deep glow of bougainvillea. Above them the ridges are spiked by the modern gadgetry of telecommunications, blurred in the midday heat, sharp against a winter sunset. Ancient watchtowers, spruced up for the first time since the Omanis or Portuguese put them there, share the skyline with aerials and dishes that, if ever required, will provide a more effective defence for the peaceful citizens living beneath them than those photogenic forts could ever have achieved.

The capital area now spreads from Seeb for 50 kms to Muscat and another 10 kms beyond to the new Bustan hotel. Half the population of Oman live here. This is the area of government, embassies, hotels, business, banking, commerce and the smart housing that goes with such things. But there is no crowding. The overriding impression is of space, the atmosphere is relaxed. Large circumference roundabouts are multicoloured with flowers and lawns. Bright white villas are festooned with flowering shrubs on grey rocky hills. Government ministries may be monumental but their architecture is variegated and inspired by Arab design. Arab design, indeed, permeates the majority of all buildings small or large and spreads to walls, windows and even the covering of airconditioning units. This is by edict of the Municipality. What might have turned into a repressive or restrictive by-law has been interpreted sensibly and variably. The result is almost wholly pleasing. Where it is not, the exceptions create an almost physical jarring to the senses. Driving towards Muscat from the airport the Intercontinental hotel (though in all other respects a memorably excellent place) rises over Qurm beach like a monstrous cube; in Ruwi the Sheraton hotel appears to have been copied from some internationally bland tower block design; and in Muscat itself the Sultan's palace, conceived in lotus-motif by an Indian architect in the early 1970s, is wholly out of context. In general, however the eye is delighted by what it sees, and occasionally, as in the Ministry of Foreign Affairs,[1] excited.

If some hotels have architecturally spoiled what has so often been surprisingly successful and sympathetic to the gaunt landscape of Muscat, the Bustan hotel, built in a small bay down the coast, is surely one of the more exciting hotels of the world. It was in fact built and designed for the Gulf Cooperation Council (GCC) summit meeting held in Muscat in December 1985 and doubles as a hotel and government conference centre. It is built in the form of an eight sided tower with a soaring 36 metre high domed central atrium decorated in inlaid marble, a mixture of mosque and palace. There are eight monarchic suites on the top floor, one for each of the six GCC heads of state and two left over – for possible institutional expansion, one wonders. The Bustan is not the only hotel which can supply the facilities required by a demanding holiday clientele. The Intercontinental, ugly though it may be in architectural terms, faces, across its own garden of lawns, palm trees, petunia beds and bougainvillea, miles of flat beach lapped by the Gulf of Oman and guarded by a warning notice – 'beware of hot sand'. As it cools in the evening the beach animates into a modern version of Monet impressionism; swimmers, walkers, joggers, the odd heron or two, some waders and a fiery sun slowly sinking towards the sand at 90 degrees to the left. Also, scattered in teams along the sands, are groups practising that great equaliser of games, football, which now provides what is almost a universal language for much of the world. The sun disappears and for miles a pointillisme of lights takes over along the coast until dawn.

Muscat makes many strong impressions upon visitors. One of the more abiding is the uncanny cleanliness of the place. There is no litter anywhere, not a plastic bag, not a piece of orange peel. The roads are clear of rubble, pavements pure. This is repeated all over the country. Garbage containers and trash cans crop up in the most unlikely and remote areas, where municipality vies with municipality for environmental achievement. It is a positive shock to see a fragment of litter anywhere. When an Omani friend flung out an empty can from the car towards, but assuredly not into, a roadside container 100 kms from the nearest police post or municipal officer I felt I would be arraigned as an accessory after the fact.

Not only outside but also inside public buildings there is this almost obsessive attention to a general well-ordered spruceness of appearance. The overall impression is slightly military, as if the Sultan himself had pinned up an Order on the palace noticeboard for the quartermaster general to carry out. That, indeed, is not far from the reality. Cleanliness and tidiness are the stated wish of His Majesty. Municipalities, therefore, have rules; they employ gangs of contract labour – mostly from the sub-continent – to ensure that everything is always spick and span.

Not only the municipalities. Government offices, hospitals and schools receive the same attention. For those of us who grumble about, but have become inured to, the dirt and filth of streets and offices in New York, London or other self-proclaimed sophisticated cities Oman in general, and the capital area in particular, is a wonder and balm. Oddly enough, although on a scale stratospherically different from today, Muscat municipality has always had a reputation for trash clearance. In this repect Qaboos has inherited and extended a tradition which one wishes he could export elsewhere.

As a tourist in Oman, which is now possible where even a few years ago it was still out of the question, the diversions offered, apart from those that belong directly to the hotel, will include visits to the old city of Muscat, to the suq and to the museums of the capital.

Muscat museums are well worth visiting. First, the Oman Museum, perched up above Qurm on a rocky outcrop near the Ministry of Information, was opened in 1974. Apart from some history, archaeology and architecture it contains copies of Victorian portraits from the Peabody Museum of Said bin Sultan (Sultan of Oman 1806–56) and Ahmed bin Naaman al Kaabi, the first Omani ambassador to the US and UK in the early 1840s. It is typically well presented and well designed, a gracious, rather serious and proud little museum.

Next, more difficult to find, is the National Museum. This is in a house in Ruwi, not far from the Falaj Hotel and the offices of the Omani Olympic Association, attached to the Islamic Library. It is quite different in flavour, somewhat offbeat and quirky, housing a rather strange amalgam of items that must somehow or other have found their way to the Ministry of National Heritage. Surprisingly, there is the inscription from above the old main gate of Muscat town, the plaque which attributed its building to Said bin Taimur, Sultan of Muscat and Oman and Dhofar and Gwadur. There is also the foundation stone of the Mission hospital dated 1909 and faded photographs of the Sultans from Turki bin Said (1871) onwards.

Quite different again is the Natural History Museum, opened in 1985 and housed in a handsome modern building next to the Ministry of National Heritage. Hanging in a covered forecourt is the skeleton of a 3 ½ ton four year old sperm whale which was grounded on an Omani beach, and, standing slightly phallicly in front of the main door, is a fossilised tree 260 million years old found in the desert. The symbol of the museum is a caracal lynx, an elusive cat that lives in the Omani desert.

The museum shows, both graphically and representationally, specimens and habitat of animals, birds, fish, insects and reptiles found in the country. Presentation is exciting and lucid, excellent for instruction of schools or other groups. There is a strong emphasis on conservation principles and all specimens in the museum have been collected from the wild with no deliberate killing of any individual creature. When later we were spectators at the discovery of a newly dead oryx in the Jiddat al Harasis the immediate reaction was to preserve the animal for subsequent use by the museum.

The Sultan's Armed Forces (SAF) museum is a different story altogether, not only, of course, in content but also in scope. Beit al Falaj fort was built in the early nineteenth century. Originally a fortified palace for the Sultan it was used as military headquarters from 1913 until in 1978 SAF moved its HQ to Muaskar al Murtafaa (MAM) out near the airport in Seeb. Pre-Qaboos it used to have that quintessential military atmosphere, part polish and efficiency, part dust and dirty socks, and the fort itself was rundown and streaked with cracks. Once Qaboos took over it was upgraded but its dispossession as HQ was inevitable and necessary. The last transformation into museum was slow in planning but the final result has been spectacular. On Armed Forces Day, 11 December 1988, it was opened. Gardens, blinding whitewash, polished brass, gleaming woodwork, all the modern gadgetry of museum design are there. In a large open space at the back of the museum are a series of life size displays and equipment including planes, missiles, vehicles, radar and ships.

This museum repays time spent in a visit. For anyone who knows anything of Oman it is revealing in different ways. Obviously a very large sum of money has been spent on rebuilding the fort and designing the exhibits. If the result is compared with, for instance, the investment by the French government in the musée d'Orsay it is to underline the same commitment, although on a different scale, to quality and inspiration.

In the second place, the SAF museum gives in surprising detail the make-up and deployment of the Armed Forces. Surprising, because if the question were to be put officially to the Ministry of Defence the answer would almost certainly, on security or some other grounds, be unforthcoming. Incidentally, the Oman telephone directory confirms the information provided by the Museum. This is a nice illustration of the nature of bureaucracy which, not only in Oman of course, will incline to suppress information even when it is already public. The civil servant will not know this because he will not have visited the museum nor studied the telephone directory.

A third, and more interesting, point. All governments are inclined, in varying degree, to communicate their own version of history. Some will suppress alternative views, others simply leave it to individual initiative to discover what the alternatives might be. The museum version of SAF's development, and more specifically of the Dhofar war, has been carefully constructed to exclude all reference to assistance from other countries and, indeed, reference to other countries in any context. The presentation as originally conceived and created was more open in this respect but nervousness in some quarters led to a complete redesign and rewriting of the exhibition. So, not only is there no reference to, or acknowledgement of, the help given by Britain, Iran or Jordan to the outcome of the war (or, in the case of Britain, to the outcome of the upheavals in the Interior in the 1950s and in the building up of SAF) but there is no mention either of Saudi Arabia (over the Buraimi incident), the People's Democratic Republic of Yemen (PDRY) or of the assistance given to PDRY by, amongst others, Iraq. The interpretation given to all these events is simple – 'Foreign powers' one of the subtitles says 'failed to destroy national unity in the Jebal Akhdar incidents; they cunningly shifted their theatre of operations to the Southern Region. A web woven by the same malign hands still tried to harm the country's security.' In other words, it was a straightforward communist plot whose outcome was a SAF victory. One recognises the sensitivities that historical events may create for current politics, but the result is that museums can be instructive places.

The last museum, a small aquarium attached to the new Marine Research Institute in a small bay between Muscat and the Bustan hotel, has no such hidden meanings but is a good place in which to take a look at the multicoloured fish that cluster in the coral along the coast.

Muscat itself is something of a museum these days. The palace, over-bearing and alien, is usually deserted. The Diwan and its satellite offices are active during office hours but then lapse into silence. The old houses, Beit Garaza, Beit Nader and Beit Fransa have been painstakingly refurbished but stand austere and withdrawn. The Ministry of Finance offices, furnished and finished in soberly magisterial style, do not fit the architectural context of Muscat and are the wrong colour. The old suq has been demolished and only one pharmacy has been left within the walls. The British Embassy is still grandly placed on the waterfront but even that, for security, is closed off with a large locked gate. So, Muscat feels unlived in, its history sucked out. It looks marvellous – bright white walls, clean cut lines, bougainvillea, lawns, polished wood and brass, arabesqued windows, flower beds, crenellations. Fort Merani has an extra tower where a lift has been installed. Fort Jalali long since ceased to be a prison. Out on the West extremity of the bay a fort has been rebuilt, carefully copied from a sketch of the harbour by Daniell in 1793. At night it is floodlit and seems as insubstantial as a set from opera. The whole place, indeed, is a bit like a theatre looking for an audience.

Outside the walls there is far more activity and life. It is a short taxi ride along the corniche to the vibrant atmosphere of Muttrah. Roads in the capital area are frequently embellished by models of indigenous life or craft. On the road to Qurm there are a couple of grazing oryx, elsewhere a coffee pot or Dhofari frankincense burner, and on this stretch of road there is a waterfall tumbling down a piece of rock that used to be attached to the rest of the hill but is now isolated by the excavation of the road. Further on, spaced around the Muttrah bay corniche, are large coloured plaques representing different birds found in Oman. They might be considered banal, but in fact are diverting and attractive.

In Muttrah the atmosphere of old Oman still pervades the suq. Much has changed, but the narrow alleys are still there, the whole area is seething with people and the shops sell as much that is impossibly useless as is obviously useful. India is predominant; coloured materials of every quality, the merchants, gold, brass and the waterfront looking to the subcontinent over the horizon. Now, of course, Muttrah has competition from supermarkets and shopping centres offering international goods at international prices. People still like the suq, however, for its atmosphere and the feeling that the process of bargaining has achieved a bargain.

After all this sightseeing back to the hotel for a swim, a shaded siesta with the rhythmic plop of a tennis match that anaesthetises its own sound, an evening stroll along the beach where shoals of sardines ruffle the lazy surface of the sea, and then that inflated ball of a sun drops safely behind the horizon before it explodes from the exertions of yet another day into a Rothko sunset.

PATROL BOATS IN PORT

The Royal Navy of Oman (RNO)[2] has about half a million square kilometres to patrol. The Oman coastline is over 1500 kms in length and the Exclusive Economic Zone for which it is responsible extends 200 miles from the coast.

Its main base is at Wudam 123 kms up the Batina road from Muscat, where there is a turning at the roundabout for the Said bin Sultan naval base. A fort has been renovated for the Wali at the turning. Said bin Sultan was the ruler who reigned for 50 years from 1806[3] and under whom old Oman enjoyed one of its more glorious and expansionary phases. Before 1985 Wudam consisted of an empty stretch of beach, a few palm trees and a small village.

In 1985 the contract was given for a new naval base to replace the existing location at the old coaling station in Muscat harbour. The base was operational in 1987 and officially opened by Sultan Qaboos as part of the November 1988 National Day celebrations. Why Wudam, an open windswept shallow beach, when the coast East of Qurm is pitted with deep water sheltered inlets? There seem to be two strands to the answer. First, that strategically the area to the North around Musandam is where the Navy is most likely to be operationally involved, so that a base West of Muscat is preferable to one East. Secondly, a social investment in the mid-Batina coast is of high value in the effort to spread development expenditure around the country and, in particular, outside the capital area.

Like everything in Oman the Sultan bin Said base is well designed, attractive to look at, tidy and disciplined. In fact its facilities would have been much enhanced if it had been constructed according to the original plan. Unfortunately its budget suffered from the oil price crisis of 1986 so that various bits of the base were deemed inessential and were postponed for better times. When we visited it in early 1990 the sports complex, reinstated by Qaboos at the official opening, was nearly complete, but there is still other building pending.

Nevertheless, to a non-nautical eye it all seemed impressive within its terms of reference. There is an operations room overlooking the jetties, a bit like an airport control tower, from which the whole area can be easily comprehended. Because of the nature of the shore the complete port complex had to be dredged out before building. The inner port has a depth of about 7 metres and the main channel, protected by breakwaters, about 8.5 metres. The naval strength consists of high-speed patrol boats and missile-carrying craft, landing craft, a supply ship and a sail training ship. Perhaps the most important part of the base – the part that has transformed the navy in the 1980s from a land-based to a self-contained seagoing operation – are the maintenance and engineering workshops and, second only to these, the training facilities. These are also inevitably the areas in which the navy is still most dependent upon expatriate assistance.

Training is the key constituent to Omanisation throughout the country and nowhere more so than in the Armed Forces. The navy has no problem in recruitment – nor for that matter do the other forces – and its commitment to training is impressive. The officer intake is spread around, with some being sent to the Sultan Qaboos University, some to King Fahd Academy in Saudi Arabia and others to Dartmouth in the UK; others go to a variety of technical and vocational colleges abroad. The training school at Wudam deals with a wide spectrum of work for all ranks including English language. The sail training ship, Shabab Oman, originally built as the Captain Scott in 1971 and well-known by now around the world, is administered by the navy, but used also by schools, clubs and educational institutes.

The workshops which have given the navy a capacity for carrying out its maintenance work look clinically clean and uncluttered. Equipment is state of the art and includes a lifting device which transports a ship from the non-tidal dock on rails to the appropriate workshop. The occasional heron looks on uncomprehendingly but impassively, as ready to fish from a concrete slipway as from the sandy beach.

The base has a large and comfortable wardroom. It has a huge area for expansion if ever required. It has its own water, electricity and sewage plants. Recycled water is used for irrigation. Four thousand people live on the base and in 1989 the hospital, catering for families as well as employees, had 34 000 outpatient visits.

A few days after our visit to Wudam a GCC naval exercise, the first ever, was due to begin. On the parade ground beneath the operations room the naval band was practising; interspersed with traditional naval tunes were the more ponderous strains of six national anthems.

MORNING IN MUSANDAM

Sheet NG 40-6E of Series K6611, Khasab, published by HMSO in 1982, gives a good idea of the crazy jigsaw outline of the Musandam peninsula. It is, however, an insufficient preparation for the extraordinary sensation of flying into Khasab by Skyvan. Flying anywhere by Skyvan is peculiar enough, but, when coming into Khasab, unreality is greatly enhanced by the sight of mountains and water out of the window. Height and distance are distorted by strong sunlight and shadows. The water, a deep ink colour and motionless within black and vertical cliffs, seems to belong to enclosed craters rather than the open sea. There is no sign of any flat surface, apart from the water itself, as the plane descends. It is with some relief that, wheeling over yet another crag, Khasab comes into focus at the end of a largish wadi. There may be equally dramatic pieces of coastline, in Norway for instance, or down in Tierra del Fuego, but even those would not have the hazy but minatory sight of Iran forming a faint Islamic horizon beyond the peninsula and islands of Musandam and the straits of Hormuz.

Khasab used to be a remote and seldom visited fishing village. The inhospitable hills of Musandam were inhabited by the Shihuh whose welcome to stray travellers was notoriously ill-mannered, if not threatening. Musandam means 'anvil', a suitably unrelenting image for a craggy area full of craggy people. Now the Shihuh, or at least those who have chosen to benefit from the Oman of Qaboos, have villas in Dubai. Khasab is a relatively thriving town, capital of the Governorate (the only one in Oman) of Musandam, and centre of both civilian and military activity. The Royal Air Force of Oman (RAFO) has its tactical advance wing in a newly-built airforce base there, the Navy has a satellite naval base on Goat island, up near the very tip of the peninsula, and intelligence support and warning is provided by radar installations on Jebal Haram, the highest point of the mountain ranges. This is the basis of SAF's command and control system for the North which helped to preserve the neutrality of the straits throughout the Iran–Iraq war.

The morning I was there I saw no tankers, no warships. The main activity came from Iranian smugglers. Whereas in the old days dhows from Dubai carrying gold to India were the main illicit trade, now it is the twin-engined grey-hulled speedboats which move videos and other electronic equipment from the Emirates to Iran. Their favourite jump-off point is Khasab, hidden from the Iranian coast but closest to it, a 45-minute trip if interception is avoided.

Most of Musandam development has taken place since 1980. Although a Musandam Development Committee was established in 1976 it was not

until its membership and mode of operation was changed in 1979[4] that
positive results began to be seen. Because of this relative neglect during
the 1970s there had developed amongst the inhabitants a deepening
dependency upon and linkage with the United Arab Emirates (UAE). Ras
al Khaima territory is only about 10 kms from Bukha and communications
along this coast are far easier to establish than from the Northern Batina
via Dibba to Khasab. Indeed, given the peculiar border divisions in that
area, Musandam geographically belongs more naturally to UAE than to
Oman. The decision to invest more seriously and extensively in Musandam
was, therefore, in part a statement to the inhabitants and to the UAE that
Musandam was Omani territory. It was more importantly, however, a
response to the heightened awareness, in the wake of the deposition of
the Shah, of the strategic importance of the straits of Hormuz. As would
become apparent during the 1980s Oman, because of Musandam, would
assume a geopolitical significance that provided it with both opportunity
and responsibility.

Anyhow, the result is that Khasab has become as active and well serviced
as any Batina town and Bukha is a respectable second. There is a small
port, hospital, boys' secondary school, banks, a youth centre, even a motel
in Khasab; in Bukha a girls' secondary school, a small hospital, and the
headquarters of the Musandam Security Force. In both places the old
forts are being repaired, if not reconstructed, by the Ministry of National
Heritage. A road between the two has been blasted out from the cliffs
and has produced a dramatic corniche; where it has been routed over a
promontory it looks as if a whole section of mountain has been removed
and then replaced with an inset serpentine ascent. On top, at the village
of Harf, a pillar box and bus shelter stand beside the road. Another route
has been engineered over the peninsula between Khasab and Dibba. In the
small bays around Khasab I was delighted to see many of the traditional
badns, their sharp prows superciliously upturned to the ubiquitous modern
Yamaha fishing boats.

I saw all this under the guidance of the Air Force station commander,
a Group Captain of great charm and efficiency. He had, like so many
Omanis, been forced to leave the country in the 1960s, by subterfuge and at
considerable upset and cost to his family, in order to be educated in Dubai.
On his return to Oman he had the rather surprising career progression of
Ministry of Social Affairs to Air Force. I asked him about the Musandam
Development Committee. 'Let's go and see the Muhafiz,' he said, 'he's
been here for several years and should know.' So we went and I found
that the Muhafiz was the son of Sheikh Ahmed bin Mohammed al Harthi
and that I must have met him as a boy when I used to visit his father at

Qabil. That was a pleasant surprise. 'Bring the file,' he said to an assistant. Back came a green leather bound book, and there was the answer to my question.

DOWN TO DHOFAR

Dhofar is different. To begin with, the beach at Salala is precisely parallel with that at Qurm but, looking out to sea, the sun sets to the right instead of the left. This may be disconcerting until a look at the map confirms that the coast at Salala is set at 180° to that at Muscat. Then again, all the palm trees bear coconuts rather than dates, and the sea pounds onto a steep glaringly white sand beach in a vicious undertow. These superficial surprises are a conditioning for the real differences.

Salala is 1000 kms from Muscat. Most of that distance is dry flat empty desert. At the end of it, Dhofar looks South and West towards Africa rather than North and East towards Central Asia. Dhofar is on the monsoon route. Muscat is lucky to get a few storms a year. The Dhofar mountains are an extension of the Southern Aden ranges, the Oman mountains are geologically on the same trend line as those of Iran. So, it is not only climate and agriculture that are different but the people, the tribes and their psychology.

Set amongst the villas and offices in Salala are productive gardens full of bananas, papaya and coconut palms. Coconuts are piled by the roadside, large smooth green fruits, not those husky kernels used at fairgrounds; the top is slashed off and a drink of coconut water is ready. The Sultan's palace takes up half the sea front, hidden behind long walls. Everywhere bougainvillea splashes over fences or is neatly trimmed into bushes. All the Sultanate ministries have smart modern Branch Directorates in Salala, and the grandest is that belonging to the Wali, who, because of the importance of Dhofar, is of Ministerial rank. Either because of the fruit growing so effortlessly in the gardens or the more sensual African characteristics appearing in many of the inhabitants Salala feels a more languid and lazy place than Muscat.

Outside Salala and away from irrigation and cultivation this becomes misleading as a response. There the countryside, except during the monsoon period, is as dry and hard as it is anywhere in Northern Oman. Nevertheless, it is still different. Frankincense may have lost much of its monetary value but it still has its biblical connotations and a certain touristic attraction. Frankincense trees look like any thorn bush but generate a gumlike juice that secretes a distinctive perfume of Arabian incense.

On the Jebal, always described simply in those terms, the tribes have immemorially been breeders of cattle. On hill and plain camels multiply. The Jebal itself, although pitted with wadis, has areas of rolling brown hill grazing that is transformed into a thick green pasture during the monsoon. This natural process has been accentuated by water drilling programmes that have created an exponential expansion in the numbers of animals that live, and eat, up there. The Jebal is now more settled than it ever has been, as can be seen from a visit to one of the administrative centres – with school, hospital, veterinary centre, mosque and commerce – but its capacity is being heavily strained.

To get the proper feel for Dhofar it is preferable to go by road from Muscat. A car may be the most comfortable, but there are also airconditioned coaches that make the journey in 12 hours three times a day. En route there are a number of hotel restaurants. At Wadi Qitbit, for instance, there is one. It is well designed, well built, well finished, set round a courtyard with a garden and fountain, surrounded by a larger garden still in the process of planting, with a large smart modern Shell station in the compound. A cattle grid at the entrance keeps unwanted camels or goats from straying into the hotel area. It has its own water and electricity plant. It is run by one of the Muscat hotels who use Indians for the purpose (who else would live out here?). American Express and Visa cards are accepted. All this provides a miniature picture of what has occurred in Oman during the last 20 years.

There is then a further 250 kms of open road to Salala. 'Danger Moving Dunes' a roadsign hallucinates. After that, nothing except for an occasional telecommunications microwave station until Thumrait is reached, where there is a large air base and army camp. Then, after traversing a moon landscape of conical hills, the top of the Jebal and the end of the desert plain announce Dhofar proper with its steep descent to the greenery of Salala.

The very greenest bit of Dhofar is Sultan Qaboos' farm. Apart from a large herd of Jersey cattle and extensive orchards of fruits and palms there is a large plant nursery and an aviary with exotic multicoloured birds. There is a modern gleaming veterinary centre and, somewhere in the midst of it all, a tall tower with Qaboos' lookout room on top, a tranquil spot from which to contemplate a sunset flaming across the plain towards the Jebal.

NATIONAL HEALTH

Nizwa hospital was one of the first batch of regional hospitals to be built in the country. It was opened in 1972 and was enlarged in 1980. It is due to be replaced as part of the next 5-year plan. It is the main hospital for the Interior region, although within the region there are six other smaller hospitals, six health centres and public health units.

I met the administrator of the hospital who, although it was at the end of what had without doubt been a tiring day and I arrived without warning, was extremely courteous and informative. The hospital covers casualty, maternity, ENT, dental, paediatrics and general surgery and has also eye, skin and orthopaedic specialists. There are 25 doctors and nurses, of whom most, if not all, are non-Omani. They deal with 800–900 outpatients a day and have 130 beds for in-patients. They have four ambulances attached to the hospital.[5]

The smaller satellite hospitals in the region generally have about five doctors and deal mostly with maternity cases as in-patients. The health centres have one doctor, probably two nurses and deal only with outpatients. Cases that cannot be handled in the region are sent to Muscat.

The hospital seemed clean, spacious and well-ordered. There was a fax machine in the office. Visiting is supposed to be confined strictly to specified hours which, if adhered to, would run wholly counter to Arab traditions. I was unable to do more than see that visitors were well behaved and orderly, even the children.

Nizwa, about to undergo in the next year or two what is described as a beautification programme, still feels like a frontier town. Much of its old world attraction has been subsumed into small neonlit stores full of bright materials and a ribbon of those noisy workshops that straighten out anything from vehicles to bedframes. The great tower of Nizwa fort has lost its self-confidence; it peers nervously towards the lowering mass of the Jebal Akhdar to ensure that modern man has not yet carved a corniche up there. Beautification, if carried out as well as it has been on the coast, may be no bad thing. In the meantime, Nizwa inhabitants are well provided with medical services and, not to be outdone by that fax machine, the local bank is efficiently equipped with an automatic cash dispenser.

At a quite different level of activity and sophistication I visited the Medinat al Haqq hospital in Dhofar, where the large regional hospital is, naturally, located in Salala. Medinat al Haqq is one of the larger administrative centres that were established on the Jebal in the course of the war. Apart from the hospital it has a deputy wali's office, a primary school, some shops, a police post (temporarily unoccupied), a veterinary centre and housing for the people in charge. It is the centre of what might be a large village but in practice is a somewhat underoccupied area. Perhaps people were far away with their cattle.

The hospital has 18 beds in two wards (12 female, 6 male), a pharmacy and X-ray facilities. It had one doctor from Bangladesh and a nurse from

Kerala, most of whose work is connected with maternity cases. Confidence in the medical service is such that a large majority of the pregnant women in the area register with the hospital. Each is given an ante-natal card which she keeps as her medical registration form, since individuals have proved to be a far better filing mechanism than medical administrators. There is an efficient immunisation service which has won the confidence of Omani women, and this hospital has a mobile immunisation team attached to it. The hospital itself is built in bleak concrete and during the monsoon it is, like everything on the Jebal, sodden and dripping with damp. Nevertheless, perhaps because it provides shelter, that is its busiest season.

Bangladesh or Kerala must seem more than one continent away for the doctors and nurses who commit their skills to outposts such as Medinat al Haqq, particularly as their commitment, however dedicated, is for the most part driven by a commercial impetus. Their problems are real. They may, for instance, feel compunction at carrying out a regulation which instructs them to report to the police any case that involves drunkenness or a traffic accident. More practically, it cannot be easy to tolerate the absence of electricity because the ministry in Salala has failed to get the diesel delivered.

The frustrations that have to be endured in Medinat Al Haqq may also exist in the Royal Hospital in Muscat just behind the Sultan Qaboos stadium, but the surroundings in which the professors, specialists, surgeons, physicians, matrons and nurses work must go a long way towards alleviating such difficulties.

The main entrance hall of the Royal Hospital is marbled and cool. There is no disorganised bustle. A reassuring calm prevails. Stone benches inset with polished hardwood break up its broad space. It is like walking into a newly built museum in Paris or Washington. Public relations assistants guide official visitors round the hospital. Visiting hours in the afternoon are strictly observed. Corridors seem endless but, once the groundplan has been mastered, are easily navigated and well signposted. Inner courtyards appear through tinted glass with elegant arches, sunburned concrete and dark shadowed lines. Wards are airy and open, sisters sit at computer terminals, nurses peer at electronic information about their patients. It is all very high tech, the greatest danger for a visitor being to trip over yet another cleaner making sure that the penultimate speck of dust is removed from ward and corridor.

There is a VIP wing kept for members of the Sultan's family and ministers. This is even more marbled, luxurious and spacious. A visiting and rest area looks out onto a hidden courtyard of flowers, fountains, tiling and water that is reminiscent of Granada. The wing was quite empty except for a nurse on the desk waiting for a royal accident.

This is a high-class high-tech hospital, a monument to 1990s medicine. 42 000 cubic metres of cement were used to build it and a further 26 000 to construct staff accommodation. It has 629 beds, accident and emergency departments, 6 operating theatres and 7 suites for radio-diagnostics; it has intensive care units, kidney transplant, fluoroscopy, computer assisted tomography; it has staff recreational facilites, accommodation for 700 staff, its own sewage plant and recycled waste water irrigating gardens and lawns. In fact it seems to have just about everything a hospital could possibly need. It took only 3 ½ years to build from the moment the contract was awarded and it was opened, after expenditure of around $250 million, in January 1987.[6]

It might be imagined that with such a mass of silent computerised calculation, with so many screens responding to so much input, with such spacious wards and with so much concentration on cleanliness, there would be no place for frustration. Problems exist, however, often exacerbated by the variety of cultural backgrounds. A vast majority of those who make this hospital work are expatriates. Specialists and physicians come from all over the world. Nurses come largely from Singapore and India. Non-medical staff come from India, Pakistan or Bangladesh. The Ministry of Health is, of course, an Omani administration. This may turn the Royal Hospital into a mini-United Nations but it can create explosive combinations of culture and command. It can also, when things go wrong, narrow the margin of tolerance between individual commitments to career, contract and remuneration.

The problems of national health in Oman are in many respects similar to those in most parts of the world, but where the infrastructure of health is of such high quality it would be tragic if imperfections in its administration degraded its usefulness. As of 1990, however, all is well and the spirit of adaptation happily prevails. In the paediatric wards the division between male and female is made not by the sex of the patient but of the parent who attends the child.

A LOT OF LEARNING

Oman counts itself as a Third World country, but its architecture and facilities are often of top first world quality. The Royal Hospital was one example, another is Sultan Qaboos University.

Imagine a massive wooden brass studded Omani traditional doorway which opens to a straight 800-metre tiled passage that bisects academic buildings and open courtyards, ends in a semicircle student centre and looks across to a huge domed and arched mosque with an elegant modernistic minaret standing sentinel at each side. Straddling the main passage are the administration block, the library, seminar rooms, theatres, lecture halls, audiovisual and television facilities, music rooms and an arts centre. Parallel to the main axis, across courtyards with trees, fountains and shrubs are the faculty colleges with their offices, equipment and seminar rooms. To the North are the Colleges of Medicine (linked in turn to the University Teaching Hospital), Agriculture and Education; to the South are the Colleges of Engineering and Sciences. Halls of residence and sporting facilities for males are to the South, for females to the North, behind the Colleges, and, in a large horseshoe beyond in a series of staggered terraces is the staff housing.

In principle sexes are segregated, not only in their living accommodation but also in their academic activities. This does not entail the extreme logic of duplication but has created a clever design compromise under which common facilities such as the library, lecture halls, theatres and seminar rooms can be entered from different sides down separate passages and, even more imaginatively, the main walkways have an upper and lower elevation for sex-separation purposes. In practice, whatever formal expression of separation exists, a natural informality has been created. Moreover, since the proportion of undergraduate females to males is around 45/55, there is a necessary and acceptable (in Islamic terms) mix in the working environment of tutorials and seminars.

The university, which opened for its first academic year in September 1986, was completed, apart from its hospital, in 4 ½ years from award of contract. The hospital was officially opened three years later. The cost of the whole complex was in excess of $500 million. The site is in the area of Khawdh about 50 kms from Muscat and inland from Seeb. In 1982 it was dry stone and scrub. The architects should be given appropriate honour for the transformation of desert into academic oasis. At least in architectural terms it should be an inspiration for Omani undergraduates.[7]

It remains something of an oasis, not least because of its remoteness from other habitation. Its nearest neighbour is the military hospital 8 kms away where the Khawdh road branches off the main Nizwa road. But also, and less attractively, it is cocooned within a security area into which it is difficult to penetrate without advance warning. Security, not without some reason, is a fetish in Oman and, Islamically speaking, there are a lot of unchaperoned girls on the campus, but this is an unfortunate first impression of academic openness.

The university faces a number of crucial challenges. These relate in various forms to the general proposition of academic excellence. In the first place there is the question of whether international or regional standards are to be observed. This in turn breaks down in practice as to whether the academic regime and, in most cases, the academic staff are chosen and administered by Europeans or Egyptians, and whether the academic courses are subject to external audit or examination on acceptable international standards. This is not a racial question but a question of academic experience and traditions.

In the second place there is the question of the language of instruction, which is English. It needs to remain English if academic standards are to be maintained and seen to be maintained at an international level. In the third place there is the question, sensitively intertwined with social and religious traditions, as to the status of women in a university milieu. Then there is the question of what are the limits, if any, to the independent status of the university itself.

These questions are not openly debated in Oman but they are inevitably part of intra-university discussion and practice. The deans have pivotal influence in determining how developments work out within their own colleges. Challenges have been made and imaginative decisions taken. It was greatly encouraging to hear about the university debates where subjects that might have been banned as sensitive are discussed sensibly and openly by both men and women students together. It was encouraging to learn that certain medical training procedures had been pronounced consistent with Islamic rules when challenged on fundamentalist grounds.

But, equally, it was dispiriting to find that in other cases academic choice and practices were being eroded and, worst of all, that academic staff were beginning to leave, not because they wanted to, but because they were being frustrated beyond endurance.

The deans are vitally important but in the final analysis it is the vice-chancellor and University Council who must take the decisions. It is unfair both on the University and on the incumbent that the acting vice-chancellor is also the Minister of Education. He is thereby saddled with an intolerable combination of responsibility and conflict of interest. At this critical juncture, when the first graduates of the university emerge in mid-1990, the vice-chancellor needs to reappoint an international advisory body similar to the one which helped to create its structure in the early 1980s which could propose either new mechanisms or the strengthening of existing ones in order to ensure the continuing excellence of an institution so excellently conceived.

It would be tragic if the clock, currently striking the quarters in Oxbridge college style over the campus, were to toll dejectedly over second-rate students taught by third-rate professors. Sultan Qaboos would be horrified at that possibility.[8]

In the academic year 1988/89 there were 303 989 students on the educational roll: that represents about 25 per cent of the total population of Oman; 45 per cent of the students were female. Since less than 2000 were enrolled at the University, a very large number were studying elsewhere in Oman: 7700 of them were girls at secondary schools. I visited Duhat al Adab girls secondary school in Muscat. I was greeted by the headmistress, elegant, smart, poised and confident. She might have been directly translated from Benenden, Kent or Mount Holyoake, Massachusetts. There were 900 girls in the school, aged 15–18, of whom 100, from Masira and the Shaquiya, were boarders. After the first year they stream to Arts or Science specialisation. Last year 180 had taken Arts, 290 Science. There were 60 teachers in the school, 10 of whom were Omanis. They have parent/teacher evenings, run their own cafeteria, have cookery classes, organise their own blood donor scheme and have an assembly for fifteen minutes every morning. The girls wear white trousers, dark blue tunics and a white headscarf. They were cheerful and very polite. I was brought a plate of cookies by an emissary from the cookery class which I had called in on.

I wondered what problems this well-designed, well-run and happy establishment had: the usual teenager emotional problems, said Mrs Makki in matter of fact tones. She had two social advisers to help with them. A greater source of difficulty were families, for whom this school was strange and, perhaps, threatening; also, of course, she added, the staff, many of whom took far more of her time than the pupils. I went off thinking that my own daughters would have been at home in this modern-minded, open and cheerful school. Can all Omani schools be like this?

I went off to see the Jabir bin Zaid secondary school for boys, the first one built in Muscat. The headmaster was a Jordanian who had been there since 1976. He was a traditionalist, authoritarian, rather quirky, generations different from Mrs Makki, but in his way as much liked and admired. The school had 975 students, with about 50 boarders. The proportion of Arts to Science was similar to that of the girls school. There were 64 teachers, of whom 4 were Omani, and the rest came from Egypt, Jordan, Morocco, Tunisia, Algeria, Sri Lanka, India, Sudan and England. There was one Egyptian social helper. Most of the problems were disciplinary. Nothing very surprising here, it all seemed a good middle of the road school with no frills.

For a complete contrast I went to see the primary/intermediate school in

Tanam. Tanam is the place, about 15 kms from Ibri into the desert, which used to be described as the Duru capital on the grounds that there was a marginally greater chance of finding the sheikh there amongst the few dry palm trees than in any other indeterminate piece of desert. Because the main oilfields were in Duru territory it was always thought that the first symbols of interior development should be installed in Tanam. And, indeed, that is where the first interior hospital was built. It was begun, amazingly enough, under Said bin Taimur. The school followed later.

It was a simple but spacious school, classrooms built round a large central play area. There were 570 children in the school, of whom two-fifths, 226 precisely, were girls. There were 12 elementary classes and 3 intermediate. The headmaster was Jordanian (he had been in Dhank for a year before arriving in Tanam), the male teachers came from Jordan with one Omani, the female from Egypt, Jordan and Sri Lanka. The children learn English from the 4th elementary year and have music and art classes in all schools. Classes start at 30–40 pupils but reduce to about 10 by the final year through wastage as the students, particularly the girls, return to their tribes for work or marriage. But, I was told, this was changing fast. The school has fifteen pick-up trucks to fetch the children from far into the desert.

The overwhelming impression was one of enthusiasm amongst the children and this seemed to transmit itself to the teachers for whom the external trappings of life were almost entirely lacking. Tanam is a dusty frontier village whose society, for people coming from Egypt, North Africa or India, must be oppressive and constricting. Their reward must be almost entirely concentrated in the continuing transformation, which must at times seem almost miraculous, that the process of education works on bedu children. Certainly noone could fail to be enchanted by a welcoming chorus in Arabic from a whole class of beautiful gazelle-eyed Duru girls spruce in their school uniforms. No wonder they are married young.

IBEX AND ORYX[9]

Those people who like deserts will also like huge horizons, unbroken skies, silence and, if they can hear it, the music of the spheres. Most of them will prefer to enjoy their deserts accompanied by late twentieth century comforts. So we were excited by the prospect of a couple of days at Yaalouni.

The Jiddat al Harasis is a large expanse of flat rather stony, very dry desert. In places it has some unappealing acacia trees and, where water occasionally settles after rain, some taller and more substantial ghaf trees. To the West the Jiddat vanishes into the Empty Quarter, to the East it stops at a steep escarpment, the Hugf, which plunges down to a flat coastal strip and the sea. The Harasis are the tribe that live on this unyielding plateau. It also used to be, in the years before 1970, an area attractive to the Arabian Oryx, the handsome white antelope with the two tall straight horns which, when seen in parallel as one, gave rise to a unicorn myth. By some Darwinian process the oryx developed a constitution and digestive system that permitted it to thrive in this environment which proved so unfriendly to most other creatures.

The Harasis, too, developed characteristics that allowed them not only to live on the Jiddat, but, apparently, to enjoy it. The whole area is, in linguistic and anthropological terms as well as geographically, a link between the Southern Arabian cultures that include Dhofar and the Northern Omani tribal areas that extend South from the interior mountain ranges. The Harasis still have their own dialect which is closer to the Southern Arabian languages than to Arabic.

The oryx story is by now well known and documented, but there is still a romance in searching the desert for a herd and finding it. They were destroyed in their natural habitat in the 1950s and 1960s, largely by raiding parties of hunters from Qatar and the Emirates. The last recorded oryx in the Jiddat was 1972. Meanwhile, in 1961, a decision had been taken that a World Herd of oryx should be established to save the species from expected extinction. This was originally planned for Kenya but for reasons of health and supervision was transferred to the Arizona desert in USA. Nine oryx were installed in Arizona and a breeding programme initiated. By 1977 the World Herd consisted of 72 animals and there were a further 34 in North American zoos.

In the same year 1977 Sultan Qaboos delivered his throwaway question to Ralph Daly, his adviser on Conservation, 'What shall we do about the oryx?' This was after a successful conservation programme had been carried out on the Arabian Tahr in the mountains near Quriyat. The outcome was the Jiddat al Harasis Development Project, part A of which was the development of the Heima area as a Tribal Administration Centre and part B was the project to reintroduce the oryx into its natural habitat in the wild.

Feasibility studies, negotiations with the World Herd and World Wildlife Fund and establishment of the base camp at Yaalouni took three years. The first group of ten animals came in two loads. Their journey was by road to Los Angeles, by 747 to Paris via Chicago, by GulfAir 707 from Paris to Seeb and by Skyvan (two per plane) from Seeb to

Yaalouni. There, on 5 March 1980, they were met by the director of the project, Mark Stanley Price, the wali and various officials. The Harasis tribesmen although they had been participating in the preparations and had been recruited as rangers to look after the oryx, only believed that they were the same animals that they had known in the past when they finally walked out of their crates and into the Yaalouni pens.

We happened to be at Yaalouni on 5 March 1990, by which time there was a count of 96 oryx in total. There also on their first return visit after leaving the project in 1987 were Mark Stanley Price, his wife and daughter. We joined Roddy Jones, the current manager, his wife, Andrew Spalton, the resident scientist in charge, the 38 Harasis who are now employed by the Project and the resident administrative staff. It was a cheerful encampment, 80 kms of desert track and 453 kms of highway from Muscat, generously appointed with those late twentieth-century comforts that accentuate the pleasures of the desert.

In the desert we met a ranger crew and sat on the sand drinking coffee and tea with them. Nearby was a pool of blue water. There had been unusually heavy rains this year so that we kept finding ponds. There were birds there and, in the water, masses of triops, tadpole-like creatures whose eggs remain dried up for ten years or more in the sand and then, when a rainpool is formed, emerge immediately into squiggling life. Frequently we could see a haze of green where grass was emerging from the sandy desert surface.

Then we saw our first oryx. They are placid unexcitable animals. This helps them to preserve fluid in their bodies and enables them to live without intake of water for weeks or months on end. A spin-off of the monsoon is that in the Jiddat thick mists roll in from the sea at night and drench the shrubs with dew. The oryx make use of this to supplement their fluid intake. There were four oryx in this small herd, two females, a male and a calf curled almost invisibly against the base of a dead acacia tree. The oryx are still known each by name, but this is fast becoming impracticable as more calves are born. The gestation period is 8 ½ months but the females will be made pregnant again only two weeks after calving. Each female, therefore, is likely to produce four calves every 3 years and will probably continue calving for around 12 years.

Suddenly we saw a different animal silhouetted on the escarpment edge. An ibex, shaggy with brown hair and horns curved almost back to its neck. We drove up to the escarpment, a vicious drop into a moonscape of greys, browns and dead white soil which, reasonably enough, the Harasis believe to be haunted. Down on a ledge below us were five more ibex, a rare sight. They stood motionless for a moment, then flicked off over the rocky outcrops. At Yaalouni there is one ibex ranger. He proved his qualification by going off alone one day, tracking an ibex, tackling it from behind, trussing it up and bringing it back to camp.

Next day we went South from Yaalouni and had a picnic under a ghaf tree. In the tree was an eagle's nest and nearby the corpses of two eaglets. Eagles are a threat to the animals owned by the bedu and these birds had been deliberately killed by a landcruiser while they were still in the dangerous intermediate state in which they had left the nest but were not yet fully competent to fly. The eaglets were already large and heavy and their talons looked like hooks of barbed wire. Later on we visited a second nest, in an acacia tree only five feet above ground, and saw a single eaglet, half-hopping half-flying, some hundreds of yards away while the parent soared off into the stratosphere. A few more days and the eaglet would be up there too.

We met another ranger team. They had sighted a herd of 14 oryx nearby. Off we went. Consternation en route. There was a dead oryx lying in the sand with a hole in its neck. Who had done this? The oryx, as indeed all other animals in Oman, are strictly subject to conservation rules. No hunting or killing is permitted.

It was quickly determined that the oryx had in fact been killed by another oryx, presumably in a fight for dominance over the herd. We found the killer, with blood over his neck and shoulders, calmly strolling with, and presumably now dominating, the herd of 14. Juma had challenged 7-year-old Fadi and won. Fadi had died because a horn had punctured an artery. This was probably accidental for the oryx does not normally fight to kill. It was, however, dramatic evidence that the oryx were, indeed, wild in the wild.

Back at Yaalouni Fadi was unceremoniously dumped into a deepfreeze and would in due course be sent to the Natural History museum in Muscat to be preserved there as an exhibit. We settled down to a relaxed Yaalouni evening. Silence and stars.

Next morning we departed for Heima and Salala. There had been 96 oryx on the Jiddat when we arrived, 95 as we left, but they would soon exceed 100. The experts reckon that when there are 300 the herd will be self-generating and sustainable provided that the hunting laws are observed. Scientifically, the next problem will be to ensure that there is sufficient genetic diversification. In future, they will be counting chromosomes more carefully than the oryx.

HAYDN IN HALBAN

'Royal Oman Symphony Orchestra cordially invites you to a concert.' The venue, it said, was the Royal Oman Symphony Orchestra Concert Hall, Halban, Seeb (map enclosed).

The map is necessary. The hall is 10 kms towards the hills from the main Batina road. When the opening concert was given many of the audience turned round in mid-desert long before they had reached the hall; they could not imagine a concert taking place so remotely from Muscat. In fact, the orchestra is attached, for administrative purposes, to the Royal Guard of Oman and their facilities are within the area of the Royal Guard training battalion whose camp at Halban is less surprising than the concert hall.

In typically Omani fashion, the concert hall would be the envy of any school and many towns in the world. Above the orchestra is their crest, crossed violins, oboe and trumpet surmounted by the royal coat of arms. Around the hall are portraits of star conductors and performers to provide inspiration. Orchestra and conductor were immaculate, the boys in tails, the girls in white tunics. The programme consisted of Bizet, Haydn, Schubert and Sibelius. It was slightly surreal.

Clearly there are advantages in being a Sultan. If you want oryx on the Jiddat you make appropriate arrangements. If you want a symphony orchestra you say to Brian Briggs-Watson in 1984 roughly the equivalent of what you said to Ralph Daly in 1977 – 'and what shall we do to create a symphony orchestra?'

Brian Briggs-Watson came to Oman to establish a mounted band for the Royal Guard. To follow this with a symphony orchestra would surely be a unique achievement. There were two possible ways of going about the task. One was to create the orchestra by remote control. This would have involved sending 100 Omanis to Vienna for seven years, writing an enormous cheque and welcoming them back as an orchestra in 1991. This was seriously considered and was the method chosen by King Hussein when he created the Jordan Symphony Orchestra. The other way was to do it indigenously, which in the long run would obviously provide far deeper roots and the basis for a continuing operation. This too would require the writing of large cheques.

So, what happened was that a special school was built in the grounds of the Royal Guard Training Battalion. Students were to be chosen young and would require not only specialised music teaching but also the normal school syllabus. Boarding facilities were needed for those who came from afar. Both music and general staff had to be recruited. And, of course, pupils had to be found.

Brian Briggs-Watson set off round Oman to find his first 100 pupils. As a general guideline not one Omani child would have ever heard a bar of classical music nor any other Western music, and the idea of a music-oriented training was totally alien, indeed without meaning. Briggs-Watson interviewed hundreds of boys. He gave them simple aptitude tests to establish their sense of rhythm, hearing and timing. Somehow he reduced his list to 100 names and, presto, he had pupils to place in his brand new school. The school had classrooms, music rooms (Brahms, Grieg, Elgar and Schubert) and instruments, two language laboratories with word-processing equipment, a clinic, dormitory accommodation and, of course, the Concert Hall.

Why should any Omani parent allow or want his child to join a school to train for a symphony orchestra? Why should the boy himself want to do this? The answer almost certainly reflected the fact that the school and the musical concept, however that was understood, were under the aegis of the Royal Guard and, therefore, Sultan Qaboos himself. The opportunity to attach oneself to the court and to obtain a guaranteed job there was not only desirable in itself but also, in practice, was seen virtually as a royal command. Total ignorance as to the nature of classical music or a symphony orchestra was, odd though it may seem, a positive help in finding recruits. Later on, as word got back to the villages, families began to accept that the advantages were not confined to being within the orbit of the Sultan but that music itself provided interest, enjoyment and status.

In 1987 Richard Pepper was appointed director of the school and orchestra. By then 37 of the original 100 had fallen by the wayside. He took in another 40 boys and 15 girls. The school uniform for the girls is in the plum colour of the Royal Guard. Boys and girls work together academically and, of course, musically. We looked in on a rehearsal by the second and first year orchestras playing together for the first time. It was a marvellous sensation to hear the ensemble improve each time they played, as the students began to feel how what they had learnt in groups fitted into the whole orchestra. This, and the concert by the senior orchestra that we had heard previously, seemed to provide a practical answer to the underlying critical question – what is the purpose of training Omani children to take up such an essentially Western cultural tradition?

There are some curious problems facing the staff. One is how to allocate instruments to children who have never seen or heard any of them. They do it mainly by physical assessment. If the child has large lung capacity he will be directed to brass; a suitable jaw configuration takes him to wind; finger adaptability may lead him to strings; and so on. In practice this seems to have worked out well.

The main problem is, however, to determine how the orchestra and the school will develop. The senior orchestra has now, in effect, graduated from the school but it remains there as the Royal Oman Symphony Orchestra. Somehow it has got to be detached from the school and take on a separate existence of its own, allowing its members variously to develop as either soloists, members of chamber groups, as music teachers or as orchestral players. Equally the graduates of later years need to be able to join the orchestra or follow their own musical careers. This will involve years of post-school (for the senior members are still of school standard, not university) training and, even more fundamental, decisions as to how classical music is to take its place in the ordinary school syllabus. There are, incidentally, facilities for music study at the graduate level in the Sultan Qaboos university but the faculty is not staffed or operational.

The orchestra school has, therefore, already achieved what most people would have thought to be impossible. It must have been an enthralling experience for Brian Briggs-Watson, Richard Pepper, his 18 international staff and the boys and girls who form the various orchestras in the school. They now have an equally daunting prospect ahead in coming to terms with the next stage of development. By the year 2000, perhaps we shall have the Royal Oman Opera Company performing Nabucco in Nizwa.

Music may have taken the headlines, but the fine arts thrive at a less fevered level. All schools include art in their syllabus. There is a network of art practice and exhibition throughout the Gulf.

The 1990 Petroleum Development Oman (PDO) calendar is devoted to young Omani artists. Their brief CVs show that many of them studied at the Muscat Youth Art Centre. This is situated in the Wadi Kebir. Next door is the Youth Theatre and on the floor above the Science Club.

There are several Youth Art Centres in Oman besides the Muscat one, in Salala, Sohar, Khasab, Nizwa, Buraimi and Sur. They are administered by the Director of Cultural and Artistry Activities within the Ministry of Education and Youth and, regionally, by the Youth Affairs Administration. This sounds formal and bureaucratic but in practice says little more than where the budget comes from.

The Wadi Kebir centre was neither formal nor bureaucratic. Students were studiously drawing, doors were hospitably open, pictures and sculptures were hung or placed around the studios and modified disorder prevailed. The centre was started in 1980. It opens in the evening for three hours. Students register for courses of three months or a year but attendance is voluntary. Seventy two were registered at the time of my visit. Teachers attend when required. Painting, drawing and sculpture courses are provided. At the end of each year there is a major exhibition held in Muscat. Judging from what I saw and from the PDO calendar every style of painting is tried out, with Arabian symbolist or figurative as the most popular. The teacher of painting whom I met had studied in London for a year, the sculpture teacher had trained in Bahrain. The Gulf area has established an active focus for art and a variety of annual exhibitions are held up and down the Gulf. It is only a matter of time before Omani, and Gulf, artists will be exhibiting in Cork street, SoHo or the Marais.

SURPRISES

Perhaps these scenes and impressions of Oman will have drawn a picture of a rather normal place with normal twentieth-century assets and liabilities. There is truth in this. What is abnormal about Oman is the fact that, within the short space of 20 years, it has become normal. However, normality itself is a highly misleading concept. Countries can no more be average than human beings, except by reference to some statistical measurement that tries to make objective rules from subjective data.

The normality of Oman today derives from its institutional structures. There exist all the government departments that are to be expected of a state – Defence, Interior, Health, Communications, Education, Foreign Affairs etc. – and, of course, all the functions that go with them – schools, telephones, embassies, armed forces, hospitals, police and so on. There are hotels, shops, restaurants, museums, conservation areas, traffic lights and gardens. All these things are to be expected; even the gardens, which are now an integral part of any self-respecting oil producing state, however lacking in water resources it may be. All this, in 1990, can be said to be normal.

One abnormality of Oman is that all these normal things are of such high design quality and that they appear to work with such efficiency and precision. I have already tried to give some impression of the quality of the material environment in Oman. It is easy to trivialise, but I found it to be a positive pleasure that all my appointments, whether with ministers or minions, were punctually met. As long as a visit was officially arranged there seemed to be no particular inhibition in imparting information. There was a pervasive briskness in the air for which I was not prepared and it seemed to illustrate a pride in Omani achievement at all levels that can no longer be taken for granted as normal in many parts of the world.

It should not be inferred from this that Oman has discovered the secret of how to run a civil service or a business. One of the many problems facing Oman is the burden of its bureaucracy and in this it can surely again claim normality. It is difficult to define the particular quality of the Omani environment, but there is, certainly, an underlying military tendency towards order. It is not that Oman or Omanis are militaristic but that Sultan Qaboos himself had a formative military experience at Sandhurst and with the British army and that this has rubbed off on the external processes of government through his own personal attitudes.

Oman has been assisted in this by another abnormality. This is the huge dependency upon expatriates for many of the services provided by government or private business. The point is that much of the external efficiency and order is carried out by non-nationals who are working, in effect, as mercenaries. They are more inclined, indeed are in a sense compelled by their contracts, to provide productive work. Omanis can manage and leave the execution to others. This is an aspect of Oman that will have to change and will bring its own problems to be overcome.

Just as this heightened awareness of an apparently smooth running Omani infrastructure is pervasive so nature provides impressions that magnify the special characteristics of Oman. The Jebal Akhdar has uniquely sloping and precipitous ravines and ranges. The creeks East of Muscat are as blueblack as ink, the monsoon in Dhofar as unexpected as a desert in Europe. Nowhere are forts so numerous or so magnificently medieval. Skylines appear like stage sets. For eight months a year the heat, when unconditioned by modern machinery, is hellish.

The combination of these and many other things gives Oman its particularity. In this catalogue of abnormality we should not forget the Omani people who are abnormal in the most attractive and acceptable manner. There are few who have not been charmed by the Omanis for their openness, hospitality and courtesy. I have met Arabs, usually from other Gulf countries, who have dismissed Omanis as non-Arabs but invariably they have never been to Oman. The GCC has had a beneficial effect in altering such attitudes.

However, it is the combination of speed and spread in the transformation of Oman that is most striking, particularly to those who knew, or even had knowledge of, the country in the time of Said bin Taimur. Perhaps the extent of its backwardness then and the degree to which infrastructure was absent were in a perverse way helpful to the process of change. It was not a question of reconstruction because there was nothing to knock down. Sultan Qaboos had a clean slate from which to construct the new Oman.

Part Two

Behind the Scenes: The
Creation of Oman, 1970–90

Part Two
Behind the Scenes: the Creation of Oman, 1970–90

FIRST THINGS FIRST, 1970–75

Background

This book is concerned with Oman and its development under Sultan Qaboos. A brief look at pre-1970 Oman may, however, be helpful for those who are ignorant of, or have forgotten, the circumstances in which Qaboos found himself when he took over the country on 23 July 1970.[1]

There were four determinants of pre-1970 Oman – the deep differences between coastal Muscat and interior Oman, the promise of oil discovery, the restrictive nature of Said bin Taimur's rule and the British connection.

The division between coast and interior had tribal, religious and psychological elements. Interior Oman was an enclosed and secretive area, mountainous and difficult of access. Its inhabitants belonged to a particular Islamic sect, the Ibadhis. There was a fundamental tribal schism between Hinawis and Ghafiris but both would combine against external influences. It was an area of fundamental tribal and religious loyalties that were based on generations of historical tradition. Coastal Oman was more relaxed and outward-looking. Its inhabitants were a mixture of indigenous farmers and sailors who had been infiltrated over the years by merchants from Iran, Pakistan and India, who gradually became indigenised themselves. Most belonged either to Sunni or Shia sects of Islam rather than Ibadhi.

Tensions between the coast and interior grew under the Al Said dynasty, whose ambitions were commercial and external and whose Sultans were little involved in the religious traditions of the interior. Latent divisions and differences were exacerbated by increasing ignorance of and disinterest in the attitudes and positions of each other. When in the late 1800s and early 1900s the Sultans in Muscat were fatally weakened by changes in international trade and politics they were saved only by British intervention but at the cost of the effective insulation of the interior from Muscat and the coast. The seeds were sown for what turned into civil war in the 1950s.

The British connection with Muscat began early. It grew out of the great imperial and commercial expansion of British interests in the eighteenth and nineteenth centuries and was closely linked to the development of the East India Company. Britain's first treaty with Oman was in 1798. For obvious commercial and practical reasons the official British connection was with the Sultan in Muscat who, when threatened from the interior, could count on British support. It is, however, important to remember that throughout the period of British hegemony in the Gulf and Indian Ocean Oman was independent. It was linked by treaty, often depended on British help and was subject to advice, but it was never colonised or otherwise controlled by British direct rule.

The lure of oil and the wealth that went with it became the catalyst for the explosive situation that developed in the 1950s. Saudi Arabian claims over wide expanses of desert, of which the Buraimi claim was the most notable, were based on all sorts of dubious tribal and border agreements but were promoted largely in the interests of oil. In Oman some of the leading tribal sheikhs of the interior saw an opportunity to obtain the assumed oil wealth for themselves by carrying out a sort of Ibadhi Unilateral Declaration of Independence, in which the Imam, Sheikh Suleiman bin Himyar, Sheikh Talib bin Ali and others, supported by the Saudis, would control the concessionary area, which had long since been granted by the Sultan to Petroleum Development Oman (then a subsidiary of the Iraq Petroleum Company). The war that ensued was, by the standards of the twentieth century, a G.A. Henty-type diversion, but its political ramifications directly affected Qaboos in 1970. The war was won by the Sultan only because of the assistance given him by the British whose moral obligation was directly descended from its eighteenth-century links to the Sultan but whose practical interest was to ensure a friendly and independent state in the South East corner of Arabia where, with luck, oil might be found by a company that was not Aramco of Saudi Arabia. As far as the rest of the Arab and LDC world was concerned Britain was up to its colonial tricks again. It would have to defend itself and Oman annually in the United Nations until 1971 and Qaboos, when he became Sultan, would have to overcome the suspicions of his fellow Arab rulers.

By 1959 the Imamate rebellion was, for all practical purposes, over, although minor incidents occurred for the next few years. Said bin Taimur was theoretically in control of a country that was more united than it ever had been. The oil company started a proper programme of work. Said bin Taimur, however, was not the ruler for the times. He was unimaginative, rigid, cautious and miserly. He had inherited a country in debt and, as a Victorian paterfamilias, he operated on the principle that, having overcome debt, he would never allow himself or his country to become indebted again, either in respect of money or any other obligations. The result was that, in terms of Omani internal policy, he trusted nobody, took all decisions and worked on the basis of restriction and constraint. In his dealings with the British, on whom he still relied for military and other support, he was meticulous in paying for what he purchased but was obdurate when he was advised to do what he himself considered unnecessary. Most of this advice related to the lifting of restrictions and to development. His argument that he could not afford to embark on such programmes became increasingly invalid as oil was discovered and, in 1967, began to be exported.

Said bin Taimur's regime was attacked on two main grounds in the 1960s. The first was his inability to administer a country in a remotely modern manner. The second was his dependence on external, that meant British, advisers and military support. Dhofar became a fertile ground for subversion. Economic dissatisfaction was used by neighbouring South Yemen to stir up political opposition. Nationalist, communist, anti-colonialist subversion began and was increasingly successful. Said bin Taimur's reaction was to clamp down further, but for military responses he was ultimately dependent upon – even though he paid them – the British.

In the end it was the interest both of the Omanis and the British that Said bin Taimur be replaced by someone with greater imagination, tolerance and respect for his people.

Qaboos Takes Over

On 23 July 1970 Said bin Taimur was deposed and signed a document of abdication in favour of his son. Qaboos bin Said inherited from his father a ramshackle country. Even the coup was a somewhat ramshackle affair. Nevertheless it was effective. Said bin Taimur was flown to London and died there in 1972, still lodged in a suite in the Dorchester hotel into which he was booked on arrival from Salala.[2]

Sultan Qaboos took over just in time. Even a few months' more of delay and there might have been no country to inherit. This may seem to over-dramatise the situation but there is solid reason for the proposition.

The threat to Oman came from two directions. The more immediately important was the military threat in Dhofar, the other was the reactionary attitude of Said bin Taimur to civil development in any part of the country. Said bin Taimur was blinkered, autocratic and had complete confidence in the principles and methods that had guided him for 38 years, but what had been virtues in the 1930s or 1940s had parted company with the realities of the 1960s.

There had for some time been revolutionary murmurs. Most ambitious Omanis had to leave the country to obtain education and jobs elsewhere. Many had gone to Kuwait, to Iraq, to Egypt and even to Russia, where university places were available to those who were prepared to learn Russian and tolerate the environment. In the 1960s there were active and passionate centres that preached, and in some cases practised, Arab nationalism, unity, socialism and many forms of anti-status quo. It was inevitable that Omanis, for all practical purposes banished from their country, should participate in activities and involvements that looked towards change and progress in their country. Effective change had to include the removal of Said bin Taimur whose inability to change himself was the point of departure for all debate on the future of Oman.

There was, therefore, plenty of potential opposition to Said bin Taimur and the regime that he directed. Most of it, however, was unorganised and disparate. Nor was it, in most cases, revolutionary in an ideological or belligerent sense. Expatriate Omanis did not, for the most part, want to shoot people or set up peoples' courts in which to commit them to trial. They just wanted to be able to return to their country and lead their own lives without the petty and pseudo-moralistic restrictions imposed by Said bin Taimur. Most of them were not, in truth, revolutionary material. Nor did they have a leader.

The nearest thing to a leader was Sayyid Tarik bin Taimur, the Sultan's brother. He left Oman in 1960, dissatisfied with the way in which the country was being governed. Throughout the 1960s his name cropped up as a potential alternative to Said bin Taimur. This was partly because he had a family legitimacy for the job, partly because his intellectual inclinations were directed towards change, partly because he had proved his point by leaving Oman. A CIA report[3] claimed that he was declared persona non grata by Sheikh Shakhbut of Abu Dhabi in 1966 for making proposals to overthrow Said bin Taimur. This report also claimed that at the same time a constitution was drawn up for Oman and a government in exile formed. Nevertheless, Tarik was no more a real revolutionary than most of his compatriots. He was not single-minded enough, nor did he work hard enough at the details of organisation. In spite of all this, and because of his perception of the military situation in Dhofar, he was getting close to action by 1970. If Qaboos had not taken the initiative Tarik, if it had not by then been too late, might have been himself galvanised into action.

The situation in Dhofar was the key to the coup. The Dhofar war had begun in a somewhat desultory fashion after the First Congress of the Dhofar Liberation Front (DLF) which took place in 1965.[4] The DLF was at first a local expression of, mainly, Nasserite nationalism, but later became increasingly ideologically motivated as the People's Democratic Republic of the Yemen (PDRY), created out of the ashes of British Aden, brought its influence to bear.[5] The political backwardness and economic stultification that grew from the policies of Said bin Taimur were a suitable trigger for spreading the appeal of the DLF. The more nationalistic Arab movements participated and supported DLF objectives, which gradually expanded and exploded, in 1968, into a far more ideological and revolutionary organisation, the Popular Front for the Liberation of the Occupied Arab Gulf (PFLOAG).[6] PFLOAG in effect took over the DLF, reformulating its objectives in strictly Marxist-Leninist terms and propagating a regime of 'scientific socialism'.

The PDRY was its home base; China stepped in to give material support in addition to that which came from Iraq and other nationalist revolutionary cells or organisations around the Arab world. PFLOAG, and more specifically its military arm, The Peoples Liberation Army (PLA), ruthlessly took over the tribal elements of DLF, squeezed them into an ideological mould and started campaigning in earnest. PLA was comparatively well equipped, demanded subservience and had clear objectives. Said bin Taimur had a small force with sparse equipment, tribes whose allegiance had been weakened through neglect and no long-term strategy. His only asset was a treaty with Britain under which he might expect military assistance but which was under strain because of his refusal to develop social and infrastructural services for his country.

By early 1970 the situation had become bleak. The Sultan's forces had only intermittent occupation of parts of the Jebal and Salala was fast becoming beleaguered. An RAF-administered airstrip was the only safe way in or out of Salala. Three things happened in the first half of 1970 that in practice sealed the fate of Said bin Taimur.

In early 1970 Brigadier John Graham arrived in Muscat to command SAF. At his first interview with Said bin Taimur he was told that the Dhofaris were evil and dangerous and must be destroyed.[7] The received opinion in SAF was that the war could only be won by force. But, even if this were true, SAF did not have the force to do it and could obtain it only from Britain. It was immediately apparent to Graham that without a change of heart and strategy Dhofar was doomed. Qaboos strongly shared this opinion and considered his father's attitude reactionary and destructive.

In March, Lieutenant Colonel Johnny Watts was asked to visit Dhofar to report on the situation. Watts had been in Oman in 1959 and had led the SAS-organised assault up the Jebal Akhdar that effectively finished the Imamate rebellion of the 1950s. By now he was Commander 22 SAS Regiment. His report was the basis of the five-point strategy that was subsequently used to win the war. The five points were: Intelligence, Medical services, Information ('Psy-ops' in the unattractive military jargon), Veterinary services, Military Operations. In other words, this was a proposal for a hearts and minds campaign similar to those that the SAS had developed in their experiences elsewhere, but adapted to Dhofar. The final report was accepted both by the military and the Foreign Office[8] as the basis on which they would propose further UK government support for the Sultan. When presented with the proposals Said bin Taimur turned them down as being inappropriate and unacceptable.

On 12 June, there was a weekend night attack on the SAF camp at Izki. Largely by luck, which included the presence of a British officer on duty, the attack was beaten off. The attackers were cleverly tracked to their own camp and in turn themselves attacked by the SAF tracking group, who took several prisoners. It was then discovered that the attackers belonged to a PFLOAG-linked organisation called NDFLOAG (National Democratic Front for the Liberation of Oman and the Arab Gulf). Cells of this group, together with ammunition and Chinese weapons, were found in Muttrah, Sur and Mutti. Here, then, was evidence of the extent to which PFLOAG was actively moving into Oman proper. A second front could have been disastrous, since SAF was already over-extended in Dhofar. In fact it seems that NDFLOAG was still not properly coordinated with PFLOAG and, more importantly that the Izki cell of NDFLOAG was not synchronised with its colleagues. The main result of the attack was to alert both SAF in Oman, Qaboos in Dhofar and the UK Foreign Office to the fact that the danger to the country was both more widespread and more imminent than had been suspected.

These were the three triggers that persuaded Qaboos and his friends that the time for action had arrived. Their execution of the coup was not particularly tidy. Reports from Kuwait were published in London (*The Times* and *Telegraph*) and Paris (*Le Monde*) on 18 June that Said bin Taimur might abdicate; Le Monde added that Tarik would be prime minister. Later there would be rumours that the coup had, indeed, been postponed. Perhaps this was post-facto rationalisation. Perhaps the 18 June reports were guesswork. Probably Said bin Taimur was anyway unaware of them. At any rate on 23 July, finally, the deed was done and, in the expressive phraseology of *Le Monde* 'Le Sultan de Mascate et Oman est destitué par son fils'.

Sultan Qaboos was only partially prepared for his new job. In 1958 he had been sent to England by his father to complete his education. First he went to a private tutor, then to Sandhurst. After passing out from Sandhurst he spent time with the Cameronian Regiment in regimental duties and a spell working in local government. During this period he also travelled round the world. All this was admirable training and background for an incipient Sultan. He returned to Salala in 1964 ready to participate in affairs of state. At this stage, however, progress was arrested when his father declined to let him do anything other than study Islam and Omani history and customs. He became a virtual prisoner in a small house[9] near his father's palace. Literally, he was unable to take any initiative or leave the palace grounds without his father's permission. A few visitors and the officials of the palace could meet him but even these meetings had an unhealthily furtive air about them. His direct knowledge of Oman and the people in the country who might be important to him was limited to those few who visited Salala and made the effort to meet him, although he learned at second hand as much as he could about the tribes and personalities of Oman. He had never visited Muscat. So, although Qaboos had had time in plenty to think about the things that he might like to do for Oman he had no practical experience of Omani management or government whatsoever.

The coup took place on 23 July. It was publicly announced on 26 July.[10] The delay was cautionary; it enabled Qaboos to be sure that his father was out of the area and that Tarik could be alerted to the success of the operation.

On 29 July Qaboos was officially recognised as Ruler by the British government, which, through some arcane reasoning or by chance, simultaneously recognised the government of the Yemen Arab Republic. On 30 July Sultan Qaboos flew to Muscat. It was the first time since 1958 that the people of Muscat had seen their ruler. Their elation was greatly enhanced by the realisation that no longer would they have to tolerate Said bin Taimur as absentee landlord, and they unrestrainedly showed their pleasure. Qaboos arrived at Beit al Falaj airport; someone had found an antique limousine that belonged to the palace; he drove to the old palace on the Muscat seafront, but soon took up temporary residence in the rather better equipped house that had been built for his father's adviser, Major Chauncy. This was the first time that Qaboos had seen Muscat and the forts of Merani and Jalali standing guard to right and left of his palace.[11]

The next day Qaboos gave his first press conference as Sultan. It was also the first press conference ever given by a Sultan of Oman. He said that a government would be formed and that he would wrest the country 'out of the days of darkness'.[12] Two days later Sayyid Tarik arrived in Muscat from Dubai to take up his expected appointment as Prime Minister.[13] Tarik had never met Qaboos who to him was a 'blank page'.[14] Qaboos knew of Tarik only as a potential alternative deposer of his father with an ill-defined reputation for supporting some form of constitutional government. Tarik recognised Qaboos as the legitimate Sultan and ruler, Qaboos needed Tarik's support and realised that this implied his appointment as Prime Minister. That was the situation on 2 August. On 3 August Qaboos left Muscat for Nizwa and the Interior to present himself to his people and be formally acknowledged by them as Sultan. He returned to Muscat and gave a broadcast on 9 August in which he made a series of policy announcements, including the appointment of Sayyid Tarik as Prime Minister. Tarik forthwith appointed 4 ministers and left the country to attend to his business abroad. He returned to Muscat on 7 September whereupon Qaboos departed to Salala for a month.

The sequence of dates is relevant in terms of the relationship between Qaboos and Tarik. It is apparent that they had virtually no opportunity between 23 July and mid-October to hold any discussion about the future of the country, about the nature of government, about the prosecution of the war or even about the definition of their own roles in any of these things. They hardly even saw each other even though they had never met before the coup. This stand-off seems to have been the result of differences in character, upbringing and temperament which proved to be unassimilable.

Tarik was easy-going and gregarious. As an exile he dabbled in nationalist politics with a variety of other Omani exiles while at the same time he pursued his own rather ill-defined affairs. He was not greatly interested in politics but his own lifestyle, and the example of autocracy offered by his brother, turned him into a constitutionalist of sorts. At the same time he had a strong sense of family tradition and rank. He was no organiser or administrator but, with a strong civil service backup and a cabinet of practical colleagues, he might have been an effective, if amateur, prime minister.

Qaboos was the opposite in almost every respect. He was stiff, formal and shy, at the same time unsure of himself but extremely sensitive to his position and the traditions of that position. Since he knew little of Muscat's political substructure he depended on and was loyal to those he did know, those who had been in Dhofar or who had visited Salala.

Qaboos needed Tarik but was nervous of him and had no real idea to what extent he could trust him. Tarik deferred to Qaboos as Sultan but was unable to create any business relationship with him. If there had been some catalyst to bring them together it is not inconceivable that they might have worked effectively together, but there was no catalyst. Down the line people were beholden either to Qaboos or to Tarik. No-one felt able or dared to bridge the gap. Given the peculiar circumstances of Oman in 1970 perhaps it should have been the business of the British Consul General[15] to have tried to do this. The British authorities, however, having helped

Qaboos to take over the country henceforward deferred to him as a ruler who, by some innate instinct or some process of osmosis, was assumed to have developed overnight presidential wisdom and virtue.

The inability of Qaboos and Tarik to work together was not, as it might have been, destructive but it created a degree of disorder bordering on chaos in decisions that concerned the structure of government, appointments and economic development. There were, fortunately for subsequent Omani development, two areas untouched by this particular disorder, the prosecution of the war in Dhofar and the operations of the oil company, Petroleum Development Oman (PDO). This was because Qaboos explicitly reserved these matters to himself. PDO was the sole source of revenue to the country and success in the war was crucial to the continued existence of Oman.

The Dhofar War[16]

Said bin Taimur handed over a country called Muscat and Oman and Dhofar, although 'and Dhofar' was seldom appended to Muscat and Oman. Qaboos was determined to create a properly unified country. This was symbolised by his decision, announced in a broadcast on 9 August, that the country was henceforth to be known as The Sultanate of Oman. He could announce it easily enough but the fact remained that Dhofar was still detached from the rest of the country and was in danger of being overcome in war by the PLA and PDRY.

On his accession Qaboos was faced with two distinct problems. One was the war, the other the social and economic development of the country. In practice this prolonged the split status of the country. It is impossible to exaggerate the situation. In the North – i.e. Muscat and Oman – the war was a distant and unknown consumer of revenues, there were no bulletins as to its course,[17] no discussion of its implications, no real comprehension as to what it was or why it was important. It was ignored. In the South – i.e. Dhofar – there was knowledge of nothing except the war, its progress and its implications for Dhofar; the North was remote and impersonal, consuming monies that might be better used in Dhofar. The North was interested only in the creation of government, business and wealth, the South only in the winning of the war and the economic development that would come with it.

So, whatever Qaboos wanted in theory, in practice he found himself a split personality within a split country; one half was Commmander in Chief of the armed forces waging war to save an existing country, the other half was Head of State trying to develop a new country. So different were the two activities that we can legitimately look at them, in the first few years of his reign, under quite separate headings.

The story of the Dhofar war is well documented, but often from a subjective point of view – whether from that of a British officer or the commentary of the SAF museum in Beit al Falaj. This is not a military history but the winning of the war was, as already indicated, integral to the continuing existence of the country and to the creation of a new Sultanate of Oman. The way in which it was won, therefore, is an important component of the development of Oman from 1970.

Strategy and tactics changed immediately Qaboos took over the country. His first decision was to offer an amnesty to all Dhofaris who wanted to return or switch to the Omani side. This was a complete reversal of the Said bin Taimur strategy of forcible suppression and conquest. No greater symbol of change could have been offered to the tribes and it was the key to all that followed. In August the first 200 Dhofaris came over under the terms of this amnesty, a potent message to the PLA that their objective of breaking down tribal allegiances was not working.

Qaboos' second decision was to seek further assistance from Britain on the basis of the report prepared by Watts earlier in the year. This implied direct support for a hearts and minds offensive as part of military operations. In practice it meant that a variety of experts, spearheaded by SAS (Special Air Service) officers and soldiers, would be provided to assist SAF under the umbrella of what was named a British Army Training Team (BATT). The terminology was important in terms of possible external repercussions since for Oman the UN was still pursuing its British connection in the Committee on Colonialism and for Britain any operational activity by SAS was always liable to political and journalistic publicity. The fact is that BATT, and within it SAS, managed to keep such a low profile that for two years there was practically no reporting of the Dhofar war in the foreign press (and none at all in Oman). However retrograde this might have been in terms of transparency it was undoubtedly helpful to the Omani war effort.

BATT was arguably one of the most positive and productive military support groups ever provided by Britain. The first contingent consisted of only 19 men and there were never more than 90. It was not the numbers that counted but their skills, leadership, resilience and adaptability. BATT did not win the war, but without BATT the first stage of the war would not have been completed so decisively or quickly.

BATT was primarily responsible for two aspects of strategy which in Dhofar were novel and created the foundations of success. One was the establishment and training of the Firqats, the other the introduction of Civil Aid Teams (CATs).

Firqats were independent military units raised from the Dhofari tribes, the Jebalis, many of them from amongst those who had previously fought with DLF and/or PLA against SAF and Said bin Taimur. Now they were to fight with SAF and Qaboos against PLA. The switch in allegiance was not difficult for them. They were fighting primarily for their tribe and their allegiance was measured by self-interest. Under Said bin Taimur there had been apparent advantage in joining DLF. When DLF turned into PFLOAG/PLA the advantage was greatly diminished, but since Said bin Taimur counted them as traitors there was no alternative to PLA. Qaboos provided an alternative and the Firqat concept gave them the opportunity to fight back to recover what they had lost under PFLOAG. Nevertheless, as can be imagined, there were many problems of re-integration for both the Firqats and for SAF. Neither trusted the other. SAF had been trained to fight the Jebalis as dissident revolutionaries. The Jebali viewed SAF as an imposed non-Dhofari army of occupation. Moreover, in agreeing to become a fighting Firqat, many Jebalis found themselves fighting against their own kinsmen who were still with PLA. The war was known by many as the War of the Families and this was no misnomer. BATT had psychological as well as military training problems to overcome.

Many of the first 200 Jebalis to take up the amnesty offer in August were the core of the first Firqat to be established. This was called Salah al Din and its fate was a lesson for BATT. Salah al Din was composed of men from a number of different tribes. Its training and first actions were successful. Then, however, it disintegrated into recrimination and mutiny. It became clear that so intensely tribal was the nature of the Jebali character that in practice they would not, except in particular instances of mutual self-interest, fight together for an indirect common interest. BATT quickly changed its tactics and began to recruit new Firqats on a tribal basis. As SAS commentators would subsequently say: you had to win the minds of Jebalis, and forget about their hearts.

CATs, the Civil Aid Teams, grew out of the activities of BATT – muddling though this may be in terms of acronyms. BATT functioned on the basis of the five points of the Watts report. On the ground they operated both in an overall HQ advisory capacity and in sub-groups in the field. Their objectives were in both cases the same; first, to improve the flow of military intelligence which, with the ejection of SAF from the Jebal, had largely dried up. Secondly, to give information to the Dhofaris about the new direction of Omani policies and the course of the war; this was done mostly by word of mouth, leaflets and, increasingly, by radio broadcast. Thirdly, to provide medical attention, both on a basic level in the field, and by providing better hospital facilities centrally. Fourthly, to provide veterinary assistance directed towards the chief asset of the Jebalis, their cows; this included the drilling of water wells and storage. Lastly, to improve the military capability of SAF by the training of the Firqats and by other means as required. SAS personnel had practised this type of activity in many parts of the world, most recently in Borneo, and possessed skills that would not have occurred to ordinary line regimental soldiers. Indeed, SAS units had many similarities to the Firqats they were training; they were very much at home in the environment of Dhofar.

CATs evolved from the activities of BATT. They would be installed in the towns and villages of the plain, and later of the Jebal, as a cross between civil government and military liaison. Typically they would consist of an administrator, a schoolmaster, a medical orderly and a shopkeeper. They would be installed once the location had been made relatively secure by military patrolling, the provision of an access route and of water. BATT would keep their lines open to the CAT and in due course a Firqat might be introduced for garrison purposes. By the end of 1970 CATs were established down the coast from Salala in Taqa and Mirbat and at the end of February 1971 a CAT was set up in Sudh after it had been taken over in a joint BATT/Firqat operation. At the end of 1971, as the war successfully progressed for Oman, CATs gave way to a Civil Aid Development (CAD) programme under the Dhofar Development Committee. This was, however, simply a more sophisticated exercise of the CAT principle, with the construction of schools, clinics, roads and housing. The principle proved itself in practice.

There is no doubt that SAS was the inspiration as well as the trigger for the success of BATT and CATs. They were also a strong influence behind the more general SAF strategy towards the war in these early days of Qaboos. The SAS officers who arrived in Salala in 1970 had one overriding impression. SAF morale was poor, which was hardly surprising in the circumstances, but it was, in particular, oppressed by the Jebal. Over the past few years SAF had gradually been dislodged from the Jebal and were now cooped up in Salala. The Jebal lowered over them. It was full of the enemy (the Adoo[18] in army terminology), but even those who were not Adoo were unsympathetic and alien. Moreover, for three months every year the monsoon blotted out the Jebal, and who knew what was being engineered up there during those months. This psychological weight, referred to as Jebalitis but which, more correctly, should have been termed Jebalphobia, hung over the soldiers, none of whom were Dhofaris and for whom Dhofar was a remote and unfriendly land. They did not think that they had joined SAF for this. Even SAF officers, many of whom were expatriate, were affected by the Jebal and by the general malaise of depression that it created in Salala.

SAS, led by Watts, knew all about Jebalitis. SAF had been afflicted by it, in different degree, during the 1950s when Ghalib, Talib and Suleiman bin Himyar retreated to the Jebal Akhdar and were deemed to be impregnably lodged there – peering down at SAF encamped in Izki and Nizwa. Major Watts, as a squadron commander, had stormed up the Jebal Akhdar in 1959. Now, as Lieutenant Colonel and commander of 22 SAS Regiment, he saw the need to repeat the performance in Dhofar. The psychological requirement for SAF was not only to return to the Jebal, but to stay there on a permanent basis, through monsoon and all.

Operation Jaguar achieved this in October at the end of the 1971 monsoon. Watts led 2 squadrons of SAS down to the Wadi Darbat[19] from Jibjat and thence to what SAF called White City and which is now Medinat al Haqq.[20] With him went two companies of the Muscat Regiment, one company from the newly formed Jebal Regiment, 300 men from Firqats, units from the Baluch Guard Regiment and some artillery. Military units never subsequently left Medinat al Haqq. They remained there during the 1972 monsoon in small numbers; during the 1973 monsoon and thereafter they were there in force. Jebalitis was cured.

Two symbolic acts took place in the aftermath of Operation Jaguar. Sultan Qaboos went up there and ceremonially opened a shop in Medinat al Haqq and a herd of 500 cattle was driven across the Jebal and down to Salala. Things were getting back to normal. Jaguar was the end of the first part of phase one of the war since July 1970. BATT activities, the establishment of CATs, the capture of Sudh and now Operation Jaguar provided sufficient evidence that Qaboos and SAF were on the offensive and could win the war. But the war was by no means won yet.

The second part of phase one lasted from end-1971 until September 1972 when General Creasey arrived to take over as Commander of SAF (CSAF). In this period two important actions took place. The first was Operation Simba in April 1972 which captured Sarfait. Sarfait was way out to the West close to the PDRY border and a PLA stronghold on their supply line into Dhofar. Its capture was politically symbolic and important but, far from Salala and base, it was militarily at risk since it could only be supplied by air. Nevertheless it was a blow to the PLA, a representative of which would later say that even though they could get supplies past the position it stopped free movement. 'It was like having someone's hand round your throat.'[21]

The second action was a daring and nearly successful operation by the

PLA to retake the offensive and capture Mirbat. The attack, on a large scale and well designed, took place on 19 July 1972. It was in the middle of the monsoon period and, therefore, unexpected. Fortunately for the garrison it was delayed, through tribal bickering and inability to keep to a precise time schedule, until after dawn. The alarm was, therefore, given. Nevertheless it was a close thing. The garrison showed exceptional bravery, for which they would later be rewarded with an array of medals, and by good fortune reinforcements were nearby in the shape of a relief unit. The balance was finally and conclusively tipped by a particularly daring support attack by 3 Strikemaster aircraft of SOAF which were piloted through the monsoon mist and rain at near ground level.

The Defence of Mirbat has entered SAF and SAS lore. It was commemmorated in a painting by David Shepherd, a copy of which hangs in the SSF (Sultan's Special Force) mess at Zeak. An Omani version of this painting, with any suggestion of expatriate involvement deleted, has a place of honour in the SAF museum at Beit al Falaj and a commentary that says: 'The battle of Mirbat is considered to be one of the decisive battles in the Southern region and paved the way for the elimination of the rebels.' It was, indeed, decisive, in the sense that the PLA was never again in a position to launch a major attack on SAF. The successful capture of Mirbat would have had a tremendous psychological effect; militarily it would have boosted PLA and depressed SAF morale, politically it would have greatly assisted PFLOAG[22] and PDRY and embarrassed Oman regionally and internationally. As it was, the PLA was discouraged and SAF felt that its new confidence was not misplaced.

The first phase of the war was, in effect, over. The second was a long slog to turn the tactical successes of 1970–72 into a completed strategic defeat of the PLA. It required different concepts of organisation, resources, planning and political coordination. In many respects the first phase, although there was a clear design, was nevertheless small-scale, local, inventive, even ad hoc. The second phase had to build a superstructure on foundations that were still, in military terms, slender. Medinat al Haqq provided a springboard on the Jebal; Sarfait was a political plus but a military minus; morale, both civilian and military, had been transformed. All this was the necessary prelude to the second stage which was signalled by the arrival, in September 1972, of a new CSAF, Major General Timothy Creasey, to replace Brigadier John Graham whose tour of duty had been so historic.

The upgrading of CSAF from Brigadier to Major General was part of Sultan Qaboos' design for this next stage of the campaign. Creasey looked around and made some quick assessments. He needed more resources and a new organisation structure. He reorganised SAF for the new requirements that would be imposed upon it. He created an Oman Brigade for the North and a Dhofar Brigade, under Brigadier Jack Fletcher, for the South; he created an HQ for the Firqats; he added two battalions to the Dhofar brigade by upgrading the Baluch Guard into the Frontier Force and the Dhofar Gendarmerie into the Southern Regiment; he strengthened the HQs of the two new Brigades; he also strengthened the support regiments of artillery, engineers and intelligence. This must have made SAF feel more like an army – 'When I arrived,' said Creasey, 'I had 4 battalions and the Oman Gendarmerie in the North and two low grade small forces in the South.'[23]

The next change that Creasey introduced was to the political control of SAF. 'On arrival I found a Defence Secretary who thought I was under his command and who controlled the budget and defence equipment programme.'[24] He suggested to the Sultan a National Defence Council which would, at least in theory, provide the political backbone to the development of policy. A decree promulgating the new Council was issued in March 1973 and its first meeting was on 9 May. Sultan Qaboos was Chairman and the members were the Deputy Defence Minister (Sayyid Fahr bin Taimur), the Minister of State for Foreign Affairs (Sayyid Fahd bin Mahmud), CSAF (General Creasey), the Economic Adviser (John Townsend), the Director of Intelligence (Colonel Dennison) and the Commissioner of Police (Felix D'Silva), with Colonel Tim Landon (Equerry to Sultan Qaboos) as Secretary.[25] Simultaneously with this reorganisation, Brigadier Hugh Oldman, who had been Defence Secretary since 1969, was retired.

The most immediately important result of the Council's establishment was a clear statement of policy announced by Qaboos. This included the defence and security of the coastal plain; the maintenance of Sarfait as an advanced frontier position; the intention to continue operations on the Jebal; and priority to be given to civil development on the Jebal. This provided Creasey with a clear mandate for phase two of the war. Creasey also turned his attention to equipment. On a mundane level he improved the quality of boots issued to the soldiers. More importantly in a long-term sense he upgraded the engineering capacity of SAF by setting up a new Engineering Services Regiment with technical assistance provided by Britain and by Jordan. He also added to the Artillery capability.

In surveying the scene on his arrival and describing the specific advantages that SAF had over the PLA he picked out for special mention SOAF and the medical support enjoyed by SAF in Dhofar. SAF had airpower, PLA did not. The Strikemasters, Skyvans and helicopters of SOAF provided a strike and transport capability that in the environment of Dhofar was invaluable. We have seen how the Strikemasters had saved the situation at Mirbat. Not only did SAF have the aircraft in support but the pilots (at this stage all expatriate) were of the highest quality and dedication.

So, Creasey had no reason to be despondent. He had been dealt a good hand by his predecessor and he now had positive political support for the next stage. He was also fortunate in having money available at the critical moment, for oil prices, rising fast during the whole of 1973, quadrupled by the end of the year as a result of oil market developments, the Arab embargo following the Suez war of October and the activities of Opec.

Nevertheless, he still had a problem. To win the war in Dhofar required more resources in men and equipment than Oman and SAF could on their own provide. Furthermore, the war was seen by Qaboos not only as a fight for Omani survival but also as part of the wider struggle against Communism and for the preservation of Arab societies. If the first phase of the war had been primarily aimed at the survival of Oman, the second phase could be legitimately argued as being also in the general interest of any Arab regime that was concerned by the revolutionary social and political aspirations of PDRY and its allies. Qaboos, therefore, sought to internationalise the war, at least to the extent of seeking direct outside assistance.

Britain was already the primary source of support. SAF benefited from Britain not only as a willing supplier of military material but also of a large number of seconded British officers (to which could be added an even larger number of contract officers); General Creasey was, of course, the senior example of this flow. In addition Britain had provided, as we have seen, BATT with its large core of SAS, together with other technical support staff. Britain was not, however, prepared to participate directly by sending army units to engage in battle. Nor, when it came to the point, were any of the Arab states prepared to provide material support to Qaboos, although both Saudi Arabia and the UAE had given limited financial assistance and Egypt was supportive at a political level. Although Oman was by this stage safely a member of the Arab League and of the United Nations, countries such as Saudi Arabia had not wholly thrown off their doubts concerning Oman and they were constrained by their uncertainty both as to the outcome of the war and of the repercussions that might be aroused amongst the more militant of their Arab colleagues, in particular Iraq which still overtly supported PDRY.

Qaboos obtained the help he needed from Iran, and later from Jordan. In early 1973 the Shah provided Qaboos with nine Bell 205 helicopters which solved the problem of supplying Sarfait; without this additional capacity the continued effort to maintain the Sarfait garrison would have severely affected other operations. Later in 1973, however, Qaboos initiated a direct approach to the Shah via Colonel Tim Landon, his equerry. The Shah reacted enthusiastically.[26] He saw the Dhofar war as an excellent opportunity to provide his own troops with battle training and experience; he was keen to make a positive move to improve his relations in the Arabian peninsula where his seizure, in 1971, of the Tunb islands had created an angry reaction; he was as anxious as anybody to prevent any Communist infiltration round the coast; and, no doubt, his sense of history gave him a proprietorial interest in Oman. The result was that in December 1973 1500 men of the Imperial Iranian Battle Group (IIBG) arrived in Oman.

Phase two of the war moved by distinct steps to its successful conclusion. At the end of December 1973 the Iranians opened up the Midway Road from Salala to Thumrait and for the next year were responsible for its defence. This provided land communication between Salala and Muscat for the first time for many years and transformed SAF transport possibilities. Simultaneously, British and Jordanian engineers were responsible for creating the Hornbeam line, a barbed wire defensive coil running 60 kms north from the coast at Mughsayl roughly parallel to the Midway Road and 50 kms to the West. Hornbeam was started on 4 December 1973 and, consisting of 15 000 coils of barbed wire, 12 000 reels of wire, 12 000 pickets and 4000 anti-personnel mines, was completed on 29 June 1974.[27] Its main purpose was to prevent PLA infiltration into the Eastern Jebal and allow civil development to take place there in comparative safety and normalcy.

The next step taken against the PLA was to create another barrier similar to Hornbeam. In October 1974 the IIBG returned to Iran and was replaced by a new unit, the Imperial Iranian Task Force. This was primarily responsible for an operation to capture Rakhyut, a small town on the coast about 40 kms West of Mughsayl, and to build from there the Demavend line which, when completed in June 1975, stretched North for about 30 kms.

In the meantime King Hussein had agreed to send Jordanian forces to assist in the war. In February 1975 the 91st Special Forces Battalion arrived and took over Thumrait and the defence of the Midway Road. On 20 April Hussein himself flew in to inspect the operation. At the end of the year he presented 31 Hunter aircraft to SOAF.

By this stage, at end-1974 and 1975, fighting was increasingly concentrated in the border area around Sarfait to which the PLA had been forced to retreat. In February 1975 Creasey finished his tour of duty and was replaced as CSAF by Major General Kenneth Perkins, to whom it was left to finish the war. The engagements in the far West of Dhofar were as bitter and difficult as any in the whole war and the SAS remained prominent in their success. On 4 December Brigadier John Akehurst, Commander of the Dhofar Brigade, issued a Special Force Routine Order:

At 1100 hrs on the second day of December 1975 the Frontier Force made physical contact with the Muscat Regiment on the Darra ridge. This is the first time since Operation Simba that ground troops have got through to the Sarfait battalion. It also represents the end of organised resistance by the so-called People's Liberation Army within Dhofar. His Majesty the Sultan was advised at 1200 hrs on the some day that Dhofar was secure for civil development.[28]

On 11 December Sultan Qaboos announced that the war was won. That day would henceforward be The Sultan's Armed Forces Day.

In reality, the war was not neatly terminated on December 2nd, 4th or 11th. A ceasefire was negotiated in the following March, but this implied no acknowledgement by PDRY, PFLOAG or PLA that they were beaten. Indeed, fighting continued on and off for years, as did the political onslaught on Qaboos' regime in Oman. SAS units remained in the country until September 1976, the Iranians until January 1979. The formal political end of the war should, perhaps, be measured from November 1982 when a normalisation agreement between Oman and PDRY was signed and from October 1983 when diplomatic relations were established. Nevertheless, December 1975 certainly signified the effective and psychological end to the war as a campaign and as the single focus of effort in the South. Dhofar was out of danger and the economic and political integration of Dhofar with Oman could begin.

The successful conclusion to the war was significant in a number of ways. The most obvious was, of course, that the threat to the Sultanate's existence had been removed. There were, however, more subtle results. Within the country, whether individuals liked it or not, it became accepted that Dhofar was indeed an integral part of the state. SAF earned credit for its achievements, so that there has been little resentment to this day that a large proportion of expenditure is annually devoted to the armed forces and security. Sultan Qaboos himself gained confidence from his personal identification with SAF and the war strategy; within the country he was recognised to have military expertise which was positively beneficial to him as ruler.

The most unexpected benefit of the war, however, was the status it gave to Oman externally. Under Said bin Taimur the country had been written off as a retrograde colonial irrelevance. Internationally it was a cypher. The war, together with the PFLOAG's threat, concentrated minds on Oman's potential strategic value.[29] The scale of the war began to impress Oman's neighbours. The support for the war given by Iran and Jordan caused Arab leaders to have second thoughts about Oman. Victory in the war gave Oman a voice in the Arabian Peninsula that could no longer be ignored as irrelevant. All this occurred simultaneously, of course, with quite different civil initiatives that were part of the process of Oman's acceptance as a genuine member of the Arab and Islamic community, but there can be no doubt that the experience of the war was a strong formative element in the rebirth of Oman as a country that could and should be taken seriously in the regional context. For instance, when the discussions about Gulf security developed in the later 1970s which ended with the formation of the Gulf Cooperation Council (GCC), Oman's opinions were influential and necessary to the debate in a way that would have been inconceivable a few years earlier and pre-1970 would not even have been sought.

The Dhofar war was a success in which many people participated. Nothing could have been achieved without the attitude, inspiration and leadership of Sultan Qaboos himself. Particularly in the early part of the war the part played by BATT was fundamental. SAF itself was transformed by the dedication and involvement of very many expatriate officers, both seconded and contract, of whom a large majority were British. SOAF, organised and led by mainly British personnel, played a crucial and daring part in both attack and supply. Iranian support was timely and effective besides giving a valuable numerical boost to the general SAF effort. The Jordanian contingent was equally supportive on a smaller scale. The part played by the Omanis themselves is self-evident, and the experience they gained in the war has since been displayed in the development and growth in sophistication of the Sultanate's Armed Forces.

The war was a notable effort of international cooperation and individual commitment. It is, therefore, all the more dispiriting that the current Omani version of the war has written out the role of non-Omani support. To say that this represents lack of confidence is hardly helpful. Perhaps it is only of any deep consequence to those who were personally involved and whose colleagues or relatives were killed or wounded (40 British officers and other ranks were killed in the campaign).[30] Perhaps it can be argued that the Omani psyche needs a reading of history that makes its reconstruction self-generated. In fact, this seems doubtful. Omanis may be proud, but they are realistic, open-minded and honest enough not to need this kind of distortion. It is to be hoped that the SAF museum, and even more the Omani history books, will one day be rearranged and rewritten to incorporate all these realities.

Developments in Muscat

It is difficult to overemphasise the general chaos of the period up to December 1971 when Tarik resigned as Prime Minister. As already described, there was no communication, let alone meeting of minds, between Qaboos and Tarik in matters of business. This was partly due to their being of different generations, partly because their experiences had been totally different, partly because the mystique of kingship lay between them. Socially they could be at ease together, but neither could deal with the other when it came to matters of governmental business. Between them there was an unbridgeable gulf of uncertainty and rank. This was not helped by the politicking and intrigues of both Omanis and expatriates, many of whom played one against the other in their effort to gain whatever advantage, material or organisational, they might be seeking. This meant that in practice those who felt themselves dependent on Qaboos made decisions in his name while those appointed by Tarik acted in his name. Since so much had to be done this was not necessarily disastrous but it led to inevitable wastage of time, temper and effort. Coordination was vestigial.

In Muscat, Hugh Oldman, the Defence Secretary, took it upon himself, once the coup had been announced, to organise a group to advise the new Sultan on what was happening and to carry out his instructions. This group became institutionalised in semi-formal fashion as an Interim Advisory Council, but its functions were vaguely defined and, once Tarik had been made prime minister and had himself appointed the first ministers, it quietly withered and vanished. It was necessary in the first instance to fill a void.

The Interim Advisory Council remains an elusive body in that there seems to have been no record of its proposals, decisions,[31] or even, membership. None of those who have admitted to membership can remember with any precision who their colleagues were; in some cases people who have been identified cannot remember that they were, or have denied being, members. The conclusion must be that indeed there was no precision and that, while there was a membership core,[32] others were asked to meetings on an ad hoc basis. Since the Council was dissolved, or dissolved itself, once Tarik was back in Oman in September, these details are anyway of little consequence. Its usefulness probably extended for no more than a few weeks, as a mechanism through which Qaboos could take some early advice and decisions on urgent matters.

One of the first decisions of Qaboos was to remove a number of the existing British expatriates who had been appointed by his father to carry out what under Said bin Taimur passed for government. This was easily done since they had all departed for their summer leave to Europe. Chauncy, Pelly, Hirst and Shebbeare duly received letters telling them that their services were no longer required.[33] Bill Heber-Percy who was Secretary of the Development Board and happened still to be in Muscat stayed on; and Robin Young, who had recently resigned as Director of Coordination in despair at his inability to do what he had been hired to do, was, in due course, reappointed and went to Salala as Director of Development for Dhofar. Philip Aldous, who had recently arrived on a temporary assignment as Financial Adviser, remained and was appointed Financial Secretary in December.

The broadcast speech by Qaboos on 9 August was the first public indication of what he intended for Oman, his first policy statement. There were three significant elements in this speech. The first was the announcement that the country would be known as the Sultanate of Oman, that Tarik was to be Prime Minister and that there was to be a new flag. This was one clear signal that the regime of Said bin Taimur was over – the symbolism of a new flag, the unity of Muscat, Oman and Dhofar and the delegation of power. The second element was the announcement of reforms and economic development which were what every Omani had been dreaming about for years. The third ingredient of his statement was the appeal to Omani exiles to return to Oman where they would be pardoned (in cases in which it might be necessary) and welcomed to participate in the expansion of the country. In his message Qaboos also expressed particular gratitude to King Feisal of Saudi Arabia, King Hussein of Jordan and Rulers in the Gulf for their good wishes, an indication of the importance he would be attaching to foreign relations.

In his speech Qaboos was specific about certain elements of economic change and development. He announced that SAF would move from its HQ in Beit al Falaj out to a new site at the junction of the Nizwa and Batina roads and that the civil airport would be re-sited at Azaiba. This would enable Muttrah to expand for commercial and residential purposes into the Beit al Falaj plain, and recognised the existing plans for greater Muttrah which had already been commissioned, but not acted upon, by Said bin Taimur. He also announced the immediate removal of some of the most irritating and negative restrictions, specifically those that limited the freedom to travel and to import and use agricultural machinery. He talked about roads and agriculture, health , education and telecommunications. Significantly, he warned about lack of water and promised a complete survey of water resources. Nor did he forget the tribes, for whose sheikhs he promised salaries.

This was a good and sufficient message for Oman in 1970. There was a special and warm reference to Tarik whose speed of return 'is greatly appreciated . . . . we have already established the vital fact that our views about the future of our country are very close indeed. We have instructed our Prime Minister to take immediate steps to form a government . . . ' Tarik appointed forthwith four ministers, of Health, Education, Interior and Justice; at the end of the year a Minister of Information, Social Services and Labour was added and soon after a Minister of Economy. Ministers were quick to create directorates and departments which gave a somewhat spurious air of bureaucratic efficiency to government. Many appointments, including some ministers, went to Omani exiles, who knew little about the country or the people in it.

Omani exiles were generally divisible into two kinds. There were those who had left Oman in the 1950s and 1960s and had found opportunities for education somewhere in the Arab world, usually Egypt, Kuwait or Iraq. Numbers are difficult to determine but figures of 12 000 Omanis in Bahrain, 14 000 in Kuwait and 50 000 in the Gulf area in the late 1960s have been suggested.[34] Some had gone to universities in the USSR, rather fewer to the UK or France. Many of them had, almost inevitably, been involved, at varying levels of complicity, in the anti-regime movements for which Tarik had been a focus in the 1960s. Tarik personally knew, or knew of, many of these people.

The other class were Omanis of Zanzibari descent. Many had fled from Zanzibar at the time of the 1964 revolution;[35] some had at that stage returned to Oman and to their original tribal areas, others, and usually those who were better educated, settled in East Africa or, perhaps, moved to Europe or the more Europeanised parts of the Middle East. Most of them were English-speaking, many of them knew no Arabic. Oman, although a far more remote homeland than for those who had actually left it, was suddenly transformed in 1970 from an unappealing backwater to an attractive alternative to wherever they had settled. Their education, abilities, and experience gave them an easy entry to a new and expanding job market.

The return of the exiles created a degree of resentment amongst resident Omanis, but this was tempered in two different ways. The first was that the resident Omanis tended to be more interested in commerce than in politics. There were widening possibilities for making money, since agencies and partnerships were, in a country that was starting from scratch, a licence for wealth. The second was that the merchant community of Muscat and

Muttrah was itself mostly non-indigenous, in the sense that its origins were Iran, Pakistan or India. To that extent they suffered, often unwittingly and indiscernibly, from that schizophrenia of assimilation – superiority in terms of perceived productivity, inferiority in terms of national legitimacy. The real indigenous Omanis of the interior, tribal and Ibadhi, were not prominent in Muscat – nor, for that matter, in Dhofar.

I have emphasised the difference of outlook between Qaboos and Tarik and the lack of real communication between them. Over the next 18 months the gulf between them in many ways widened, but in a perverse sense became less relevant. When Qaboos said in his broadcast that 'our views about the future of our country are very close indeed', this was an expression of hope or expectation, or simply an assumption, rather than the result of any discussion (for which, as has been described, there had not been any opportunity at that stage). In the weeks and months that followed there never was any discussion of objectives, of methods or of policy. Qaboos quickly arrogated to himself the portfolios of defence, finance and oil. Foreign Affairs was, as we shall see, shared between Qaboos and Tarik but with no great clarity as to where any dividing line resided. The rest was theoretically in the hands of Tarik as Prime Minister, although in practice Hugh Oldman, the Defence Secretary, involved himself in the attempt to coordinate and initiate development projects.

Tarik's ambition may well have been to be Minister of Defence, not Prime Minister. His earlier experience in Oman was with SAF. There he felt at home, but SAF and Defence were out of bounds for him. Even when Qaboos was absent from the country and he was technically acting Head of State he was excluded from SAF and the Dhofar war which were firmly in the hands of the Defence Secretary and Commander of SAF. His SAF experience, however, had not made him a manager or administrator. At heart he was an amateur who was out of his depth in the world of organisation, analysis and execution of programmes or ideas. He had no secretarial or administrative back-up, not because it was not available to him, but because he neither wanted nor asked for it.

As prime minister, therefore, he was not a success, nor as a constitutional reformer. He soon lost what urge he had ever had for systemic reform. This originally seems, however, to have been genuine enough. In an interview with Eric Rouleau[36] in May 1971 Tarik is quoted as saying: 'I am a democrat. Nothing beneficial will be accomplished in this country without a constitution and parliament' and again 'Fundamentally I am a socialist and republican. I believe that all monarchies are in the end condemned to disappear.' Although he admitted to ideological differences with Qaboos, in practice this did not seem to matter. Things happened in spite of the philosophical differences and lack of coordination between Tarik and Qaboos. His innate sense of family loyalty and propriety, together with his sociable and extrovert nature, gradually changed his relationship with Qaboos into one of rather remote and easy-going tolerance. The break with Qaboos occurred largely because of interference in his areas of responsibility, not through any personal distaste. Whatever he may have privately felt, Tarik never criticised Qaboos in public.

For all his failings Tarik was not a failure. In the first place the fact that he was there as prime minister, part of the new Omani system, was invaluable for Qaboos' image in the Gulf and the Arab world. Tarik's reputation, whether deserved or not, was such that, if he had not been there in Muscat, Qaboos' position would have been weakened and questioned. Secondly, the achievements of the government in the sphere of economic development, however detached from the direct influence and inspiration of Tarik, were, if not coordinated, at least obvious and measurable to Omanis. More positively, however, Tarik was directly influential and active in developing Oman's foreign relations.

Social investment that took place in the Tarik era was mostly in education and health where the priority was greatest. Clinics and primary schools were opened almost in competition. Precision is lacking but by end-1971 there were 20–30 new clinics and 10–15 new primary schools; 6 hospitals were being built, in Sur, Sumail, Nizwa, Sohar, Buraimi and Rustaq. Primary school students had grown from 900 to 7000 (of whom 1100 were girls), outpatient admissions from 24 000 to 56 000.[37] A free health service was announced.

Infrastructurally, there were three main developments, a road up the Batina to Sohar, the Port Qaboos project at Muttrah (foreseen under Said bin Taimur's development plans but never initiated) and the new international airport whose site was moved from Azaiba (as announced in the 9 August broadcast) up the coast to Seeb. In mid-1971 the Greater Muttrah Development Authority was set up. Building of offices and houses was widespread, land purchase and allocation quickly developed, as it always does, into a focus of influence and patronage and Sultan Qaboos' first palace was under construction in Seeb. Salesmen, contractors and contacts descended on Muscat; the carpet-baggers had arrived.

On the economic and social front, therefore, developments were much as could have been predicted or expected; there was not much planning, but plenty of execution. Foreign relations, on the other hand, required planning in order to achieve anything. Qaboos and Tarik, and in this their vision coincided, had the objective of integrating Oman into the mainstream of Arab and international affairs, of re-establishing it as an independent country with its own weight and influence. The first necessary steps were to join the Arab League and the United Nations.

Tarik made one appointment that influenced the course of events in Oman in a way that he could never have predicted and certainly would not have chosen. He took on as an adviser on foreign affairs Omer Barouni. Barouni had been a minister and diplomat under King Idris, but had left Libya for Beirut at the time of the Qaddafi coup. He was an expert on the history and practice of the Ibadhi religion and in this capacity got to know Tarik. His job was specifically to help in preparing Oman's application to join the Arab League. It was he who introduced Robert Anderson, Ghassan Shakir and Yahia Omar to Qaboos in London in the summer of 1971.

It has to be remembered that, as far as most Arab countries were concerned, Oman in 1970 was under the influence, if not the direct control, of Britain. They assumed that the coup which had replaced Said bin Taimur with Qaboos had been planned and executed by Britain. It was apparent that Britain was heavily involved in the Dhofar war and they could see, and often had to deal with, British advisers in Muscat. However well disposed they might be to Qaboos, about whom they knew nothing, they had no reason to believe that he was not in practice under the thumb of the British. Tarik and Barouni had a large job of information and persuasion in front of them.

In the UN the 'Question of Oman' [38] that was debated annually in the 4th Committee was shelved in autumn 1970 by a resolution that recommended reconsideration of the status of Oman's independence after a year. This was a hopeful beginning. At the end of the year Barouni organised an Omani Friendship Delegation that would lobby for support for Arab League membership. This was led by the Minister of Education, Sheikh Saud bin Ali al Khalili (from a well known Imamate family), and it went to Yemen, Saudi Arabia, Iraq, Syria, Lebanon, Jordan, Egypt, Libya, Tunisia, Algeria, Morocco and Kuwait. In March 1971 the Minister of Health, Dr. Asim Jamali, took a second delegation to Cairo to present Oman's formal application for Arab League membership. PDRY objected and consideration of the application was postponed until September.

In May 1971 four Friendship Missions set out from Oman. One went to Kuwait, Saudi Arabia and Yemen; a second to Iraq, Syria, Lebanon and Jordan; a third went to Libya, Egypt and Sudan; and the fourth to Tunisia, Algeria and Morocco. At the end of May, Oman made official application to the UN to become a member. In June, Arab delegations at the UN decided to wait for the Arab League decision before supporting the application. At this stage Saudi Arabia was still unprepared to support Oman in either organisation, partly for historical reasons, partly because of outstanding promises and support to the exiled Imam who was based in Saudi Arabia.

In September the Arab League agreed to accept Oman as its 17th member. Opposition still came from PDRY, but the decision was finally swayed by a change of position by Saudi Arabia as a result of agreements reached in Beirut between the Imam and the Sultanate. On 4 October 1971 the Security Council unanimously decided to recommend the Assembly to admit Oman as a member. This was the result of an appeal by Dr Jamali to the Syrian delegate, a friend of his, whose term of office was just ending and whose proposal was accepted by his colleagues as a kind of leaving present. With the added authority of the Security Council's recommendation Oman was officially admitted by the General Assembly on 7 October as the 131st member of the UN. Voting was 117 in favour, one against (PDRY) and two abstentions (Cuba and Saudi Arabia). Immediately prior to the vote consideration of the 'Question of Oman' was formally concluded, as recommended by the 4th Committee, by a vote of 115 in favour, two against (PDRY and Cuba) and one abstention (Saudi Arabia).

This was a successful end to hard lobbying for Omani recognition, but one loose end remained. The attitude of Saudi Arabia was still ambivalent, as displayed by its abstention votes in the General Assembly (where to be linked with Cuba was a peculiar and unique experience for the Kingdom). This end was tied up in December when Sultan Qaboos made an official visit to Riyadh. He was received as king ('Jalalat') and Oman was recognised by Saudi Arabia. The claims of the Imam, supported by Saudi Arabia, were finally buried.[39] Saudi recognition did not, however, imply acceptance of boundaries which would remain an outstanding issue for another 18 years.

Oman was a member of the UN, not least through the efforts of Tarik. It was ironic, therefore, that almost the first UN vote in which Oman was involved led to the final break of Tarik with Qaboos. The vote concerned the question of Chinese representation at the UN; Ahmed Makki, who had been left in New York as Oman's representative to the UN, received instructions first from Tarik, then from Qaboos, as to how to cast his vote. The instructions were opposite. Diplomatically, he was ill when voting took place. On 21 December Tarik wrote his letter of resignation to Qaboos. It was accepted. There was no recrimination. Tarik wanted to become a roving ambassador and in February he became Personal Adviser on Diplomatic Affairs and Senior Ambassador.[40] In that capacity he remained active. He headed an Omani delegation in talks with Iran on the median line in the Straits of Hormuz and he accompanied the

Sultan on a number of missions, to the Arab Summit Conference in Algiers in November 1973, to Iran in March 1974 and to the US in January 1975. He died in December 1980.

The immediate cause of the break between Tarik and Qaboos was, therefore, the UN China vote. There were, however, other deeper reasons. There was the fundamental difference in outlook between them; there was the lack of communication; pre-eminently, however, there was the infiltration into Oman of the 'mafia' (as they would inevitably be called) which had in the first place been effected by introductions made by Barouni.

Little has been written about the 'mafia', but there have been rumours in abundance, coded hints, a few press articles and, for those who lived in Oman, a rich source of anecdote. Over the years angles of vision have altered, certainties have blurred and assessments have been reassessed. Above all, perhaps, it is now clear (as it was probably always clear to those who saw clearly) that Oman's experience is not greatly different from that of most other countries, a factor that may be dispiriting but has to be taken into account by all of us.

The bare facts are relatively straightforward. Barouni knew Ghassan Shakir, a Saudi business man living in Beirut, and Yahia Omar, who was a fellow-Libyan exile from Qaddafi, living and doing business in Rome. Robert B. Anderson, a former Secretary of the Treasury in the Eisenhower administration, at this time a business man, had contacts with Shakir and, perhaps, also with Omar. Shakir was well connected in the Middle East. He had been to Victoria College where he was in the same class as King Hussein; he graduated from Cambridge University in 1957 and was associated with his father's bank, Banque du Liban et d'Outre Mer; his father had been a banker and adviser to the Saudi royal family; he was married to the daughter of a prime minister of Lebanon; he was well known in Beirut in the years when it was the hub of Middle East business and dealing; he was 'a great fixer and highly efficient in getting things done'.[41] Robert Anderson had a variety of business interests and contacts worldwide including undefined relationships with the CIA, with which Yahia Omar was also widely believed to be linked. Anderson alleged that his role in Oman was arranged in part by Shakir in order 'to consult on ways to improve their economy' and get Oman 'out from under the dominance of the British'.[42] He admitted later that he had voluntarily reported information about Oman to the CIA but said he had no 'official responsibilities'[43] on behalf of the agency. Certainly, several of those who were recruited as advisers to the Oman government had at one time had CIA connections and Jim Critchfield, who later came out to Oman as representative of the contracting and consulting firm

Tetra Tech, had been head of CIA's Near East Division in the late 1960s.

CIA attributions are by definition indefinable, but the reputation of the CIA is such that, once an attribution has been made, it is open to all kinds of rumour, fancy and intrigue. Nothing can be confirmed, nothing denied; or, if it is, it cannot be believed. This, then, was one result of the introduction of Anderson, Shakir and Omar. When Anderson said that one of his objectives was to get Oman 'out from under the dominance of the British' that was sufficient evidence for many people to assume there was a guiding hand in Langley, Virginia. Because the CIA was known to function independently of the normal line of government the US *charge d'affaires*, Clifford Quinlan, could say 'I discovered that the CIA had connections with Robert Anderson and Omar . . . I didn't know what representations they were making to His Majesty in the name of the US. They were unofficial representatives of the US government'.[44]

The facts about CIA involvement will not be known and, ironically, if they were recorded, they would not necessarily be believed. Such is the effect of 'intelligence' upon the intellect. Nevertheless, it is possible, based on as much evidence as one can gather, to come to conclusions which at least satisfy oneself. There is an arguable case for supposing that the introduction of Shakir and Omar into Oman was a constructed scheme of the CIA to further US interests there. It is true that the takeover by Qaboos coincided with the removal of British forces from the Gulf and that this created a void in an area of strategic importance; it is true that the removal of Said bin Taimur provided an opportunity for the US to obtain influence in an area that had effectively been denied to it; it is true that Oman might have been seen as an opportunity for US military interests, even for US business. This does not, however, prove that the CIA were involved in a takeover operation; if they were, it was wholly unsuccessful and remained uncoordinated with other US policy in Oman, but that does not prove anything either. The case for such a plot, however, seems weakly circumstantial and unpersuasive even for unrepentant conspiracy theorists.

What is inherently more probable (and also fits the facts) is that Shakir and Omar saw an opportunity or, more likely, were presented with an opportunity by Barouni. Tarik in particular, but also Qaboos, were anxious, as we have seen, to widen and legitimise Omani relationships. The British, useful in some respects, were useless to them in promoting their image in the Arab world or in the US. They needed Arabs to help them in Arabia, Americans in US. That was why Tarik recruited Barouni. Barouni led Qaboos to Shakir, and Shakir brought in Anderson and Omar.

This happened in England in summer 1971 while Qaboos was on holiday in London. Also involved in this phase of introductions was Major Tim Landon, by now equerry to Sultan Qaboos. Landon had been at Sandhurst with Qaboos, went to Oman as an Intelligence Officer and was in Salala at the time of the coup. He has remained ever since one of Qaboos' close associates and confidants, one of the background architects of modern Oman.

Shakir, Omar and Anderson operated on two different planes, the diplomatic and the commercial.[45] To both they applied Lebanese principles and practice. This created shockwaves in the British expatriate circles of Muscat; for the Omanis it provided new and exciting opportunities to make money. As a general rule the British advisers tried to create organisations, methods and systems but saw them by-passed and rolled aside by the ministers and other authorities to whom they were responsible. The disorder that already existed as a result of the gap between Qaboos and Tarik widened as the 'mafia' took remote control of contracts, planning and expenditure.

Tarik, although half responsible via Barouni for the introduction of the 'mafia', was suspicious of their motives and their personalities. He found himself increasingly sidetracked and ignored as they took over effective direction of affairs. Two episodes showed Tarik how the wind blew. In October 1971 the Sultan announced that Anderson would handle on his behalf the offshore oil concession; this had already been given to Wendell Phillips but was withdrawn on a technicality. It was subsequently granted to a consortium led by Sun Oil. In November, Anderson introduced Conrad Black, husband of Shirley Temple, to take over the Oman Fisheries concession in the name of a company called Mardela, an arrangement for which Oman would pay Mardela rather than vice versa. Tarik had no part in these decisions; indeed, he was ignorant of the them until he heard of them, like everyone else in Muscat, through the local gossip network.[46]

On the diplomatic front the 'mafia' were efficient in executing what was in effect the marketing of Qaboos. They had between them useful contacts throughout the Middle East and these were put into motion. Sultan Qaboos' first official foreign visit (Tarik went with him) was in October 1971 to Iran where he attended, as a king, the self-glorifying celebrations of the Shah at Persepolis to commemmorate the 2500th anniversary of the death of Cyrus, founder of the Persian empire. The flamboyance and extravagance of the occasion may have helped to confirm in Qaboos a taste for the trappings of power which anyway form an integral part of the exercise of Arab kingship.

More significantly, and as the culmination of Oman's acceptance in the Arab League and United Nations, Qaboos was officially invited to Riyadh in December. Anderson would claim that he was responsible for arranging this visit,[47] but Shakir was also prominent. It was after this visit that, on 14

December, Saudi Arabia, having abstained in the UN votes, finally recognised Oman. During 1972 Shakir and Omar followed this up by organising official visits to Jordan in June and to Egypt and Libya in late November and early December. They themselves were part of the Omani delegation, described as 'Advisers for Political and Economic Affairs'. This series of visits was important for Qaboos in consolidating himself and Oman as part of the Arab community. He has since maintained close contact with Jordan; partly this may be the empathy of king for king, but Hussein's practical support for Oman in the Dhofar war cemented a friendship that has been significant to Qaboos. Similarly, Qaboos has shown steadfast friendship for Egypt, particularly in the post-Camp David period when he was a lonely supporter of Sadat's policies. In the case of Iran, Qaboos' early links with the Shah no doubt encouraged him to request help in the Dhofar war and he has been careful ever since to maintain relations with the regime in Teheran.

The end of 1971 was the first milestone in the progress of modern Oman. The attempt to work with Tarik as prime minister was over. The 'mafia' was established. Oman was regionally and internationally recognised. Down in Dhofar, even if unknown in Muscat, Operation Jaguar had successfully established SAF on the Jebal. Development projects were visibly under way. Omanis felt confident and free. If there had been time it would have been a good moment to draw breath.

Neither Oman nor the Omanis, however, had time to draw breath. There was too much to do and too many opportunities. For the next three years there was a giddy progression of projects, plans, advice, imports, building, consumption, ministers and experts. The mixture of order and disorganisation continued.

Order was represented by expatriate-inspired planning, which counselled OECD-type restraint and care for the traditional business controls of balance sheets, profit and loss accounts and debt management – bankers and executives in suits. Superimposed upon this were quite different attitudes and compulsions – the urge to get moving quickly and make up for lost time, an assumption that resources were available for everything that needed to be done and an instinct that OECD-imported systems (so often, in practice, brought by Britons) could be placed prominently on a shelf and then left there to collect dust. On balance, these fundamentally opposite approaches produced remarkably satisfactory results.

Qaboos himself was, of course, ultimately responsible for what happened. He was always, and will always remain, open to criticism by one group of people or another. That is the prerogative of an absolute ruler and Qaboos is an autocratic ruler. These first years were the period in which he was finding his feet. His years of forced withdrawal in Salala had given him plenty of time in which to decide on broad priorities but it was only through experience on the job that he could learn how to balance one set of demands against another, one group of people against another, one system against another. His first priority[48] was to provide education to his people, 'a must and a right'; then health and 'according to our means' communications and all the rest of modern infrastructure. He was 'horrified by the prisons'. And, above all, he sought to unify the country. Qaboos was clear about these priorities and he made sure that action was taken quickly to achieve what was needed. Expense was not a relevant constraint. Qaboos was not an accountant and he assumed that oil revenues would pay for what was required. That assumption, and a fundamental disregard for the sources of money and the mechanisms under which it is traded, led Qaboos into some critical situations and the criticisms that go with them, but partly by luck and partly by management he emerged unscathed.

In an autocracy power is in the hands of those who have access to the ruler. Qaboos must have been aware of this by observing how his father managed the country from his palace in Salala; if not, he certainly learned it once he became ruler himself. So, individuals and institutions varied in influence and, at the next level, other individuals and groups varied their attachments and dependences. The hub of activity was, naturally, in the areas where money was to be spent, where contracts were negotiated.

Control of the exchequer was the key position – which is why Qaboos kept it to himself; but this did not prevent the developments surrounding Development displaying the contrast between order and disorganisation. In March 1972 an Interim Planning Council was established. This was an all-Omani committee which, although its nomenclature suggested Development, had no terms of reference other than the implied task of dealing with contracts. It was implied by the inclusion of this phrase in the decree which established it: 'As a result of this decision the existing Tenders Committee is hereby cancelled. The Interim Planning Council will succeed it with the inclusion of the Secretary for Financial Affairs.'[49] This committee lasted only until September. It did no planning, and supervision of tenders and the granting of contracts proved to be so productive of jealousy and recrimination that it was disbanded six months later.

In the meantime two appointments were made; John Townsend as Economic Adviser and Dr Riad Rais as Economic Adviser for Development and Planning. Rais was brought to Oman from Beirut by Shakir with whom he had been associated in Jeddah. Townsend had been in Oman in 1969 as chief representative of Whitehead and Partners and had prepared a development plan for Said bin Taimur; more recently he had completed a survey on the structure of government and an Economic Survey 1972 which provided the only respectable statistics and proposals for economic planning and organisation.

Townsend has recorded his version of events in his book[50] written soon after he left Oman in July 1975. At the time it was resented by the government for its frank criticisms of people and systems and in this respect it was too close to events; but his record shows with great clarity how Western and Arab personalities and cultures clashed in the process of creating the structures of state.

In September 1972 the Supreme Council for Economic and Development Planning was established with Sultan Qaboos as President, Sayyid Thuwaini as vice-president, Rais as member and Townsend as Secretary. This time the Council had some positive terms of reference, it set up a a Centre for Economic Planning and Development and contacted UNDP and other UN agencies.

A number of complaints were made about the activities of Rais and he was dismissed in April 1973. Anderson resigned soon after for what were described as health reasons.[51] Shakir and Omar remained in their advisory capacity. Townsend's position was temporarily strengthened and it was in theory further consolidated by the fact that Oman had become on 27 December 1971 the 117th member of the IMF and World Bank[52] and that in 1972 it became a member of the IFC (February) and IDA (June).[53] IMF and World Bank teams visited Oman and made their comments. International bankers visited and made their assessments of Oman's creditworthiness. The end of isolation and the opportunities for commercial dealings meant that the realities of the Omani situation were becoming known. The risk in doing business there began to be calculable.

In spite of this, the Supreme Council in practice lapsed once Rais had departed, and in April 1973 a General Development Organisation was created. Power, and particularly the control of contracts, became more diffused. The Palace Office and the Diwan grew in importance and influence. The Minister of Communications and Public Services had a mandate that included posts and telegraphs, water, power, housing, civil aviation and ports. At the end of 1973 the General Development Organisation in turn disappeared and a Minister of Development was appointed whose responsibilities covered planning, oil affairs, town planning, industry, commerce, fisheries and agriculture. At the end of 1974 the concentration of influence in these two ministries was again dispersed by the creation of the Ministry of Public Works, the Ministry of Petroleum, Minerals, Agriculture and Fisheries and the Ministry of Trade and Industry; also the Sultan created two new Councils, the Finance Council and the Development

Council. All this shuffling and reshuffling represented the reality of power sharing rather than reorganisation for efficiency.

Economic development, the handling of contracts and disbursement of expenditure were, then, the inspiration for internal political and financial machinations in this period. These became more frenzied and profitable as the oil price, and therefore revenues, multiplied. At the end of 1973 the massive Opec-inspired oil price increases were automatically picked up by Oman as the terms that companies gave to Opec producers were offered by PDO to the Sultan. The result was that state oil revenues increased from RO 50m in 1972 to RO 61m in 1973 to RO 291m in 1974 with oil production virtually static in those 3 years[54] (the Riyal Omani (RO) is tied to the US dollar; the rate of exchange was 0.345 to the dollar until 1986 and since then has been 0.384).

This revenue increase, resulting from factors wholly extraneous to the Sultanate, was a piece of luck for Qaboos, an accident of timing that could hardly have been better designed for a country in the early stages of development. Simultaneously with demand outstripping the supply of funds revenues were, as if by magic, expanded by a factor of five. It was, however, not only luck but a challenge to profligacy which was eagerly taken up. By the end of 1974 Oman was in financial crisis.

There were, however, other developments of significance that occurred before the end of 1974. Above all there was, hidden away in Dhofar and unknown to, or ignored by, the majority of Muscatis the successful progress of the war. This has been described earlier. By the end of 1973 the first contingent of Iranian troops was in Dhofar. In March 1974 Qaboos made a state visit to Iran during the course of which the Shah promised the use of a squadron of Iranian Phantoms as further assistance in the Dhofar war. This meant that a suitable runway was required. A contract was forthwith given and a 4000-metre runway and base was completed by the end of the year at Thumrait at a cost of over RO 50m. Later in the year an integrated air defence system based on 28 Rapier guided missile units, radar and ground installations, together with 12 Jaguar strike aircraft, was ordered from the British Aircraft Corporation (BAC) at a cost of around RO 160 million.[55] The balance between military expenditure, civil development expenditure and available resources, even when boosted by the oil price increase, was skewed beyond the capacity of an expatriate adviser (or an ambassador if he had so chosen) to restore. In due course it would be the bankers who had to bring some degree of order into an increasingly chaotic and dangerous financial situation.

*   *   *

Although the war was for the most part remote and confined to Dhofar, PFLOAG activity in Northern Oman itself did not end with the failed operation against Izki in June 1970. Political and military infiltration and organisation continued, as became apparent in December 1972 when the security forces uncovered a plot that could have had serious consequences. Seventy-seven Omanis, including eight women, were arrested and caches of Chinese weapons and ammunition were discovered. In the following June a trial was held in Muscat to which the public were denied access: 74 of the defendants were found guilty; 19 were sentenced to death, but 9 were reprieved at the last moment to join 23 others sentenced to life imprisonment.[56] The manner of the trial and its result was distasteful to many, particularly as the public announcement at the end combined the news of the trial, sentences, executions and reprieves in one broadcast. A second plot was discovered in early 1974; 52 Omanis fled across the border to Abu Dhabi, were extradited and were committed to trial in June; one was sentenced to death, the rest to various terms of imprisonment.

What should be made of these episodes? Was there any real risk of a PFLOAG revolutionary success in Oman? No; but it was a reminder to Qaboos and those close to him that there was an opposition, that PFLOAG had its supporters in the country and that they should not take for granted that the regime was without its critics. Most of those critics were no more revolutionary than the expatriate Omanis had been in the 1960s but, amongst some of those who found the beneficiaries of the new regime either unworthy or undeserving, there was sympathy for the activists. In the event, it was a splutter of reaction; nothing was sustained, and the intelligence and security organisation was strong enough to ensure that trouble would be stifled.

One other internal security flurry should be noted, not because it had any serious consequence (it had none) but because of its unique nature. In late 1970 there were some persuasive security reports that activists, believed to be Iraqi-trained or, possibly, Iraqi, had infiltrated into Musandam. This set off alarm signals because of the strategic threat that unfriendly forces could exercise from the peninsula. Since SAF had no presence at that time in Musandam and no expertise for the sort of operation needed, an SAS operation was set up in which simultaneous seaborne and parachute landings would take place. For the first time ever in an offensive operation the SAS made a freefall drop, landing in the Rawdha bowl.[57] No Iraqis or any other revolutionaries were there, but a survey was subsequently made of Musandam which formed the basis for later development plans.

Back in Muscat the landscape began to change. In early 1972 the Falaj, the first proper hotel in the Sultanate, was opened to the great relief of visitors and hosts. In June the Muscat and Muttrah municipalities were merged and began to spread into what is now the capital area stretching up to Seeb. In September Seeb International Airport[58] was opened although an official inauguration by the Sultan was delayed until the end of 1973. In early 1973 Qaboos moved out to his new palace in Seeb. In May the Muttrah corniche was opened. In mid-1973 the company that would build Medinat Qaboos was set up and in November 1974 the first houses were being sold. Decrees were formalised and published in the Official Gazette. The first number was actually published on 27 April 1972, although the Law setting it up was dated February. In the following March the Official Gazette Department was transferred from the Palace Office to the Ministry of Interior. The first Decree concerned the definition of nationality. A large number of decrees recorded appointments (they still do). Many give the flavour of current social or international concerns. In June 1972 there was an Israeli Boycott decree,[59] a signal of how Oman was integrating into the Arab League. A year later commercial links with South Africa were banned.[60] In November 1973 it was forbidden to fire guns anywhere in the Sultanate, in December a Department for the Collection of Omani Heritage was established[61] in the Ministry of Education and Tourism and in the following February it was announced that a Society for the Collection of Omani Manuscripts was operating.

Meantime, the internationalisation of Oman continued. Qaboos visited Jordan in June 1972, Egypt and Libya in November. By mid-1972 Oman had 9 embassies abroad.[62] In June an American charge d'affaires arrived in Muscat. In July the Sultan issued a decree on territorial waters, the continental shelf and restricted fishing rights.[63] During 1973 Qaboos was at the Non-aligned Conference in Algiers and he returned there in November, accompanied by Tarik, for the Arab Summit. During the year an IBRD mission came to Muscat and gave advice on restructuring and strengthening some of the ministries.

Social developments were not overlooked. A decree was issued covering hygienic provisions for pharmacies and drugstores. In December 1973 a Traffic Law was introduced. Also in December the Oman National Housing Development Company was established[64] and in March 1974 a Housing Loan decree was issued under which Omanis could borrow up to 60 months' salary with repayment up to the age of retirement. In May a Prison Law was published. Colour television was inaugurated in November on National Day. At the end of 1974 a census was started with UN assistance to cover the capital area, Sohar, Sur and Nizwa.

The merchant class were meanwhile enjoying boom times. Total imports into Oman jumped from RO 14 million in 1971 to RO 136 million in

1974;[65] government recurrent civil expenditure rose from RO 10 million to RO 60 million and development expenditure from RO 20 million to RO 128 million.[66] Most of this was handled by Omani business men who set up agencies and, in the case of building and specialised equipment, partnerships with expatriate firms. Every level of fortune could be, and was, made. There were dangers, of course, since, in the end, everything depended on the management of government revenues but this seemed, as so often it has seemed to so many in similar circumstances, a minor risk.

It may seem surprising that within four years there was such a quantity of government in Oman and that, allowing for lapses of quality, so much had been achieved. This was primarily due both to the energy of Omanis in important posts and the efforts of an extensive group of expatriates. As already indicated these two groups did not necessarily approve of, or even trust, each other but the net result was positive. In the Palace the key advisers to Qaboos were Colonel Landon, the Sultan's equerry, Colonel Said Salim, Director of the Royal Court and Sayyid Hamad bin Hamoud, the Minister of Diwan Affairs.[67] To these should be added Ghassan Shakir, Yahia Omar and Anderson. Legal Affairs were in the hands of Tom Hill, an adviser brought in by Anderson, who was author of many of the early laws.[68] Dr Asim Jamali, Minister of Health, was involved in so much else that he was widely expected to follow Tarik as prime minister until Qaboos decided not to appoint another.[69] Abdul Hafiz Salim Rajab , as Minister of Communications and Public Services, was ubiquitous and influential; he had been educated in USSR and had a Russian wife which was grist to the conspiracy theorist mills. Karim Ahmed al Harami was Minister of Development; he had arrived back early in Oman from Dubai where he had known Tarik. John Townsend, the Economic Adviser, was an expatriate anchor in the area of finance but the force of Omani expenditure gales inevitably loosened his ability to keep a grip on Oman's cash flow. SAF was essentially a separate organisation and the Defence Department was closely overseen by Qaboos himself. That left Foreign Affairs where, as has been seen, responsibility was widely shared between Qaboos, Tarik, Shakir and the more internationally astute Omanis such as Ahmed Makki, Yousuf al Alawi and Asim Jamali. At the end of 1973, however, a far-reaching appointment was made when Qais Abdul Munaim Zawawi became Minister of State for Foreign Affairs;[70] and his elder brother Dr Omer Zawawi in the next year became a political adviser to the Sultan.

One significance of Qais Zawawi's appointment was that he was the first businessman to become a minister; this created problems of putative conflict of interest which have never disappeared from the Omani scene. More importantly, it firmly placed in the limelight of government a person, and a family, which has been a constant and influential participant in the development of Oman's economy and foreign policy. The Zawawi's father, who originated from Saudi Arabia, had looked after the affairs of both Said bin Taimur and his father in Karachi. Omer studied medicine (against his will) in Cairo and Beirut and practised for a time in Saudi Arabia. He then did a course on medical economics at Harvard (economics being the subject that interested him). After his father died he went into business in Saudi Arabia and came to Oman in 1971.[71] Qais was sent by the family to Muscat in 1967 and was established strongly in business when Qaboos took over and, as with others who were already in situ, was well placed to expand his interests. The family has owed its influence partly to its long service to the Al Saids, strengthened by the relationship that was then built up with Qaboos' family,[72] and partly, of course, to their own characters and capabilities.

Sultan Qaboos, encouraged by his advisers, dealt with the conflict of interest difficulty in a practical way. It was accepted that Qais Zawawi should not have to give up his business interests on becoming a minister. If a minister was permitted to be a businessman it was logical that a civil servant also could be. If, however, Oman was to be an open society it was necessary to define a code of conduct.

Two important decrees were, therefore, promulgated in 1974. The first, number 22/74 dated 20 May 1974 and published in the Official Gazette of 1 June 1974, laid down the rules for signing contracts or agreements.[73] It was designed to ensure that all contracts conformed to financial policies and budgets and to legal requirements; a system for countersignatures was also included. The second, number 43/74 dated 25 November and published in the Official Gazette of 15 December 1974, dealt with conflict of interest. A memorandum attached to it reads as follows:

> The aim of this decree is to avoid a conflict or opposition of interests and to prevent the misuse of public positions in granting government contracts.
>
> In order to achieve this aim, this decree forbids government officials to possess business with the exception of any which they had in their possession before taking up public positions or before the issue of this decree. Notification should be given by a government official of any interests he officially possesses. By this decree government officials are also forbidden to use their influence on behalf of commercial enterprises or to work as brokers for any commercial enterprises.

Furthermore, the decree stipulates that the government may not enter into any contract with commercial enterprises in which government officials have an interest without obtaining written authority from His Majesty the Sultan.

It is also forbidden by this decree for any government official to accept private positions without the Sultan's approval or to accept awards or gifts from those having trade connections with the government.

The decree allows the Sultan to dismiss any official from his post who contravenes the law or to fine, imprison or to award any other punishment to any official, in addition to the punishments stipulated by the Penal Code. All awards received by a government official contrary to this decree will become government property.

In the text of the decree the definition of interest is in fact even more stringent:

Interest in a Commercial Enterprise – Means possession of 10 per cent or more in the profit and loss of any commercial enterprise or being an owner, partner, director, treasurer, person responsible or employee of a commercial enterprise. Any interests possessed by a husband, who is a government official or his parents, children, brothers or nephews or nieces, will be considered as the interests of a government official for the purposes of this law.

So, the rules of conduct for the Sultan's employees were clear enough. Many critics would claim that they were observed by only a minority of those to whom they applied. Firm evidence is non-existent. No prosecution has ever been brought under the relevant section of the Penal Code and there has never been a register of interests. Rules are effective only if rigorously upheld by authority; these rules were inspired by and written in the language of Europe, but the legal practices of Oman as an Islamic state were not designed to interpret and manage such regulations. Lapses occurred; some were blatant, some were hidden and, as time passed, attitudes towards business, business morality and the regulations themselves altered. The introduction of the laws was applauded, but they were viewed with a degree of cynicism as additional factors that needed to be taken into account in dealing with business matters rather than as a strict and practical guide to conduct.

As it turned out greater strictness and more effective control was precisely what was needed, and was lacking, during 1974.

SECOND THOUGHTS, 1975–76

The year 1974 ended in a blaze of expenditure and commitment to expenditure. Much of it, however, was unbudgeted and many contracts were, in effect, open-ended. Projects were added, often from the direction of the Diwan, without warning and without consultation. It was not that the projects were intrinsically undesirable but that there was no proper control of their number, value or terms. There were two main reasons for this. One was that nobody had any clear idea of the ongoing status of government cash flow nor of its borrowing capacity, the second was that the Financial Secretary (at this time Townsend) was an expatriate whose authority was limited by the fact that he was an expatriate. He was, nevertheless, able to impress upon Sultan Qaboos the need for restraint and a decree was issued in July 1974 which froze the commitment to new capital projects until 1976.[1] This was the theory, but in practice Qaboos himself negated the effect of the decree by ordering the integrated air defence system for RO 160 million two months later. This was an example that a number of ministers found it easy to follow.

Statistics show what took place, but they are only partially useful in trying to understand what was happening. Table 1 shows what was the statistical position, but the figures do not give the flavour of the scene where a desalination plant budgeted at RO 20 million cost over RO 100 million,[2] where the cost of a hotel increased from RO 4.5 million to more than RO 10 million and where short-term loans were regularly being raised to tide over expenditure needs for the days and weeks prior to quarterly receipts from PDO of oil revenue. The situation became critical in early 1975 when the government found itself unable to pay around $45 million of loan repayments.

In early February 1975 the Finance Council, which had since November 1974 consisted of Qais Zawawi, Yahia Omar, Ghassan Shakir and Townsend, approached Morgan Grenfell in London to sound them out on the possibility of raising a $400 million medium-term loan to tide the country over its financial difficulties. This led to a study team being set up by Morgan Grenfell with Hambros and the British Bank of the Middle East (BBME) to look into the current financial position of Oman and to make proposals as to how best to proceed. Morgan Grenfell had established a position In Oman in 1972 when it was felt that links should be set up with merchant banks, and in 1973 they raised a loan of $35 million for the government, the first external financing that had been arranged. Hambros were not far behind with a $25 million loan. BBME was the oldest established commercial bank in the Sultanate and, although there

TABLE 1   *Revenue and expenditure, 1973/1974/1975*

RO millions	1973	1974	1975
Revenue	68.6	303.2	387.7
Expenditure	108.4	349.2	509.5
of which			
– defence/national security	42.0	117.7	241.0
– civil recurrent	20.2	68.9	81.5
– civil development	29.5	142.9	173.0

SOURCE: *SYB* 1986, Table 215.

were now others doing business, was still the largest and most trusted by the Sultan.

The study, and the final report,[3] had a number of effects, some less predictable than others. It took place, it should be remembered, at a time when rumours, suspicions, conspiracies and accusations were swirling around Muscat. What precisely was the influence of Omar and Shakir? What was their relationship with the Zawawi family? How did Landon fit in ? Who got what out of contracts? Who decided what projects should be undertaken when? What control did Townsend have, or want to have? What was the state of the country's finances? Was oil production in decline?

And there were other, perhaps more sinister, matters being discussed around Muscat. First, the perennial question of the CIA and US intentions towards Oman rumbled on. This was fuelled by the visit of Qaboos to Washington in January (of this year, 1975) during which he met President Ford and Secretary of State Kissinger. The US agreed to provide 10 launchers and 120 TOW missiles and there were press reports that there had been discussions on a US request for rights in Musandam and Masira. At the same time, a second study on Oman's finances was being discussed with Chase Manhattan Bank. Did all this imply a US takeover in Oman?

Secondly, on a different tack, there was the question as to whether the Arab states, led by Saudi Arabia, were going to' 'buy out' Oman. Stories about loans, at almost every level of magnitude, from Riyadh, Abu Dhabi, Tripoli, even Teheran, were abundant; Omar and Shakir, after all, were supposed to be the fixers for such things with their multifarious Arab connections. Did this imply an Arab nationalist future for Oman?

Lastly, even more ominous, there was the ultimate conspiracy theory, a Russian plot. Those who saw, or chose to see, this possibility pointed to those in the government who had been educated or otherwise trained in USSR, particularly Abdul Hafiz Rajab, the Minister of Communications.

If Russian subversion in Oman was probably admitted by most people to be near the fringe of reality, nevertheless the atmosphere in Muscat was such that nothing could be ruled out.

The study team had to pick their way cautiously through this tangle and try to piece together the reality of Omani finances and politics. Their conclusions and proposals were diplomatically phrased but, for those who understood the code, they pulled no punches. The main recommendation was, as might have been predicted, more expert staff and greater control over expenditure. The prescription, however, required reference to the symptoms of the illness. Organisationally, the institutions directly responsible were the Development Council[4] and the Finance Council,[5] both under the chairmanship of Sultan Qaboos himself. The members of the former were Qais Zawawi as vice-chairman, five ministers and a representative from the Finance Ministry. Qais Zawawi was also vice-chairman of the Finance Council, with Shakir, Yahia Omar and Townsend as members.

In terms of expenditure the report[6] drew critical attention to a number of areas. The first covered those in which Qaboos himself clearly had some responsibility, the Ministry of the Diwan whose expenditure was nearly 100 per cent in excess of budget, and the Office of the Economic Adviser whose expenditure was RO 21.2 million against a budget of RO 1.6 million – 'the difference is accounted for by unbudgeted payments of some RO 20 million made for special purposes on the express instructions of HM the Sultan'.

The second area was development expenditure in general, where analysis showed that in both 1972 and 1973 the deficit (amounting to RO 42.9 million for the two years) was about 35 per cent of disposable income. In 1974 the deficit was RO 42.6 million and the 1975 budget proposals provided for a deficit of a further RO 88 million. Particular projects picked out for mention were the BAC defence contract, the desalination plant, a number of road projects and the Intercontinental Hotel, together with other contracts which had been signed but not included in the 1975 budget, specifically the Salalah airport extension and Masira desalination plant.

The report was forthright about the Finance Council when it drew attention to three relevant points:

1.   Without in any way denigrating the skills and contributions made by present members of the Council many, if not all, by the nature of their other responsibilities, spend much of their time outside Oman. HE the Deputy Chairman is additionally burdened by his duties as Minister of State for Foreign Affairs.

2.   Whilst present members of the Finance Council provide undoubted

and valuable experience in international, political and legal affairs, we believe they may not have had the benefit of the detailed financial and accounting experience necessary to carry out all the functions under their Terms of Reference.

3. We believe that the Finance Council must be provided with more frequent and detailed information an all aspects relating to the finances and economy of the Sultanate.

It went on to recommend additional expert members and a permanent secretariat for the Finance Council. It also proposed additional experts be recruited for the Development Council and the Ministry of Finance. It supported a continuing role for the Economic Adviser.

The report, finally, turned to the short and medium term cash position, details of which the team had spent three weeks trying to tease out from often conflicting and semi-submerged information. They were able to conclude that 'the source of the current cash crisis arises particularly from expenditure committed between November 1974 and January 1975' and that the peak requirement for borrowing facilities would be around RO 130 million in mid-1975. For the medium term the report made it clear that it would in no way be feasible for Oman to raise a loan of $400 million from international markets in present circumstances but that provided the proposed remedies were taken the economy would recover and strengthen.

The report was delivered to the Finance Council. It seems doubtful that many others ever saw it. The immediate result of the report was that BBME, in a move of far-sighted calculation, advanced Oman a short-term loan of $150 million; this, together with a loan from the Arab Bank, covered the immediate cash flow difficulties. Further alleviations to the financial position came from a $100 million Saudi loan for road and other developments in Dhofar and from the continuing strength of oil revenues.

Oil revenue had been one of the major problems for the study team in piecing together their analysis of Oman's finances. There was no other appreciable source of revenue to the government; oil accounted for 96 per cent of total revenue in 1974 and by 1980 it was still well in excess of 90 per cent. It only dropped below 90 per cent in 1983. In their meetings in Oman, however, the team was handicapped by not being allowed to speak to PDO (nor the Ministry of Defence, the largest individual spender). Oil revenue for 1975 was estimated by the team at RO 325 million, by the Ministry of Finance at RO 365 million. Zawawi made reference to a new contract with Shell[7] which would enable Omani oil to be sold to greater advantage in a world market which was by then in heavy competition. RO 365 million was finally accepted, but without great confidence, by the team. In the end, 1975 oil revenue turned out to be RO 373 million.

In practice, however, the crisis was over by the time the report was finished.[8] The report, and the probing and analysis which went into its writing, was greatly more important for the psychological change it set in motion than the figures it generated. The figures were, of course, important in making it possible for the BBME to make their loan and in giving the Councils reason for introducing austerity measures, but the report and the knowledge that it was being drawn up provided the necessary jolt to bring about a fundamental change of attitude amongst the Omani policy managers.

From 1975 Ghassan Shakir and Yahia Omar took a less direct role in Omani business, ministers and merchants lowered their expectations of commercial gain, or at least were less frenetic about the amassing of wealth. A brake was put on the wilder aspects of project initiation. Even though the report was confidential its existence was public knowledge. Those who were implicitly criticised in the report knew that the bankers knew what had been going on. They knew that the international banking and financial system would not bale them out unless changes were introduced. They knew that, unless these changes were made, they would themselves be on borrowed time. They realised that their own interests must be made to coincide with the interests of Oman. This was a radical change of attitude and it percolated through the system in a number of ways.

One casualty of the report was the Economic Adviser, John Townsend. This was in spite of, perhaps even because of, the support given by the report to his position and, by implication, to himself. Although this was at the time seen by many to have been a decision dangerous to the hope of future economic stability for the country it was probably beneficial. This was not because of any criticism of Townsend himself but because it was no longer appropriate to have a European expatriate in such an exposed position. It was by now essential that decisions, whether of policy or execution, should be seen to be made by Omani citizens. Of course, there remained many expatriates all over the government, within the private sector and attached to diverse advisory bodies but they implemented, did not take, decisions that were essentially Omani. For four years expatriates had been organisationally responsible for many of the top policy decisions but had increasingly been unable, because of the submarine currents of Omani politics, to discharge the terms of that responsibility. It was time for them to be removed from the firing line.

They had to be replaced, however, with as strong and resilient a structure of Omani responsibility as could be erected. The message of the report was clear. The Finance and Development Councils were enlarged and made more professional. Terms of reference and control systems were refurbished. Budgets were more rigorously drawn up and work on the first 5-year plan was begun. Some of these systems were already in the pipeline before the report was submitted but the atmosphere in which they were to be carried out was changed. They were underpinned also by the results of studies that had been initiated during 1974 under a World Bank Technical Assistance project. Of particular importance in the current context was the introduction of a Development Law[9] which laid down systems for the annual budget, the 5-year Development Plan and gave terms of reference to the Development Council. The leader of the study team was Dr Sharif Lutfi, an Egyptian, who stayed on in Oman for many years as head of the Development Secretariat.

Another law which emerged from the process of audit which was implicit in the mounting of the study was the Law for the Organisation of State Administration.[10] This has been one of the most influential and fundamental laws that has been decreed. Not only did it set out the structure and responsibilities of government but it has remained ever since, with periodic amendments, the basis of Omani government. The Law covered general statements as to the authority of the Sultan and the responsibilities of his Ministers and the extent of their delegated powers, the role of the Council of Ministers, Special Councils, Ministries and the Diwan of Legislation[11] and in an Appendix the specific responsibilities and duties of the Special Councils and Ministries. Although there have been many changes since 1975 to the number and delineation of responsibility of individual ministries the main elements of government have remained.

Laws and structures are one thing, the execution and use of them another. The fact that the government went through 1975 without further financial crisis was not wholly the result of the study and report. Already before it was initiated the World Bank team under Dr Lutfi had recommended the creation of the Development Council which, together with the Secretariat under Dr Lutfi himself, was established on 17 November 1974. Their first undertaking was the preparation of the Development Law which was quickly followed by a circular to all Ministries asking for their submissions for the first 5-year plan. At the same time they set up the committee[12] which was responsible for the subsequent publication of the Law for Organisation of State Administration.

Nor did the financial study and report – nor, for that matter, the activities of the Development Council or Finance Council – necessarily prevent further financial problems. Controls were improved but they were not impervious to manipulation. The weakest link in the chain of financial control was, almost inevitably, the Diwan itself. In any autocracy, and particularly in an autocracy whose traditions are based on the ability of the tribal chief to look after his people, it is not easy for the civil servants, still less the courtiers, to define what a ruler should or should not spend. Nor is it easy for the civil servants to know what expenditures derive from the ruler's own decisions and what from the influence of the courtiers. It was not particularly surprising, therefore, that in 1976 there was a second, but much more limited, crisis that concerned the financing of the Diwan. This too was the subject of a study and report by Morgan Grenfell whose main findings related, as with the broader government study, to strengthening the systems and controls over the granting of contracts and their execution and of setting up an effective organisation within the Diwan.

Qaboos himself seemed, in an almost Reaganesque manner, remote from and generally unaware of the extent of the problems. Partly this was due to lack of experience and disinterest in money and finance. That is, he was not trained to read accounts or deal with the intricacies of bank rates, loan financing, currency backing or repayment scheduling. More than this, however, there was the intuitive psychology of the Arab ruler, whose job depends more on spending than on husbanding resources. In this respect his father, Said bin Taimur, was aberrant and, although for much of his reign he had little to spend, was reviled for not spending it. Perhaps Qaboos has reacted against his upbringing, perhaps he has reverted to a more natural mode of Arab rule; maybe there is a combined effect. At any rate Qaboos is by nature a spender.

This has undoubtedly created criticism, particularly amongst the more puritan of his expatriate well-wishers. It has also caused problems for the state exchequer as has been described. However, it seems inappropriate to blame or criticise Qaboos for this except in one important respect. To manage an Arab state a ruler needs advisers (ministers, businessmen, technocrats, politicians) whom he can trust and who are themselves able and willing to manage. He must also know when an adviser is overstepping the invisible line of proper management and advice and act accordingly. Qaboos has had many excellent advisers and he has deflected a few of the less good from their offices, but there have been some who have been allowed to operate on the wrong side of that invisible line for longer than Oman, with its limited resource base, can safely tolerate. It is towards this, rather than the propensity to spend, that criticism may be directed towards Sultan Qaboos.

*   *   *

By 1976 the shape of the Omani state was in main outline mapped out. There was, of course, much still to be filled in, some lines were indistinct, some would be redrawn, but a pattern had emerged. The two fundamental achievements of Oman's first five years were, firstly, the ending of the Dhofar war and, secondly, the establishment of a workable structure for economic and social development for the Sultanate.

The ending of the war meant that the integration of the Southern region into the Sultanate could proceed. Civil development within the province had begun on two different levels. There was the ground roots work done by the CATs but there was also the beginnings of infrastructural development that went back to the first days of Qaboos (planning had in fact taken place while Said bin Taimur was still ruler) of which the largest projects were Raysut harbour and the early road programmes carried out by Taylor Woodrow, who established a partnership with the Omani company of WJ Towell. Robin Young, who went to Salala as Director of Development in 1970, was an active initiator of development projects and coordinated his work closely with that of the Defence Department, the Wali and the CATs. This was institutionalised with the creation of the Dhofar Development Programme in October 1972.[13] This body became responsible for a large proportion of the Sultanate's early development expenditure. Published statistics do not show the breakdown of civil expenditure regionally from 1971–75 (the 5-year plans do give this breakdown for later years) but, according to Townsend,[14] nearly 25 per cent went to the Southern Region (his figures seem to include some military expenditure) and this would be consistent with the 1976–80 first 5-year plan which estimated the Southern Region as recipient of 27 per cent[15] of the total. Bearing in mind that the total population of the Southern Region is less than 10 per cent[16] of the total Oman population, the South seems to have gained a comparative advantage from the integration objective, although it was, of course, starting from a scarcely measurable base.

Expenditure does not, however, necessarily imply any depth to the integration process and this was still shallow in 1976. Communications were still sparse and safety could not be assured. Although the ending of the war had been announced on 11 December 1975 a ceasefire was only arranged, with the political assistance of Saudi Arabia, in March 1976. Although Dhofaris from the South were quickly brought into Government and were influential in the Palace, a return movement to Salala of Omanis from the North was sluggish and at this stage largely confined to the military. Qaboos had, correctly enough, seen the need to create a national

1. The Royal Hospital, Muscat: Accommodation Block

2. (above) Ministry of Foreign Affairs, Muscat

3. (below) Rusayl Industrial Estate, Headquarters Building

4.　(above) Sultan Qaboos University, Muscat

5.　(below) Sultan Qaboos University, Muscat

6. Sultan Qaboos University, Muscat

identity that spread all over the Sultanate but it was not something that could be achieved by decree.

As for an overall development programme the first 5-year plan 1976–80 appeared in September 1976.[17] Of course, none of the revenue or expenditure figures turned out as planned.[18] It would have been chance if they had. What was important was that Ministries had plans and spending budgets which were internally consistent and tied to overall state objectives. These were contained in a Resolution dated 9 February 1975 of the Development Council which was attached to the 5-year plan and included in its text in abbreviated form in Chapter 2. It was predictable in content but to the point. It stressed the need to diversify the economy, particularly in the areas of mining, manufacturing, agriculture and fisheries, and to spread investment regionally. It underlined the need to deal with the problem of water resources. In the foreword there was a summing-up: 'This is the first Five-Year Development Plan to be prepared for the Sultanate. Its main objective is to ensure the continued healthy growth and modernisation of the economy, to diversify the sources of national income and to raise the standard of living of different population groups living in the various regions of the country.'

Not everything in the Sultanate was defence and economics. In the same Gazette that published the Economic Development Law was a Law for the Organisation of the Scout movement in Oman.[19] In July a Publications Law[20] was issued which laid down strict rules for both publishing locally and for the distribution of foreign publications. 'Publications may not be imported from abroad before approval is obtained from the Directorate of Printing and Publications', said Article 33; and article 34 was more threatening, 'It is absolutely forbidden to bring into the Sultanate any publications, the subject matter of which disturbs security or touches national feelings, or if they offend public morals and decorum.' Article 36 lists various categories about which 'it is forbidden to write or to copy, print, publish or distribute' and these include in subsection 2 'any matter which is against the person of His Majesty the Sultan, or against the order of the state or is harmful to it, or is damaging to the highest interests of the country, or inviting the adoption and propagation of destructive principles.' Not an encouragement to authors.

More liberally, 84 Baluch soldiers were granted Omani citizenship in October 1975,[21] and consistent with a continuing care for ecological conservation in the Sultanate, crayfishing was banned between 1 May and 15 August each year to permit breeding to take place.[22] Oman was on course for its development years.

GROWTH, 1976–90

External Affairs

The US Connection
Strategically Oman is a valuable piece of real estate. It takes up most of the Eastern side of Arabia facing Iran and the Indian Ocean, and the Musandam peninsula stands like a rocky watchtower enfilading the entrance to the Gulf itself. Since the second world war the Indian Ocean, the Gulf and Iran have been an integral geographical part of the cold war, one slice of potential geopolitical threat. That meant a US interest in the area.[1]

In practice, the US was prepared, during the 1950s and 1960s, to commit its concerns for Oman and the Gulf to the care of Great Britain whose influence in the area had been paramount for a century and more, whose military and political presence was firmly entrenched and whose dependability was not questioned. This did not extend to the Indian Ocean, however, where Britain clearly no longer had the resources and capability to carry the weight of geopolitical responsibility.

The focus of interest within the US establishment in the Indian Ocean was the Navy. This began in the late 1950s with analyses that led, first, to the need for an Indian Ocean fleet and, secondly, to the need for a base for such a fleet. The primary compulsion was the need to contain Soviet expansion but the secondary, and more immediate, concern was the disintegration of hitherto friendly regimes and their tendency to become not only unfriendly to US interests but positively supportive of (and supported by) Soviet policy.[2] Where the disintegration had not taken place the US interest was to preserve the status quo, for instance in Saudi Arabia, the Arabian peninsula and Iran. Naval thinking led logically to what became known as the 'strategic islands concept', the idea that a base should be established on Diego Garcia in the Chagos archipelago, a remote collection of islands 1500kms beyond the Southern tip of India and 4000kms from Muscat.[3] The concept was slowly and rather ill-temperedly translated into reality. The Chagos archipelago had to be formally detached by Britain from Mauritius and turned into what became, by Order in Council in November 1965, the British Indian Ocean Teritory (BIOT)[4] which could then be leased to US. The inhabitants, around 1000, had to be removed, amidst adverse publicity, to Mauritius. Robert McNamara, by this time US Secretary of Defence, disliked the whole idea and refused to pay Britain for the lease. In February 1967 a request to Congress for $26 million to create an 'austere support facility' on Diego Garcia was turned down. Finally, however, in 1968 there was agreement, McNamara having in the meantime left the Department of Defence, to an 'austere communications facility'. 'Austere' was the euphemism employed by the naval authorities to persuade suspicious members of the administration that their real intention was not to establish a full-scale naval base there.

Two developments occurred to change US attitudes to the Gulf area. One was the announcement in January 1968 by the British Government that they would withdraw their forces from the Gulf by the end of 1971. This was one of the most fundamental geopolitical decisions relating to the area that was taken in the postwar years. It upset an existing balance and radically changed the attitudes of the main actors. It led directly to US policy that established the 'twin pillars' defence strategy based on Iran and Saudi Arabia backed by US indirect support and supplies. The later, and far more traumatic, occurrence was the oil embargo that followed the 1973 Arab-Israel war. This was not only a generalised blow to Western energy security assumptions but directly affected US naval operations in the Gulf and Indian Ocean. The 'act of recognition by senior policy makers that events in the Persian Gulf area could directly affect American security in a profound manner was, in itself, a major watershed in US strategic thinking'.[5]

The effect upon Oman of the 1968 decision was not immediate but US policy from now implied greater interest in Oman. In 1970 President Nixon reviewed Gulf policy and concluded that the 'Persian Gulf problem was primarily political, not military'. Policy was to be based on the 'twin pillars' of Saudi Arabia and Iran; there should be a group of three ships kept in the Gulf; diplomatic representation should be expanded; the lower Gulf states should be encouraged to maintain reliance on UK for their security needs. In place of a military presence the US would assist regional states to develop their own security forces through arms sales and advisers while providing technical assistance for development purposes. US policy derived wholly from cold war attitudes and was directed against the perceived threat posed by the USSR. Gary Sick makes the point that there remained a minority, but strong, group which wanted to take a stronger line but that in practice Vietnam kept the military too busy to be able, even if it had been agreed, to divert resources to the Gulf area.

One result of this new US debate was the appointment in July 1972 of C. J. Quinlan as *Chargé d'affaires* in Muscat.[6] Prior to Quinlan's arrival there had been no representation whatsoever since 1915 when the last consul had departed. Said bin Taimur's only link with the US had been through the investment company to which he had entrusted, but never used, the money realised by the sale of Gwadur for £3 million to Pakistan in 1958. In 1958 a new Treaty of Amity, Economic Relations and Consular Rights replaced the original US 1833 Treaty with Oman. It was the intention then to open an embassy, but the equipment designed for that purpose was transferred to Yemen. Nothing further was officially done until Quinlan arrived in 1972, although there was without doubt a CIA interest in maintaining information about and connections with Oman.[7] A resident ambassador, William Wolle, was appointed in July 1974 after further assessment had been made on the importance of the country to US interests.[8]

The culmination of this first phase of US attention towards Oman was the visit of Sultan Qaboos to Washington in January 1975. This created a firm basis for future US agreements and links with the Sultanate and resulted in the provision by the US of some TOW missiles and launchers to Oman, which had been declared eligible for Foreign Military Sales (FMS) in January 1973.[9] It would also have been natural for the facilities at the Masira airbase to be put on the agenda of the Washington meeting, for Masira was a desirable stepping stone to Diego Garcia and, in general, to the Indian Ocean, the Gulf, Iran and Pakistan.

Masira island, off the coast of Oman between Ras el Hadd and Dhofar, had provided an air refuelling facility for the British for many years. In 1932 a landing ground and oil depot were constructed as part of the link between RAF Commands in Aden and Iraq. A Civil Air Agreement was signed between Oman and UK in 1934[10] and this was replaced post-war by a new Agreement signed on 5 April 1947[11] covering airfields at Salala, Masira and Gwadur for which UK paid the Sultan £6000 per annum. Both Agreements were specifically civil although their main importance was in fact military. Also on Masira there was a relay station for the World Service of the BBC. This was opened, as the British Eastern Relay Station, on 1 June 1969.[12]

The Masira facilities were handed back by Britain to Oman in March 1977.[13] US interest in negotiating for landing rights and usage of Masira island as a transit base was one of the reasons for US interest in Oman when the British announced their plans for withdrawal from the Gulf. Press reports suggested that the matter was raised with Sultan Qaboos in January 1975 although no progress was made. In 1977, when the British departed from Masira, reports were even more numerous, but any suggestion of an agreement was consistently denied by Qaboos who was himself engaged in sensitive security negotiations with his Gulf colleagues. Qaboos did, however, add that transit or refuelling could be permitted to any friendly nation,[14] and this is precisely what happened in the case of the US. An agreement,[15] informal and loose, was reached with the US Embassy whereby US planes, in particular long-range P3 surveillance aircraft, could, by prior arrangement, refuel and transit at Masira. This was later extended to the temporary use of Seeb while improvements and repairs were being made to the Masira runways.

As the Diego Garcia facilities were developed and as it became clear that the foundations underpinning one of the US 'twin pillars' were beginning to crumble the level of US anxiety intensified. The thinking that led to the formation of the Rapid Deployment Force (RDF) was under way by July 1977; in 1978 Brzezinski ordered planning to be accelerated; in April 1979 the National Security Council (NSC) entered the scene and this was followed by a major Pentagon involvement that led finally in June to what was known as the Wolfowitz Report.[16] Although the report has not been published and is unavailable on the grounds that it was never completed a heavily expurgated copy of Part 1 can be seen in the National Security Archive in Washington, which obtained it under the Freedom of Information Act.[17] An annotation makes it clear that Part 2 was never prepared.

However, an article by Richard Burt in the *New York Times*, 2 February 1980, describes and discusses the report to which, at least in part, he clearly had access at the time. Oman and Djibouti are specifically mentioned as necessary bases for a US response to Soviet action in the area although at this stage (June 1979) an approach had not yet been made to them. The report seems to have been accepted as the rationale and basis for US policy in the area.

It can hardly have been coincidental that it was at this same time, November 1979, that the Musandam Development Committee suddenly swung into action and handed over the contract for development, which turned out to be both military and civil, to the US firm of Tetra Tech International.[18] Control of the project on the Omani side was, significantly, vested in the Diwan.

In December of the same year a Pentagon team visited Kenya, Somalia and Oman to discuss the question of military access to facilities in those countries. Later in the month Afghanistan was invaded by the Soviets. On 23 January 1980 President Carter, as part of his State of the Union message, enunciated, much to the surprise of the Gulf States who had not been informed of it, the Carter Doctrine – 'An attempt by an outside force to gain control of the Persian Gulf region will be regarded as an assault on the vital interests of the USA, and such an assault will be repelled by any means necessary, including military force.'

Funds for the RDF were budgeted, facilities at Diego Garcia further improved, negotiations for access facilities intensified. The headquarters of the Rapid Defence Joint Task Force (RDJTF) as it was now called became operational on 1 March at MacDill Airport Base in Florida. The principle

of an Access Agreement with Oman was agreed in early February, its terms
agreed in principle during a visit of Reginald Bartholemew, Director of the
Bureau of Politico-Military Affairs, to Muscat in April and officially signed
on June 4.[19] The US naval presence in the Indian Ocean rose to around 25
ships, including two aircraft carriers and 150 planes. By the end of 1980,
as Gary Sick[20] puts it: 'Not only was the US military presence [in the Gulf]
at its highest level in history but there was also an underlying conviction
that this region represented a major strategic zone of US vital interests,
demanding both sustained attention at the highest levels of US policy
making and direct US engagement in support of specifically US interests.
That was without precedent.'

Oman had been firmly dragged into the world of geopolitics. The
Department of Defence, quoted in the New York Times, made this clear
to anyone who had doubts: 'Our principal objectives are to assure continued
access to Persian Gulf oil and to prevent the Soviets from acquiring political
or military control directly or through proxies.'[21] Ronald Reagan, who took
over the Presidency from Carter in January 1981, doubled expenditure
on the RDJTF and, on 1 January 1983 reconstituted it as the Central
Command. He assumed, and spoke of but did not define, a 'strategic
consensus' in the area. It was undefinable since the Gulf Cooperation
Council (GCC), established in May 1981, had a defence policy which
was formally based on non-alignment. However unrealistic or idealistic
this attitude might have appeared in the midst of the Iran-Iraq war it was
hardly consistent with the idea of a 'strategic consensus', particularly as
the unspoken military assumption behind the words was that access ought
to mean access for land as well as naval forces.[22]

The US Access (or Facilities) Agreement with Oman was signed on 4
June 1980 in an exchange of letters between the US ambassador, Marshall
Wiley, and the Deputy Prime Minister for External Affairs, Qais Zawawi.
The main text of the letter reads:[23]

> I have the honor to refer to the recent discussions between our two
> governments regarding a framework for bilateral cooperation relating
> to economic development and trade, and to defence equipment, training
> and development, in order to enhance the capability of Oman to
> safeguard its security and territorial integrity, and to promote peace
> and stability.
>
> As a result of those discussions and as part of this framework, agree-
> ment was reached on the use of certain facilities in Oman by the United
> States in accordance with and subject to implementing arrangements as
> may be agreed from time to time by our two governments.

As part of the negotiation with Oman the US also signed an agreement, on 19 August, to set up a Joint Commission on Economic and Technical Cooperation.[24] This was, formally, a ten-year renewable agreement with a review clause stipulated after five years 'and every five years thereafter'. Although the 'implementing arrangements' referred to in the main Facilities Agreement were not published they too seem to have included the five-year review clause.

The details of the Access Agreement have not been published, but the main elements concerned with upgrading of the airports, prepositioning of supplies and access to the facilities on a prior approval basis are common knowledge. What is less well-known is the side-letter to the main Agreement in which there is a formal undertaking by the US of support for Oman in case of aggression against the country. This is the only such written undertaking to any country in the area,[25] if President Truman's letter of October 1950 to King Ibn Saud is excluded.[26] It is a measure of the importance that the US attached to the agreement that they should have accepted the commitment in the case of Oman. It is also a comment on Omani attitudes that they should have insisted on it.

Each year the Assistant Secretary of State must present proposals for Foreign Military Sales (FMS) and Economic Support Funds (ESF) appropriations to, amongst others, the Senate Foreign Relations Committee. An indication of US official thinking on the country under consideration is, therefore, recorded in these documents. In 1983, Nicholas Veliotes made the following case:[27]

By providing modest military and economic assistance we demonstrate that we are prepared to support the very real security needs of this strategic country which shares a common border with Soviet-backed South Yemen and which has granted the US access to military facilities. Our military facilities in Oman are crucial to any effort to halt aggression in the Gulf area. Our FMS programme provides funds to assist the modernisation of Oman's armed forces so that they would have the means to help to defend these facilities.

In an effort to broaden our relationship with Oman beyond its security aspects, the US-Oman Joint Commission was established in 1980 in conjunction with the facilities access agreement. We provide $5 million every year in ESF grants to fund the operation of the Joint Commission, feasability and design studies, technical assistance and training. A $10 million loan program has thus far concentrated on water resources and is programmed in fiscal 84 for school construction.

The reliability and importance of Oman was stressed. 'Oman's agreement to permit access to its facilities represents a key asset for the US Central Command,' said Secretary of State Schultz in 1985,[28] and he repeated this in 1986,[29] 'The security relationship we have built with Oman is a vital element of our Central Command strategy.' In 1985 Richard Murphy added a point:[30]

> A significant increase in FMS credits is requested to help Oman bear the cost of upgrading and modernising its air defence capability as part of a collective effort by the GCC. The continued threat of military attack by Iran has required Oman to increase defence expenditure in recent years to approximately 48% of budgeted expenditures, one of the highest levels in the world.

The amount of money being requested from Congress each year was around $40 million for FMS and $15–20 million for ESF.[31] The FMS funds were earmarked for improvement of the runway, fuel storage and other facilities at Masira, and a variety of construction projects including runway improvements at Thumrait, Seeb and Khasab. The quantity of supplies prepositioned at these centres reached very large proportions by the end of the 1980s.

ESF funds created problems and misunderstandings. Qaboos made a state visit to the US in April 1983 in the course of which President Reagan assured him that the ESF programme would be increased to the level of $20 million per annum. In practice, Congress was inclined to reduce the level of all aid appropriations in the later 1980s and this was applied to Oman along with other countries. This did not improve the US reputation and standing in Oman and did nothing to make the 1990 review negotiations easier. On two occasions, in May 1984 and in April 1986, vice-president Bush visited Oman to help smooth relations and to take note of the uses of US military and economic aid. In his statement on 19 May 1984, at the end of a trip to East and South Asia, he said[32] '. . . we consider him [Qaboos] to be an inspiring leader, a statesman whose advice we seek and remember and, above all, a friend.'

Military attitudes and statements were, as can be imagined, more direct than those of the State Department. The Commander of the RDJTF was Lt. General P. X. Kelley. In February 1981 he faced a House Committee on the Budget, some members of which seemed sceptical of the expenditures and objectives of the Force:

> 'While we have significant airlift capacity in the Military Airlift

Command, it is not sufficient to put a capital R in Rapid' he said.[33]

'What is your mission?'

'My mission includes any contingency outside of NATO. We are focused primarily for the near term on SW Asia and that includes any contingency there, sir. We are not a Third World intervention force. We are a force to contend with anything up to and including the Soviet Union outside of Nato.'

'Some qualms have been raised about the reliability of some of those countries being mentioned as stations for prepositioning supplies, like Kenya, Somalia and so forth. Does this give you some concern?'

'Sir, that is a question above my pay grade.'

'You say you are a strictly operational HQ?'

'Yes, sir, maybe that is one of the misunderstandings. I command the RDJTF HQ. Now when we have a crisis the forces are then assigned to me, but in normal peacetime operation they belong to another commander. As an example, the Army and Air Force units belong to a unified commander USINCRED. The Navy and Marine forces belong either to CINCLANT or CINCPAC. But I want to emphasise that once my operation order is approved by the Joint Chiefs of Staff and then they give me the order to execute, all of these commanders in chief have a requirement to provide me with these forces and they, in fact, become supporting commanders to me' . . . 'People, sir, are not hard to move . . . the problem is moving equipment . . . to give a gee-whiz figure, one C-4 loaded with ammunition, which is high density cargo, equals 500 C-141 sorties but the problem is I have got to wait for the C-4 to get there because it is slower; and I may need that ammunition tomorrow.'

At the end of the report, the civil servants were able to deal less colourfully with a few written questions:

'What kind and level of threat will trigger an RDF response?'

'An RDF deployment is dependent upon the decision reached by the National Command Authorities,'

was the straight-faced reply. Of course, the statements and responses given in public hearings are peculiar to the circumstances in which they are made. They are primarily designed to achieve departmental objectives or satisfy departmental critics within a highly politicised environment. There is no equivalent or comparable process in Oman and, therefore, no evidence exists, except as hearsay,[34] for what Omani official comment might have been. It seems incontrovertible, however, that Sultan Qaboos saw that it was in his interests to conclude an agreement with the US. The economic element was useful but only secondary. It was the military content that was important.

The Omanis needed re-insurance. The Iran-Iraq war was threatening in that either side represented potential danger. The GCC was an element of insurance but it was of only limited and partial value. Qaboos was realistic as to its limitations as a political, military or economic source of strength. He had always relied primarily on Western – mostly British – support, but knew the boundaries of British resource. He knew without having to read congressional records that the US strategic interest was primarily concerned with the Soviets and oil security. He realised that US military authorities wanted land base access and that this was unacceptable to Arab opinion. He knew that his fellow members of the GCC and Arab League did not want to see direct alliances with the US, but he had already parted company with them over the Camp David Agreements and was one of very few overt Arab supporters of Egypt's peace treaty with Israel. He saw the Access Agreement as an opportunity for Oman; an opportunity to gain US support at a time when he had a strong negotiating hand and could impose conditions on an agreeement that he knew the US needed.

The conditions on which the US gained access to Omani military facilities were, apart from the important side-letter of support in case of aggression, that they must seek prior political approval and clearance for any proposed use of the facilities, and that they should themselves be responsible for any upgrading of the facilities which they needed for their own purposes (this was the basis of the FMS appropriations). The Omanis were tough on the prior approval condition. They had every reason to be, since the condition was flouted, even before the agreement was signed,[35] in April 1980 when the US airforce used Masira, without any prior warning or request, in their secret and botched attempt to free the embassy hostages in Teheran.

Later, in 1985, when the first review of the Agreement was being discussed, tension on this point was exacerbated.[36] The Omani side sought to strengthen the conditions of access while the US military took the line that, since they had built and paid for the improvement of the military bases, they should have unconditional access to them. US diplomacy in this instance was assisted neither by the military component in the negotiations nor by the media[37] which coincidentally picked up the stories and rumours connected with Robert Anderson, the CIA, Ghassan Shakir and Yahya Omar in the early 1970s and gave them a prominence that seemed to Omani sensitivities a direct attack on the Sultan and his close advisers as well as an effort to bring pressure on the negotiations. The military were particularly incensed by the presence of General Watts,[38] the Chief of Staff, as leader of the Omani negotiating team. They assumed[39] that the British government was pulling strings behind the scenes. This was a total misreading of a situation in which Watts was, not without some Omani subtlety, told to fill the role for which he had been employed and which he then carried in the interests of his Omani political superiors. The British government played no part at all; they would not have been able to do so even if they had wanted.

So, although there were dissatisfactions on the US side, these were mostly of their own making and reflected an inbuilt military insensitivity. In practice the agreement has worked satisfactorily for the US, particularly during the critical times of the Iran-Iraq war, and has, equally satisfactorily, given Oman a low-key and two-way international involvement which has lifted it well above the ranks of the smaller LDCs. This status was earned in timely fashion, for the changed appearance of the geopolitical world since Gorbachev and the economic collapse of the Soviet Union has altered the negotiating strength of Oman.[40]

This was apparent in the 1990 Review in which the prior assumptions of both the US and Omani negotiators had to be modified. The reduction of ESF credits from the $20 million level still rankled with the Omanis and there were differences of opinion relating to some practical details of the Access Agreement. The main point at issue was, however, the wish of the Omani side that the side-letters covering US undertakings of support to Oman should be incorporated in the main agreement. A first round of discussions in March was inconclusive. The underlying interest of both sides was, however, to reach agreement and an extension of the Access Agreement for a further ten years was signed on 1 December 1990.[41] The side letters remain outside the main agreement. The Economic and Technical Agreement and the Joint Commission administering it was also renewed for ten years with ESF credits on a 'best efforts' basis of $20 million per annum.[42]

Americans sometimes feel that their influence and credit with Omanis is less than it might be and that the British, for instance, continue to maintain an ease of access that is no longer consistent with their reduced capacity to influence events. The fact is that US business interests have not penetrated deep into Oman, except in areas directly connected with Defence and the Access Agreement. Partly this is because of the small scale of the market, partly because the ESF credits are not large enough to have more than a limited effect. In spite of this, the Joint Commission has its own permanent staff and offices in Muscat which gives it a certain sense of immediacy that other countries' joint commissions, which meet only periodically for discussion of possible aid programmes, do not have. The red meat of US interest is, however, the military side of the agreement and, in spite of the occasional lapse of military judgment, this has been managed in an atypically restrained manner. The 150th anniversary of the arrival in New York, on 30 April 1840, of the Omani sailship 'Sultanah', with Ahmed bin Naaman on board as ambassador of Said bin Sultan, was celebrated both in Muscat and Washington and can be seen in this context as a symbolic seal of current friendship.[43]

Gulf Cooperation Council

To play a part in the geopolitical scene gives, even for a minor actor, a certain kudos. For Oman, however, its backyard is Arabia and the Gulf. That is its primary focus of attention.

Oman's first concern, in 1970, was Saudi Arabia. Creating a relationship with Riyadh was not straightforward. There was a long history of Saudi expansionism to overcome as well as the more recent examples of Saudi attitudes – Buraimi, Saudi support for the Imam's rebellion, the presence of the Imam in Saudi Arabia and real doubts as to what the outcome of the Dhofar war would be. As has been seen, Qaboos managed this to good effect and his reception in Riyadh by King Feisal in December 1971 confirmed that a new relationship was in existence.

It did not mean, however, that the old problems were at an end. The most blatant and difficult matter to settle was the border. The problem was not the precise delineation of the border, but the Saudi claim, which was periodically repeated, for a large chunk of Omani territory. Even the establishment of the GCC did nothing to weaken these claims which, although they were never followed up by any public or private campaign for negotiation or compromise, nevertheless did nothing to discourage latent Omani suspicions as to the reality of Saudi policy. It was, moreover, distasteful to the Omanis that such claims should be made when outwardly the Saudis acted as friendly colleagues.

The border claim in one way served as a Saudi reminder to Oman as to where real power lay in the Gulf. It also seems to have reflected a division within the Saudi royal family over more general policy questions. It was a way in which one part of the family could express its opposition to the ruler. On the one hand it was difficult for the ruler to drop the claim entirely, on the other it was understood that the claim would not be followed up in any serious manner. For Omanis it was an embarrassment and cause of considerable sensitivity that they should be used in this way as a symbolic shuttlecock between factions of the Saudi royal family. It was, therefore, a relief and a considerable achievement for Omani diplomacy that the dispute should have been settled.

It was settled in two meetings between King Fahd and Sultan Qaboos. First, Qaboos invited Fahd to stay on after the December 1989 GCC Summit held in Muscat. He remained for a two-day visit at the end of which an announcement[44] was made that both countries had agreed to demarcate their border. This was followed by a state visit made by Qaboos to Saudi Arabia from 20–22 March 1990, during which the border agreement was signed.[45] This represented the formal end to Saudi-Omani differences and symbolised the recognition by Saudi Arabia that Oman had a valuable independent voice that was positive and useful in Gulf politics. It may be thought curious that this realisation was delayed so long but Arab disputes, particularly when concerned with borders, are notoriously difficult to settle. This can be counted a notable achievement.

Beyond Saudi Arabia was the Gulf in general. Before Qaboos took over as ruler, most of the Peninsula ignored, and was ignorant about, Oman. An exception was the UAE, and particularly Abu Dhabi, where Sheikh Zaid had already had relatively close contact with Said bin Taimur, and where the Sultan had a certain status even if he had no influence. Further North another exception was Iraq whose menacing revolutionary campaigns had for years included not only subversive propaganda against Oman but also the training and financing of Omanis abroad. Fortunately Iraq was a long way away. As has been seen, Qaboos relatively quickly established relations with the Gulf countries and also with Iran. In 1976 expediency overcame sentiment and diplomatic relations between Iraq and Oman were established in February. By this time the question of some formal cooperation between the Gulf states was becoming a matter of increasing urgency.

The Gulf by the mid-1970s was in need of therapy. It had been suffering for some years from an identity problem activated by the withdrawal of British forces from the area in 1971. This became more severe as the pretensions of the Shah expanded and Iraq became more strident. It was fuelled by the sudden influx of wealth as oil revenues multiplied in the wake of the 1973 Opec oil price takeover. Some sort of formal alignment seemed appropriate, but this raised the disturbing question of what its scope or content should be.

There were three countries jockeying for power. Iran had effectively assumed control over the waters of the Gulf but seemed prepared to leave the peninsula to the Saudis. Both countries were massively supported by the US and, in return, represented the 'twin pillars' of US policy in the area.

Iraq – revolutionary, extreme, ambitious to make its leadership mark in the
Arab world – was a threat to the more peacable countries of the peninsula
and had been, through history, a rival to, and often at war with, Iran.

In March 1975 Iran and Iraq signed a treaty that settled the explosive and
long-standing border dispute in the Shatt-el-Arab. The Saudis forthwith, as
Safran puts it,[46]

> endeavoured to use Iraq to frustrate the Shah's schemes to institution-
> alize his hegemonic aspirations through a Gulf collective defense pact,
> and to use Iran to check Iraq's aspiration to become the center of an
> alignment of the Arab countries of the Gulf. They also strove to play
> on the rival aspirations of the two powers in order to restrict the
> position of either one among the Gulf emirates and to assert their own
> predominance there.

In the same month, March, the Shah proposed a security pact grouping
all the Gulf states and repeated this in July after a visit to Teheran by Crown
Prince Fahd.[47] The Saudis prevaricated but later in the year, in the course of
an Islamic conference in Jeddah, agreed with the other Gulf states certain
principles that included the exclusion of the superpowers from the region
and the denial of military bases to them. In March 1976 King Khaled made
a royal visit to all the Gulf states. He was followed within a few weeks by
the vice-president (as he then was) Saddam Hussein of Iraq.

Already at this stage Oman was developing its own policy towards Gulf
security which it would reiterate over the coming years, a policy based
on a degree of self-generated Gulf defence capability but linked to and
supported by external (in practice US and to a lesser extent UK) guarantees.
It was many years before the policy was, in spite of themselves, accepted
by the other Gulf states. Their perception of threats from the USSR was
considerably less developed, and their fear of an Arab backlash against
themselves greatly more developed, than that of Oman.

In October 1976 Prince Naif, the Interior minister, made another official
Saudi trip to push for an internal Gulf security pact, but Kuwait and Oman,
from opposite ends of the Gulf and for opposite reasons – Kuwait through
fear of Iraq, Oman from its links with Iran – insisted on a full Gulf
conference. In November 1976 a foreign ministers' conference was held in
Muscat with Iran and Iraq included. There were varied proposals, including
Oman's linkage ideas, but no agreement. As the Omani Minister of State
for Foreign Affairs put it:[48] 'There was a situation, or better an atmosphere,
which did not make joint defence cooperation possible at present.'

There was a continuing jockeying for position in 1977 as Iran established a series of bilateral agreements in the Gulf, starting in January with an agreement with Oman to withdraw a part of the Iranian forces from Dhofar.[49] Iraq responded with a similar diplomatic offensive in the Gulf, in particular by reestablishing relationships with Kuwait which had been, not for the first time,[50] the recipient of Iraqi threats and force in the previous August. As 1977 moved into 1978, however, the attention of the three main Gulf powers was wrenched by a number of developments into other directions. Afghanistan was taken over by a Marxist regime; Ethiopia was successfully campaigning against Eritrea; PDRY slithered further left in an internal coup; the USSR was seen behind, and supporting, all these movements. This was followed by the Camp David agreements, signed in September, and a quickly deteriorating internal situation in Iran.[51] Iraq stepped in with a call for an Arab Summit, held in November, and orchestrated an anti-Egypt coalition in what was essentially a bid for leadership of the Arab world. As Iran and Iraq moved towards war, and Israel and Egypt towards peace, Iraq's position seemed increasingly strong. It enunciated principles and appeals with which it was difficult for Arab states, least of all those in the Arabian peninsula, to disagree. Even Oman supported the condemnation of the Camp David agreements at the Baghdad Summit of 2–5 November, although it absented itself from the March 1979 Summit at which Egypt was thrown out of the Arab League and never supported any subsequent hostility towards Egypt.

In September 1979 Oman again proposed the formation of an organisation that would, with Western participation, protect navigation routes; Iraq quickly counter-proposed an Arab security pact. In Taif in October Saudi Arabia managed without difficulty to have both proposals shelved. In January 1980 President Carter, responding to the Soviet invasion of Afghanistan a month earlier, announced the 'Carter doctrine' and on 8 February Saddam Hussein riposted with the Charter for Pan-Arab Action, which called for non-alignment and rejected any foreign military presence on Arab lands. Oman ignored the Iraqi charter and five days later agreed the principles of the Access Agreement with the US. Iraq condemned Oman: 'By granting facilities to the US Qaboos has excluded himself from among Arab patriots and from among the non-aligned regimes.'[52] Saudi Arabia was typically embarrassed by the Iraqi Charter, partly because it was still trying to remain even handed between Iran and Iraq, partly because of its huge military dependency upon the US.

The outbreak of war in September 1980 led to some clarifications. It was immediately assumed that Iraq would quickly win the war, an outcome publicly supported by most Arab countries. Saudi support was typically cautious, however, and lines were kept open with Iran. Specifically, Saudi

Arabia supported mediation through the offices of the Islamic Conference
and a meeting was held in January 1981. A mediation commission was set
up which made proposals for a settlement but this was turned down by
Khomeini and the revolutionary leaders in Teheran.[53]

Soon after the Islamic Conference and while the mediation commission
was in progress the Saudis took initiatives to establish what became
the Gulf Cooperation Council (GCC).[54] On 4 February the six foreign
ministers met in Riyadh; on 9 March they met in Muscat and approved
the statutes; on 25–26 May 1981 the heads of state met in Abu Dhabi and
formally launched the organisation.

Although security was at the top of every individual agenda and had
been at the centre of political negotiation for the past ten years it was
mentioned neither in the objectives of the organisation (article 4) nor in the
communique issued after the meeting, except to say that 'the security and
stability of the area is the responsibility of its peoples and states'. Indeed,
in the communique it was specifically stated that

> they also affirmed their total rejection of any foreign interference in
> the area whatever its origin and called for the necessity of isolating
> the whole area from international conflicts and in particular keeping
> away military fleets and foreign bases for their interest and that of the
> world.

None of the members had any difficulty in turning a blind eye to
the Facilities Agreement between Oman and the US, to the presence of
US AWACS aircraft in Saudi Arabia, to the various military support
agreements that existed between Gulf states and the Western powers and
to the naval vessels that were even then steaming around the Gulf. The
unwritten and unadmitted clauses were as important as those that were
signed.

The GCC was off the ground, but its main thrust was inoperative.
At the February meeting in Taif the Saudi security proposal was for
bilateral agreements between members; Oman still wanted joint protection
for navigation in the Hormuz straits; Kuwait admitted no external threat.
These positions were repeated in March and May.[55] At the end of August,
at a Foreign Ministers conference, again in Taif, Oman restated its position
in a formal paper which said that in view of Soviet activities in the region
the Gulf States should give priority to cooperation with the US and other
Western countries.[56] Its military clauses provided for setting up a joint
naval force for the protection of the Gulf; for holding periodical joint
manoeuvres; and for unifying the GCC members' aerial defence systems.

The Omani position was consistent and remained consistent. It gradually obtained de facto support. In January 1982 the first reports of a GCC Rapid Deployment Force proposal emerged; in October 1983 the first Peninsula Shield joint exercise took place; when the tanker war began with Iranian attacks on Kuwaiti and Saudi tankers in April 1984 the mood openly changed and in June a decision was taken that the GCC would be responsible for the 12-mile limit (this became known as the 'King Fahd line'). The implication was that the international community was responsible beyond the 12-mile limit. This outcome was in practice almost precisely what Oman had been so unpopularly proposing for the preceding eight years. The final seal of approval for the Omani policy line was the GCC decision to allocate nearly $2 billion over twelve years to Oman for upgrading their military resources.[57]

Within the GCC Oman has exhibited its independent line over a range of issues, the most important relating to external relations. Its alliance with Iran and acceptance of Iranian support in the Dhofar war was anathema to many in the Gulf, particularly Iraq and Kuwait. If Arab states had been prepared to help Qaboos in the early years, perhaps he would never have called upon the Shah; but they did not. Oman's proposals for a Gulf security pact allied in some practical manner to the Western powers was, as has been seen, a concept that other Gulf states did not want to support, but which, in the later stages of the Iran-Iraq war, they found themselves seeking.[58] When Sadat signed the Camp David agreements Oman attended the first Baghdad Summit in November 1978 which decided 'not to endorse' those Agreements. They did not, however, attend the second, in March 1979, which suspended Egyptian membership of the Arab League and severed diplomatic relations with Egypt.[59] Oman not only maintained diplomatic relations with Egypt but Qaboos and Mubarak exchanged visits in February and May 1982. Moreover, Qaboos tried, to no avail, to persuade King Hussein and others to restore relations with Egypt.

In internal defence matters Qaboos consistently maintained his close links with Britain and welcomed the presence of British officers and technical staff within SAF. In 1980 he signed the Access Agreement with US in spite of opposition from other Arab states. He refused to be deflected from what he saw as the correct course for Oman and was prepared to maintain consistency on issues on which others either compromised their positions or sought to make him compromise his. Critics might claim that Omani policy was only possible because Oman was remote from the centre of activity, but the fact remains that over time Qaboos has been vindicated. His influence has been as a result greater than was ever expected and has grown, not diminished, over time.

After its creation in 1981 the GCC was dominated, during the rest of the 1980s, by developments in the Iran-Iraq war, but this did not mean that all its members felt identically about the war. Traditionally the UAE and Oman, amongst GCC members, had the most open relationship with Iran. In the case of UAE this was based on trading and family links; the relationship of Dubai, for instance, with Iran was comparable to that of a Greek trading colony with Athens in the fifth-century BC. In the case of Oman there was a long history of relationships, from that of colony in the early centuries AD to the recent military links forged out of the Dhofar war. For the other GCC members the situation was different. Kuwait, although it had similar trading and family links as Dubai, was overshadowed by the Iraqi claim to its territory and a realpolitik that demanded it support Iraq. Saudi Arabia had been in contention with Iran for political influence in the Gulf, but was torn by a schizophrenic nervous fear of both belligerents. Bahrain had barely escaped the colonising grasp of Iran in 1969 and was now, with Qatar, firmly under the grip of Saudi influence.

Within the GCC it was, therefore, Oman which was able to engage in the most practical even-handed approach to the Gulf war. It had to establish this principle within a few days of the start of the war when Iraqi planes landed in Oman with the intention of using it as a base. They were told to leave. From that time onwards Oman was consistent in working to maintain links with Iran in spite of pressures on the GCC to express exclusive support for Iraq.

Later, in 1986–87, when the tanker war was at its peak Oman was able to keep its control over the Hormuz channel and ensure safe passage for ships entering and leaving the Gulf by a mixture of firmness and civility and by strictly distinguishing between national and international rights and obligations. Iran, even if it felt inclined to, could not fault Omani policy and practice and it knew that, if there was any question of challenging Oman, the reaction would be immediate and that, if necessary, Oman would be supported by the foreign naval presence which by then was in place.

Oman never broke its dialogue with Iran, even though Oman withdrew its *chargé d'affaires* from Teheran in October 1982, and the result was positive in both directions. There were occasions when Oman was able to act as agent between Iran and US for the repatriation of Iranians wounded or killed in clashes in the Gulf. Arrangements could be made in proper Islamic fashion without publicity and without, therefore, any escalation of tension. Iran, for its part, recognised that to have at least one interlocutor who was impartial and scrupulous was an advantage to be preserved.

Although the GCC was inevitably caught up in the backwash of the Iran-Iraq war and Gulf security was, as has been noted, the inspiration behind it, it was formally created with political and economic objectives. This is not the place to make assessments about the achievements, failures or successes of the GCC itself. Its economic integration and trade policies have in practice provided few benefits. Oman, however, benefited early on from one of its more useful political initiatives, the brokering of a peace treaty between Oman and PDRY. This was led by Kuwait with the assistance of UAE. An accord was signed in September 1982 and an agreement on principles that should govern relations between them was reached at a meeting in Kuwait in November. This led in July 1986 to an agreement to exchange resident ambassadors. In 1988 the PDRY President made an official visit to Oman, and Oman has subsequently even extended limited aid to PDRY.[60]

For Oman the benefits of the GCC[61] have been largely in the political arena. It has enabled Oman to know its neighbours and its neighbours to know Oman. Without the continual contact which has occurred through innumerable GCC meetings covering consultation between ministries on countless subjects this degree of understanding could never have been created. Moreover, it has been through these meetings, even though they have often led to nothing productive, that the Omanis have created a reputation for both creative and plain speaking. The process of self-learning within the GCC has in some ways parallelled that of European nations in the EEC.

Security
Security has been a constant background refrain to discussion of Oman's position in the Gulf and its relationships with the GCC, Iran, UK and US. Security aspects represent an important component of Omani foreign policy. Geography, in particular the territorial waters in the straits of Hormuz, has given Oman its international significance, but Qaboos has used this as an asset on which to build his own structure of influence. In different circumstances he might have decided to depend wholly upon external support, either from an Arab or Western source. Circumstances, however, were such that, because of the Dhofar war and because of the threat presented by PDRY, Qaboos possessed a military resource far larger and more organised than might have been expected. The combination of geography and the Dhofar war enabled him to work from strong foundations and he was further assisted by Oman's traditional links with the British armed forces which, although almost entirely responsible in the early days for the effectiveness of SAF, had always been firmly under the command of the Sultan.

With the Dhofar war effectively over by 1976 Qaboos set about

TABLE 2　*Expenditure on defence and national security*

	Expenditure RO millions	as percentage of total govt. expenditure
1976–80	1449	43.4
1981–85	3247	41.2
1986	665	35.2
1987	584	36.3
1988	589 (est.)	37.6

SOURCE: *SYB* 1986, Table 215 and *SYB* 1989, Table 222.

equipping and strengthening SAF for a role which would combine defence security and offensive preparedness and give Oman a voice and a vote that, with muscle power behind it, would be of significance. As an indication of this intent it is instructive to look at the expenditure committed to 'defence and national security' since 1975 both in absolute and relative terms. 'Defence and national security' covers police and special forces but the commitment to the armed forces – supplemented by US payments under the Facilities Agreement – has been large and consistent (see Table 2).

Expenditure does not necessarily imply efficiency or effectiveness. Qaboos himself was trained at Sandhurst and has never lost his feel for military discipline or quality of personnel and equipment; nor for the trappings of pomp that show off that discipline and quality. The result is a force that looks good and, as far as can be judged, is good. Since 1975 the army has had few practical opportunities for active operations, although operations on the PDRY border in 1987 and 1989 have led to questions and concerns about the army reaction to incursions in that area. The actions were small-scale and probably inspired by local tribal ambitions rather than by any governmental policy but they demonstrated a distinct lack of planning or coordination on the Omani side. The navy and airforce, however, proved themselves professional and proficient during the Iran-Iraq war. The problem for the future is related more to organisation and command coordination than to equipment.

Oman's military forces, of course, have, in the final analysis, only a limited capacity to defend or attack although they cover, if inevitably with no great depth, a wide range of capability. The army has an armoured regiment, artillery, armed reconnaissance, field engineering, an airborne regiment and, under the Royal Household, a Special Forces regiment. The navy has missile craft, patrol boats and amphibious craft. The airforce has two squadrons of Jaguar fighter aircraft, one squadron of Hunters, training and transport aircraft and two squadrons of helicopters. There are about 30 000 persons in the armed forces.[62]

If Oman's armed forces seem like a miniature version of the British army this is no accident. They were built up during the 1970s and 1980s with a strong input from Britain which sold equipment and provided an extensive back-up of technical, personnel, training and staff appointments – officers who were seconded from the British army or who contracted direct to SAF. Until 1987 the Chief of Staff was British, the last one being Lieutenant General John Watts, by then much promoted from the relatively junior officer who had led the Jebal Akhdar attack in 1959; only in 1990 did Omanis take over the posts of commander of the navy and air force.

It would, however, be misleading to imagine either that Britain controlled the Omani forces or that the military connection was the only British relationship with Oman. The link has certainly been a strong one although it has inevitably weakened over time. In the case of the navy, for instance, replacement of the existing corvettes with a larger version that will provide a deep-water capability is likely to come from France. The overall relationship with Britain, however, is unlikely to weaken, at least while Qaboos remains in power. His own personal experience of Britain and the British has given him confidence in their advice and judgment. This has occurred at many different levels, from the friendships that he has with members of the British Royal family, the prime minister and ministers through to the military, diplomats, bankers and ordinary professional people. This has given Britain a preferred position amongst foreign countries, a position which is reflected by large numbers of Omanis from a broad spectrum of experience and activity who have personal links with Britain.

For historical reasons the British position has been strong in the security context, but Omani foreign policy has consistently broadened its base over the years. The US connection has been described. Oman needed this insurance while the Cold War was being fought since it saw itself, with some reason, as being an outpost in that war, an outpost, moreover, that was directly threatened.

Although the Dhofar war was militarily over, and a ceasefire was agreed in early 1976, this did not mean that the threat of political retribution from PDRY suddenly subsided. On the contrary, it carried on at least until the end of 1982 when, under the mediation of the GCC, Oman and PDRY signed a joint declaration of principles designed to govern relations between them. During these years PDRY carried on a virulent political campaign against Oman and received strong support, in particular from the USSR and Cuba. In August 1981 PDRY announced a tripartite cooperation agreement with Libya and Ethiopia, a pact with potentially sinister implications even if such agreements seldom produce their potential. These were the years in which the USSR invaded Afghanistan and were heavily involved with Ethiopia against Somalia and Eritrea, when the Horn of Africa seemed to be a Russian, and communist, springboard to threaten the Arabian peninsula. Qaboos had good reason to be nervous of the threats implied by these convulsions, never mind the dangers later posed by the Iran-Iraq war.

Qaboos has on a number of occasions managed to surprise onlookers with his policy decisions. In May 1978 he established diplomatic relations with Peking,[63] as a counter to USSR/PDRY activity, the first Gulf state to do this. In September 1985 Oman and USSR (only six months into the Gorbachev era) established diplomatic relations[64] in a move that pre-empted others and took them by surprise. Decisions such as these illustrate Qaboos' independent view of the world and of Oman's place in it. There is clearly no question of taking advice from others, whether the UK or US or his GCC colleagues, any of whom would have probably urged cautious indecision at the time the decisions were made.

If many of Omani foreign policy decisions are made with a keen eye on security consideration others seem to exemplify Qaboos' fundamental predilection for a world ruled by consistency, good sense, decency and friendliness. It is not his fault if most of the rest of the world fails, or is unable, to follow such an essentially hopeful view of things, but at least Oman can do its best. Qaboos' strength in his international relations, and perhaps this extends to his internal political attitudes as well, is rationality and lack of emotion. This may not generate excitement but it supports stability.

So, Omani contacts are by now spread far beyond the natural or traditional areas of the Arab League, Islamic Conference Organisation, Britain and the US. By 1990 Oman had diplomatic relations with 91 countries and belonged to 24 international organisations and specialised agencies.[65] It was firmly slotted into the international system.

Economy and Infrastructure

Oil

The motor for Omani life and development has been since 1967, is now, and will remain, oil. The operating company of the main producing concession throughout this time has been Petroleum Development Oman Ltd. (PDO), in which the majority ownership was, until 1974, Shell. Since 1974 the Oman government has been majority owner, with Shell, as a minority shareholder, providing technical and managerial services.[66] It has been a beneficial and satisfying partnership, in which good fortune and good timing has also played its part.

Oil production in Oman has twice seemed to be declining and has twice been supplemented by development of new fields. These developments have in both cases resulted from renegotiation of terms between the government and PDO and from the availability of new technologies. In the early 1970s it quickly became clear that the original Fahud area could not sustain production at its opening rate of around 300 000 b/d. In 1975 the development of fields in the Ghaba area boosted production from a low of 291 000 b/d to around 350 000 b/d. In the early 1980s development of the Southern fields restored production from a low of 282 000 b/d in 1980 to 400 000 b/d by 1984. Since then production has continued to climb and by the end of 1990 had reached 700 000 b/d.[67] PDO oil reserves increased from 2.5 billion barrels in 1980 to over 4 billion by 1988; gas reserves in 1988 were over 9 ^{12} cubic feet with production at around 450 million cubic feet.[68]

By any standards this has been a successful operation. It has, however, required a large and sustained commitment and effort in terms of technology, people and investment. This has taken place because of a solidly based mutual trust between Sultan Qaboos, his oil minister, Said Shanfari,[69] and Shell. Qaboos early on understood that oil was the pre-requisite for Oman's development and he kept its ultimate management firmly in his own hands. It is fair to say that the PDO operation in Oman has been, in its relatively small way, as smooth and successful as any joint oil venture.

The relationship between Shell and Oman has lasted over 20 years already and there seems no reason why it should not continue. Certainly the current plans are in the same mould as previous developments. In 1990 PDO announced a huge new project to develop Lekhwair over the next 5 years.[70] This will increase production of the Lekhwair field from 21 000 b/d to over 100 000 b/d with an investment of $500 million and the drilling of 126 new production and 47 water injection wells. Other investment will include 75 wells in Yibal, 100 wells in Nimr and the continuation of a high technology programme for research and the practical application of Enhanced Oil Recovery techniques in Marmul and other fields.[71] All this is being supplemented by an 'enhanced Omanisation programme' which aims to have PDO 90 per cent Omanised by 2000 and which has already in 1990, for instance, involved training at university level for 350 Omanis in the UK. Even though the cost of producing Omani oil is high by the standards of the Middle East its cost is still only about $4/bbl.

Oil revenue for Oman has, therefore, been dependent partly on a

TABLE 3   *Oil revenues: actual and inflation corrected (1980–88)*

	1980	1981	1982	1983	1984	1985	1986	1987	1988
Oil prod. '000 b/d	283	328	336	389	416	498	560	582	619
Revenue RO million	1096	1341	1216	1278	1305	1510	929	1195	994
Revenue (inflation corrected)	1096	1303	1238	1305	1374	1519	802	942	698

SOURCE: *SYB* 1989. Oil production and oil revenue figures from Tables 171 and 222. Inflation correction calculated by applying the unit value index of imports, all items, Table 220, and *SYB* 1986, Table 213.

continuing technological and managerial effort and more immediately on the state of the international oil market. Apart from the crucial element of price Oman has benefited from a crude oil quality, and a location outside the Gulf, that has been attractive to consumers. Price, however, has been the main determinant of revenue and the two huge increases in 1973/4 and 1979/80 came at particularly fortuitous times for Oman. The 1973/74 price increase allowed Oman's initial infrastructural development to take place, while the 1979/80 increase financed a second wave of investment and expenditure that transformed the country from what was still a frontier-type economy in the late 1970s to the fully-fledged sophisticated oil state of the late 1980s. This transformation, and the high costs implied by it, was, of course, hit hard by the greatly reduced oil price levels from 1986 to mid-1990, by the reduced value of the dollar against most other leading currencies in those years and by the inflation[72] that followed the devaluation of the Omani riyal by 10 per cent against the dollar in 1986. Prior to 1985 the rate of exchange had been RO 0.345 to the dollar, from 1986 it has been RO 0.384. Oil revenue in 1988 was worth only 64 per cent of the 1980 revenue and 46 per cent of 1985 revenue (see Table 3).

This was, of course, in line with other GCC members but the management of such reduced revenue has needed strong nerves. The argument that the reduction was from an abnormally high base is theoretical rather than practical.

Oman never joined Opec. This was because Qaboos wanted to be sure that he kept absolute freedom of manoeuvre in his oil policy. He did not want to risk any interference in an area that was so crucial to Oman's existence. This was entirely consistent with his early decision to keep oil policy and relationships within Oman under his own control. It was a wise decision for he benefited (and suffered) from Opec decisions without being responsible for them or being caught up in their political fallout. In the 1980s his position shifted slightly. On the one hand Oman became marginally implicated with Opec through its GCC membership – to the extent that, when it suited Saudi Arabia to obtain GCC support for its Opec oil policy, Oman was part of that support. More significantly, however, Qaboos backed initiatives in 1988 for non-Opec solidarity with Opec.

An initiative along these lines was clearly in Oman's interests as oil prices juddered at a low level from 1986. It arose from an invitation in Spring 1986 from Opec to a number of non-Opec oil producers to attend an Opec meeting as observers. The original five observers were Angola, Egypt, Mexico, Malaysia and Oman although others would be added from as diverse direction as Moscow and Texas. Oman became actively involved in the non-Opec initiative in 1988. Qaboos favoured this initiative which was spearheaded by Shanfari and supported on a technical level by his adviser on petroleum affairs, Hermann Franssen. The idea was to obtain commitments from non-Opec countries to a degree of voluntary oil production restraint in order to strengthen the will of Opec members to reduce their own production. Although there was never any formal agreement from either side the diplomatic activity and publicity created by the proposals had an occasional positive effect on the oil market. For Qaboos it was a useful exercise. It gave Oman a high profile in a plan which, although never likely to be effective, was received sympathetically by a wide spectrum of diverse interest. As an exercise in non-confrontational diplomacy on a subject of evident importance to Oman which at the same time had a credible international potential it was well suited to Qaboos' wish to project his country as a positive and independent force for balancing opposing interests. Moreover, although there were occasional conditional commitments to reducing oil production, the statistics of 1988 and 1989 show that there was minimal practical diminution of Omani oil production or sales.

Finance

Oil has provided the major part of Omani revenue. It has been supplemented by loans and grants from a variety of international sources, government and commercial. Oman has spent its revenues under three main headings – defence and national security, civil recurrent and development. Since 1980 it has also transferred a proportion of its oil revenue into a State General Reserve Fund (SGRF). The way in which this process has been managed can be understood, at least in general terms, by studying the 5-year planning documentation and the annual Statistical Year Books. Three

5-year plans have been created as the basis for economic development of the state, 1976–80, 1981–85, 1986–90. As described above the first grew out of the early years of trial and uncoordinated expenditure. The second, full with expectation, coincided with the oil price increases of 1979/80. The third was amended in time to take account of the oil price collapse of 1986. The fourth, now published, looks forward to the third decade of Omani development.

The 5-year plans have demonstrated Omani economic and social intentions, the statistical year books provide evidence of how the intentions were translated into action.

Study of these documents[73] shows a notable consistency in distribution of overall expenditure between categories and of development expenditure between sectors. Both the first two plans were fortunate in obtaining more revenue than expected as a result of oil price movements, 20 per cent in the case of the first, nearly 10 per cent in the case of the second. Changing trends over the years provide few surprises. The share of civil recurrent expenditure is rising, an almost inevitable result of a huge government activity and an increasing infrastructure to maintain. In the past few years, as revenue remained relatively static, the squeeze has been on development expenditure. More significantly, the breakdown of expenditure by ministry shows that the main growth area is the Royal Diwan, the cost centre that has always been the most difficult to control. During 1981–85 the Diwan was responsible for 12 per cent of all development expenditure and 13 per cent of civil recurrent; in 1988, admittedly a year in which development expenditure had sunk to only 18 per cent of total expenditure, the Diwan was responsible for one third and its share of recurrent expenditure had risen to 14 per cent. In terms of combined development and recurrent expenditure the Diwan had become larger than any other ministry. In 1988 it was responsible for spending RO 140 million.[74]

Numbers are notoriously misleading unless anchored to a foundation of relevance and experience. Nevertheless, some indication of Omani statistical achievement is necessary. GDP was RO 105 million in 1970, RO 2000 million in 1980, RO 3000 million in 1987.[75] From 1971–85 government investment in Electricity and Water has been over RO 400 million, in Roads over RO 500 million, in Education RO 200 million, in Health over RO 100 million. Total government investment in development in these 15 years was nearly RO 4000 million, total expenditure on Defence and National Security over RO 5000 million. GNP per capita in 1987 was recorded by the UN[76] as $5810 which put it at the top of the Upper-middle-income category, number 92 out of 120 countries with a population in excess of 1 million.

The transformation of the numbers into social development will be dealt with in the next section. They raise, however, some more immediate reactions. The first is that the Omani economy remains almost entirely reliant on oil revenue. Efforts to diversify the economy and to 'develop new sources of income to supplement and eventually to replace oil revenues' [77] have remained unproductive. In 1987 the total of customs duties, corporate tax, fees and taxes and payments for services made up only 11 per cent of total government revenue; and nearly half of it came from heavily subsidised income from electricity and water charges.[78]

Omani balance of trade has been healthily positive but is dependent on oil for plus or minus 90 per cent of its export earnings. In 1988 the only other exports with a value in excess of RO 1 million were fish (RO 19 million), copper cathodes (RO 17 million) and limes (RO 2 million).[79] By 1988 there were only 39 companies with a capital in excess of RO 5 million;[80] of these only 12 were in productive industry, with 24 in construction, finance and hotels. The largest single investment after oil has been in copper for which the Oman Mining Company was set up in 1978. Half of the original investment of over $200 million came from a grant from Saudi Arabia, but the project, although efficiently managed and producing high quality cathodes, is uneconomic except on a marginal costing basis and has limited reserves of ore. A jetty, built in Sohar specifically for copper export, has never been used.

The potential for minerals in Oman is optimistically foreseen in public documentation but it is likely to be a chimera. A diversity of minerals undoubtedly exist in the mountains. Oman 1989[81] mentions chromite, manganese, laterite, iron and nickel; also coal, asbestos, gypsum, limestone and marble. There is a small marble processing factory at Rusayl but the chances that any of the other minerals are commercially extractable seem slim.

Efforts to develop private local industry have been made, but the result has been limited. Apart from oil and housing the total private contribution to capital formation has been negligible at RO 125 million in the period 1976–80 and RO 278 million in 1981–85.[82] The 1986–90 plan showed no expected increase. The instruments by which the government has fostered economic activity have been the creation of specialist banks and the development of the Rusayl Industrial Estate.

The three government-backed banks set up to encourage local investment are the Housing Bank,[83] the Oman Bank for Agriculture and Fisheries (OBAF)[84] and the Oman Development Bank (ODB).[85]

In ten years of operation, from 1979–88, the ODB[86] has provided financing amounting to RO 50 million to 253 projects whose total cost was nearly RO 150 million. In 1988 26 projects costing RO 14 million received ODB financing worth over RO 4 million. Of the 26 projects 12 were under RO 100 000. Any project in excess of a cost of RO 5000 is considered. Loans are made at a preferential rate of interest (6% in the capital area, 5% outside) with a grace period of 1–2 years. The Bank has paid-up capital of RO 10 million, of which 40 per cent is held by the Government, 40 per cent by regional institutions and banks, 20 per cent by Omanis. In the *Times of Oman* of 13 September 1990, ODB announced that RO 5 million of 5-year bonds would be issued to help finance investments and development projects. Bonds would be valued at RO 1 and be issued through the Muscat Securities Market.

The Oman Bank for Agriculture and Fisheries deals for the most part in small business.[87] In 1988 its twelve branches approved loans totalling RO 6 million for nearly 1200 projects, of which 950 received less than RO 5000 each. At the other end of the scale 2 projects received RO 1.5 million. Loans are heavily subsidised, with, for instance, small loans for fishing boats attracting only 2 per cent interest with repayment over 3–4 years. The Bank has paid-up capital of just under RO 13 million.

The Rusayl Industrial Estate was opened in 1984 and officially inaugurated by Sultan Qaboos on 4 December 1985. In the second 5-year plan RO 21 million was allocated to its development and further RO 10 million in the third plan to its expansion.[88] It has its own power supply generated by natural gas and, nearby, housing and services for those working on the site. It is 45 kms from Muscat and 6 kms from Seeb International Airport on the road to Nizwa. In October 1988 there were 48 different industries established at Rusayl, including the marble factory. Similar industrial estates are planned for Sohar, Raysut, Nizwa and Sur and will be developed during the fourth 5-year plan.[89]

Agricultural production is encouraged not only by the Oman Bank for Agriculture and Fisheries but also by the government-inspired marketing organisation, The Public Authority for Marketing Agricultural Produce (PAMAP).[90] This organisation has imaginatively publicised itself with the logo of 'Green Oman', which is spread over its products, its marketing outlets and transport. From 1981–85 PAMAP invested nearly RO 8 million, and a further RO 5 million has been allocated to it for the period 1986–90.[91] By 1989 PAMAP had established 6 distribution centres and 17 collecting centres, with a headquarters and main distribution centre at Ghala in the capital area. PAMAP also has a food processing unit which produces pickles, lime powder and frankincense. PAMAP buys fruit and vegetables from farmers at prices that are, in principle, fixed weekly by headquarters. It sells both locally in the market and sends bulk to Muscat. The distribution centres have limited refrigerated storage capacity. Turnover is difficult to establish but the Nizwa centre appears to be handling 300–400 tons of vegetables and fruit per annum.[92] The operating cost of PAMAP is not published, but it seems certain that it must be heavily subsidised, well beyond the cost of capital. PAMAP provides a necessary service and incentive to farmers in Oman given that the development of agriculture is a government objective. The extent to which this should be an objective is another question.

Although most industrial and agricultural investment incentive derives from the government the private sector has not remained wholly idle. At the end of 1988 there were 22 commercial banks licensed to operate in Oman, of which 9 were local and 13 foreign.[93] Most local banks are majority owned by family groups, some with participation by members of the Royal Family. A proportion of shares will be held by the public which in practice means the larger merchant families. Cross holdings between banks, companies and individuals are common. There exist two other companies with potential investment capacity, Oman Investment and Finance Company and Oman International Development and Investment Company (Ominvest). The former deals primarily, however, with the collection of accounts for the Ministry of Electricity and Water. Ominvest is the nearest to a merchant bank that exists in Oman, but its share capital is only RO 8 million held as to 80 per cent by 80 shareholders, with another 1400 holding the balance of 20 per cent. Because of the lack of internal investment opportunity 40 per cent of the assets are, in fact, held abroad and much of the Omani investment is in insurance and finance. The problem of investment opportunity is common to all Gulf banks including, for instance, the Gulf Investment Corporation, the investment arm of the GCC, so that the lists of investments in the annual reports of these companies tend to be short and of little diversity.

Oman now has a stock exchange, the Muscat Securites Market, opened in May 1989, which should theoretically help the investment process, but its activity is still rudimentary. A random example of a day's trading, taken on 22 October 1989, shows that on that day the volume of trading was RO 21301 representing 8864 shares and 6 contracts.[94] There were 49 quoted companies. The scope for individual investment in Omani companies is not extensive.

All this is, by any standards, small-scale. Industry, in particular, heavily subsidised by the state as it is, remains marginal. Investment opportunities are extremely limited. Encouragement by the government, however, both through diverse subsidy and continuing exhortation is seen as a necessary element in the process of job creation and diversification of the economy.

Oman is faced with the problems common to most LDCs, a vicious circle of economic justification, opportunity, size of local market, subsidy, resources, training and the graduates emerging from the educational system. Its one asset has been that, in common with other Gulf oil producing countries, it has had more money available than most other LDCs with which to break into the circle, but in the longer term this too becomes part of it.

Oman's cash flow from oil has been healthy, but it has not been forgotten that saving and borrowing are both part of economic life. In 1980 the State General Reserve Fund (SGRF) was established by Royal Decree 1/80 as a separate entity to be managed under the direction of the Financial Affairs Council.[95] Its assets were to be composed, primarily, of 15 per cent of oil revenues and, secondarily, of annual surpluses on current account. Withdrawals were permitted for financing a deficit in the state budget. SGRF accounts are not published, although a net annual withdrawal figure is quoted in the Statistical Year Book. This shows that from 1980–84 the balance was in favour of transfers to the SGRF, from 1985–88 of withdrawals from SGRF. The total of net withdrawals from SGRF has exceeded net transfers to SGRF by RO 265 million in those nine years.[96] This raises the question of what remaining balance there may now be in the SGRF. This is further complicated by the change in treatment of the SGRF transfer/withdrawal figure between the Statistical Year Books of 1987 and 1988 – up to 1987 it is treated as a reduction/increase in total revenue, from 1988 it is treated as a below the line item in balancing the surplus/deficit on total expenditure. It is, therefore, unclear whether or not the surplus on current account recorded in 1980 and 1981 would qualify, under 1988 statistical practice, as a potential addition to SGRF funds.[97] There is also an unknown figure representing interest income arising from SGRF investments. Current SGRF balances cannot, therefore, be calculated from published documents; nor can SGRF annual receipts from oil, since the 15 per cent allocation of oil revenue is itself subject to variation and has, during the low price era, fallen to only 5 per cent. The belief is that SGRF assets are not allowed to fall below about RO 1 billion, but this cannot be substantiated from published information.[98]

Oman has borrowed money consistently since the first loan agreement with Morgan Grenfell in 1973. Loans have since arrived from diverse quarters; many from Saudi Arabia and Gulf institutions, from World Bank sources, from commercial bank sources and the eurodollar market. It may be noted that the terms that Oman has been able to negotiate have in most cases been very competitive. From 1976–86 the total of net grants and borrowings is recorded as nearly RO 400 million of grants and over

RO 500 million of borrowings.[99] From 1983–88 long-term loans taken up amounted to just over RO 1 billion, with repayments over the same period of over RO 500 million.[100] Oman's total debt in 1987 was recorded as $3.8 billion and its debt service as $660 million.[101] It is planned to keep the current borrowing level as a ceiling which should not, at least for the next few years, be exceeded.

Investment
During the course of the first two 5-year plans and three years of the third, that is from 1976–88, the total of development money spent by the government on services and infrastructure has been close on RO 3 billion (excluding a further RO 1 billion which has been spent on civilian projects under the military budget): 80 per cent of this RO 3 billion has been committed to 10 areas of social infrastructure – to Roads (20%), Electricity and Water (16%), Education (9.5%), Town Planning/ Municipalities (7%), Post and Telecommunications (6.5%), Health (6%), Housing (6%), Airports and Ports (4%), Agriculture and Fisheries (3%), Irrigation and Water Resources (2%) (see also Table 10).

Money is one thing, but the quality of services and their effect on society, assuming it is possible to measure it, is more relevant. In at least one respect the quality of Oman's investment expenditure produces the highest praise from those who have seen it. This is in its physical presentation – architecture, construction and design. Roads are immaculately engineered, signed and maintained. Hospitals are imaginatively designed and well built. Schools are attractive and well-equipped. Low-cost housing manages to look like medium cost housing. Tele-relay stations are neatly ranged over the country and merge into the landscape. Municipalities plan roads, roundabouts, trees and open spaces and then keep them clean, tidy and colourful. There is electricity in every corner of the country and water is available in remote places. The outward and visible manifestation of Omani expenditure is impressive and pleasant to the eye.

The bricks and mortar of infrastructure are, moreover, administered and managed with considerable efficiency. This is to a great degree due to the input of non-Omanis. Expatriates fill, in particular, the intermediate and manual levels of activity. The statistics give an indication of the dependency on non-Omanis in the economy. In the civil service,[102] for instance, total numbers more or less doubled between 1980 and 1988, but the proportion of Omanis to non-Omanis remained similar.

Non-Omanis are listed under the following nationalities [103] – Egypt, Sudan, Jordan, India, Pakistan, Sri Lanka, Philippines and 'other'. In 1988 the largest groups were Egyptians with a total of 9667 (33% of the total)

and Indians with 6643 (22%). Predictably enough the majority of Egyptians
were in Education[104] (8313, split 55/45 between men and women) and the
largest group of Indians were in Health (2749, split 36/64 between men and
women). Most of the Sudanese (872 out of 1175) and Jordanians (754 out
of 778) were in Education. At the other end of the scale the Ministry of
Foreign Affairs was all Omani except for one Egyptian and five Indians.

Another measure of dependence upon expatriates is the statistic on
Labour Cards issued to non-Omanis working in the private sector.[105] In
1980 there were 132 618 and in 1988 248 870, an increase of 88 per cent.
The majority were employed in two sectors, Construction (33% in 1988)
and Trading/restaurant/hotels (32%).[106] Over 90 per cent came from India,
Pakistan and Bangladesh.[107]

Bricks and mortar, administration and management do not necessarily
add up to production or output. It is instructive, therefore, to see what, at
least in statistical terms, has been achieved.

Within the Ministry of Education, general education, that is the main
public education system, has more or less tripled in size between 1980
and 1988. Within the Ministry of Health there has been a similar increase
measured in the number of doctors and nurses. Asphalted roads have been
doubled in length, from 2102 kms to 4247 kms,[108] the consumption of
electricity has multiplied by nearly five times and water by nearly four
times. Details are shown in Tables 4–6.

Before trying to determine how these statistics relate to the reality of
Omani society there is a general point to be considered. That is the extent
to which development has been spread regionally over the country and how
it relates to regional population concentrations.

In size, Oman is huge, around 300 000 square kilometres, but five-sixths
of this is desert.[109] There has been no census so the population is not
known, but 1.4 million Omanis[110] and 0.3 million expatriates seems to be
generally recognised as a reasonable 1990 estimate. The country is split into
seven regions for planning and statistical purposes and Table 7 gives an
idea of how development has been spread round the country. 'Live births'
may provide an approximate indication of the population distribution. In
the case of the South, at least, the 7 per cent seems consistent with its
estimate of 100 000 within the assumed total of 1.4 million. During the
period 1976–1985 the total of government investment was distributed in
the proportion of 52 per cent to the Capital area, 12 per cent to the South
and 36 per cent to the remainder of the country.[111]

Without pressing the point unduly it would seem that the regional
distribution of infrastructure throughout the Sultanate has been successfully
achieved. The fact that the main specialist hospitals and the university are

TABLE 4   *Education statistics, 1980 and 1988*

General education		1980	1988	percentage increase 1988 over 1980
Primary	– schools	237	370	56
	– students, male ('000)	56.4	122.4	117
	– students, female ('000)	27.3	106.3	289
	– teachers	3107	8308	167
Preparatory	– schools	114	267	134
	– students, male ('000)	7.8	30.7	294
	– students, female ('000)	2.3	20.3	783
	– teachers	847	3890	359
Secondary	– schools	12	66	450
	– students, male ('000)	0.7	7.5	971
	– students, female ('000)	0.2	7.7	3750
	– teachers	101	1150	1039
TOTAL STUDENTS ('000)		94.8	294.9	211
TOTAL TEACHERS		4055	12860	217
Ministry of Education recurrent expenditure (RO million)		32	105	228

SOURCE: *SYB* 1986, Table 219 and *SYB* 1989, Tables 8, 226.

sited in the capital area may be a matter of complaint to those in other regions but it can hardly be doubted that they are best placed where they are.[112]

There can be no doubt that the importance of regional development is well in the minds of some of the ministers. The Minister of Planning, Mohammed Moosa,[113] intends to split government investment planning in future between the 7 regions. The Minister of Health, Dr Ali Moosa, has already restructured his ministry on a regional basis with eight directors general (Batina region has been split into two) each responsible for a regional budget and development plan. Logically this will lead to regional capitals with devolution, to at least some degree, of responsibility away from Muscat and into the regions. This has already happened in the South, and to a lesser extent in Musandam, partly because they are so remote from the capital and partly because they have both been subjected to special development treatment with their own Development Councils – in the case of the South this still operates, in the case of Musandam it is now concentrated into the responsibility of the Governor. Regionalisation brings with it, of course, the danger of increased bureaucracy and decreased

TABLE 5   *Health statistics, 1980 and 1988*

Ministry of Health	1980	1988	percentage increase 1988 over 1980
Hospitals	28	47	68
Health centres*	50	86	72
Preventive health centres	29	94	224
Beds	1784	3316	86
Doctors	294	907	209
Nursing staff	857	3260	280
Number of out-patients ('000)	3123	5702	83
Number of in-patients ('000)	108	177	64
Ministry of Health recurrent expenditure (RO million)	19	61	221

SOURCE: *SYB* 1986, Tables 37, 38, 219 and *SYB* 1989, Tables 37, 40, 41, 226.

* Under 1988 definitions

TABLE 6   *Electricity and water statistics, 1980 and 1988*

Electricity '000 KW/h	1980	1988	percentage increase 1988 over 1980
Consumption			
– Muscat	586 841	2 419 396	312
– South	115 908	321 118	177
– rest	26 865	800 051	2878
– TOTAL	729 614	3 540 565	385

NOTE: The lowest monthly consumption (mid-winter) and the highest (mid-summer) are 50 percent lower and higher than the mean, i.e. the highest monthly consumption figure is 3 times the lowest.

Water million gallons			
Consumption			
– capital area	1532	6109	299
– South	542	1757	224
– TOTAL	2075	7866	279
Ministry of Electricity and Water recurrent expenditure (RO million)	33	97	194

SOURCE: *SYB* 1986 Tables 91, 99, 219, *SYB* 1989 Tables 100, 106, 226.

TABLE 7   *Regional distribution statistics by percentages (1988)*

	Live births	Hospitals No.	beds	Govt. schools	Tel. lines	Social housing cost–up to 1988	Reg. cost – up to 1988	OBAF loans	Letter boxes
Muscat	25	17	43	15	57	58	32	10	28
Dakhiliah	12	17	12	12	6	7	9	11	13
Dhahirah	8	9	5	12	5	7	10	6	10
Musandam	2	6	3	2	1	2	1	–	14
Batina	29	19	11	28	14	8	24	48	15
Sharquiya	17	21	14	16	8	10	13	21	14
Janubiah	7	11	12	15	9	8	11	4	6
TOTAL No.	41384	47	3316	703	83032	112m	35347	6.1bn	426

SOURCE: *SYB* 1989, Tables 43, 37, 11, 96, 57, 160, 209, 93.

ability to take decisions, but in a country the size of Oman the need to give a regional as well as national identity to people who are by tradition and nature tribal and individualistic can usefully take precedence over the centralising tendencies of those with ministerial power. In the end it is, of course, the quality of ministers and civil servants which will determine whether either centralisation or decentralisation works.

Education and Health

Statistics themselves can illuminate or mislead. One of the most notable developments in Oman has been the attention to women's education, not only within schools but also as regards health and job opportunity. Table 4 shows that, although overall the number of boys in government schools exceeds girls by 54/46, in secondary schools there are actually more girls than boys. At Sultan Qaboos university the proportion at end-1988 was 60/40 in favour of boys but, excluding the Agriculture and Engineering faculties which were almost entirely male-dominated, the rest showed a 50/49 bias in favour of girls. It is significant, perhaps, that about 25 per cent of girls, both those at Sultan Qaboos university and those following university courses abroad, are studying either medicine or science.

Apart from general education the Omani government has applied itself to technical and other specialist education and training. Listed in the Statistical Year Book[114] are Islamic education (8 schools with 849 students), Agricultural, Industrial and Commercial secondary schools (one of each with a total of 706 students), 5 intermediate teacher training institutes (with 908 male and 745 female students), an Institute of Health Science (with 123 male and 146 female students in 1990), the Institute of Bankers (with 200 students) and the Oman Technical Industrial College (with 325 male and 228 female students). In addition, of course, there is Sultan Qaboos University with, in 1988/89 academic year, a total of 1051 male and 768 female undergraduates. In total there are more than 300 000 students recorded as being in government educational establishments of one sort or another in 1989, that is in excess of 20 per cent of the total population of Oman. There is still, however, a long way to go. In 1988/89 there were nearly 230 000 students in primary education, only 15 000 in secondary. There were, however, nearly 3000 at university, a relatively healthy 20 per cent of those coming out of secondary education.

None of these figures necessarily indicate quality, although they certainly show government determination and student enthusiasm. The problem is all too common – how to ensure that the paper qualification, particularly if it is degraded by a weak control system over external comparisons, can be translated into practical use. This is pre-eminently the problem with the output from technical and specialist secondary education and the university where examinations and standards need to be measured against international, or at least regional, equivalents. What is often lacking in these courses is proper comprehension of the theory and sufficient practical on the job training. Courses tend to be accelerated for students whose real need is more, not less, training. Laboratory technicians, for instance, are on a 3-year course (plus 4 months of additional English language learning) which in the UK would be 4 years. Their qualifications and capabilities are necessarily less even if their titles are the same.

Quality is not as difficult to determine in the area of health. Much of the medical input, as has been seen, depends on expatriates, but the initiatives to meet the challenges of what medicine is able to provide come from the government. The Minister, Dr Ali Moosa, is a man of strong purpose, himself a chest surgeon who did his postgraduate work in the UK. He has set to with enthusiasm to reform and renew the organisation and practice of health in Oman. As indicated, he has taken the regional approach and has appointed eight Directors General who are based in Muscat, Sohar,

Rustaq, Nizwa, Ibri, Sur, Khasab and Salala. The Directors General are not necessarily doctors; their main qualification must be the capacity to lead, and all will be subjected to additional managerial training. Each region is to have a main regional hospital which will in most cases be of a new common design; it will concentrate on outpatients, emergencies and accidents, and maternity and paedriatic sevices, but will have 200 beds available for in-patients. Regional health support will come from new polyclinics, approximately one to every 20–30 000 people, and health centres where there are less than 10 000 people within a 15 km radius. Health centres will concentrate on prevention and education, making use of the existing highly successful National Health Programme. Dr Ali Moosa intends to double the size of the Institute of Health Science to improve the output of Omani nurses, laboratory technicians, radiographers and other technical staff. He foresees most of the expatriate doctors coming from India or Arab countries, not because there is any opposition to Europeans but because they are now difficult to recruit and expensive to employ. He will keep under central ministerial control personnel, planning and supervision and the Royal Hospital which will be the main provider of tertiary treatment. At present the University hospital (opened in 1990) is under the control of the University. Although there is coordination with the Ministry it needs to be integrated into the medical system, probably as part of the tertiary service, if there is not to be waste and duplication.

The National Health Programme (NHP) in Oman has been outstandingly successful in reducing infant mortality and preventing disease. There are seven separate programmes run under the overall Programme: Expanded Programme of Immunisation, Control of Diarrhoeal Diseases, Acute Respiratory Infections, Oral Health (dental) programme, Prevention of Blindness, Mother and Child Health and Control of Tuberculosis.The NHP is part of the Preventive Medicine division of the Ministry but the Director of Curative Medicine, Dr Musallim Albualy, himself a paediatrician who trained in England and worked for many years in the US (he has been in Oman since 1981) has also been deeply involved and interested in its success. From 1985–90 it was, somewhat surprisingly, run by an ex-SAS officer, Sean Brogan,[115] who applied principles not only of organisation and management but also of information technology to the task. The result has been spectacularly successful and, apart from the medical statistics of the programmes, he left behind a series of Standard Operating Manuals covering the individual programmes which were produced in bulk from his own computer and desk top publishing set-up. It is reckoned that 85 per cent of the country by 1990 was covered by the NHP, that TB had reduced by 50 per cent in five years, that infant mortality was down from over 100 to under 40 per 1000 births. After a polio outbreak in 1988 WHO discovered from the extensive and accurate documentation held by the NHP that their own procedures for the LDCs (used by Oman amongst many others) needed to be modified.

The NHP works primarily by the education of mothers. They are briefed when they attend a clinic in any health centre or hospital in the country and checking procedures are carried out whenever they attend with their children after birth. In addition NHP runs supervisory teams which work out of health centres and keep an eye on sanitation in the home and villages and recheck that immunisation has been carried out correctly. The key to the success of the NHP has been that it works on a 'horizontal' basis from health centres in the regions where its systems are integrated into, and are automatically carried out by, the overall system. The result is that mothers, who themselves hold their own health cards, are the first to ensure that all the tests, checks and immunisations are carried out.[116]

One of the inspiriting Omani reactions to modern life is the way in which they want the best of what is going and then set about getting it. It reflects, or is anyway consistent with, the attitude of Qaboos himself who, as has been seen, takes it for granted that he should have the best orchestra, palace, armament, band, garden, hotel or hospital. His more imaginative ministers take the same line. Sometimes it may lead to waste, but more often it produces something unexpected and appealing.

Telecommunications

Health and education produce examples of surprises and excellence. So does the Ministry of Posts, Telegraph and Telephones (PTT). The Minister, Ahmed bin Suweidan, bubbles with enthusiasm. He has every right to do so since he has graduated to minister from a humble Ibri background in which, as a boy, he became fascinated by electrical gadgets. One day he decided, although he had no educational qualification, that he would become a wireless operator with SAF. Ten years later he was appointed as wireless operator to Captain Landon, the Intelligence Officer in Salala. So, he was a participant in the drama of 23 July 1970 and later went to Muscat to help set up communications in the Royal Palace. He has a highly sophisticated TV and Radio monitoring system in a studio attached to his large and exotic cliffside house in Muscat and his objective for PTT in Oman is that it should always be at the forefront of technology.

The General Telecommunications Organisation (GTO) is a separate government-owned corporation.[117] It was originally funded by government with RO 50 million loans but is able to, and does, borrow in its own right. Since 1987 it has been paying significant dividends to the government.

The GTO implemented RO 81.5 million of projects during 1981–85 and planned a further RO 93.8 million for 1986–90 of which RO 92.1 million was to be covered by self-financing.[118] It has satellite and microwave links into and round the country and is in the process of completing a fibre optic circuit between the regions and connected to the UAE. It is setting up a new satellite station in Ibri for connection to the Intelsat Atlantic as a complement to the existing station at Al Amirat connected to the Arabsat Indian Ocean link. Telephones exist in nearly every village of Oman and a special design of cardphone is being developed to overcome the dust and humidity problems that affect ordinary cards.

There is a certain pleasure in finding such an enthusiastic urge to provide the best of whatever is available. No doubt it is in one sense a response to a psychological impulse to prove that the country and its people are modern, forward-looking and capable, perhaps more capable than the providers of technology, of holding their own in a bright new technological age. A case can, perhaps, be made for attributing many Omani and Arab attitudes to an inferiority complex or, more simply, to an innate fascination with gadgetry that diverts attention from the rigours of geography and traditional living. Equally, however, this can be argued to be too cynical, a reaction of envy by those who are not able to aspire to what Oman, through the luck of the oil draw, can achieve. There are dangers too, of course, as the people of Kuwait discovered to their cost in August 1990.

Society

Participation

The most immediate changes to Omani society over the past 20 years have clearly been those that relate to health, education and communications, the three areas of basic human need which were denied to Omanis by Said bin Taimur. There are, however, other developments in Omani society that should be addressed.

However benevolent, Sultan Qaboos has autocratic powers, just as his colleagues have in that most exclusive of organisations, the GCC, the club of oil-producer kings. For years they have been described as an anachronism, but their replacement, whether by a process of revolution or democratic development (or, as in the case of Kuwait, by invasion), has generally been an external rather than internal debate. Nevertheless, tentative movements towards forms of participation in the formulation of policy and decisions have taken place in Oman, even if they may seem marginal to those on the outside who demand democracy for those inside.

Qaboos himself is not at all apologetic or defensive about his own power.

On the one hand he takes it for granted that his position is grounded on the legitimacy of inheritance and tradition, on the other he is insistent that there is an adequate process of feedback and opportunity for the percolation of opinion to have its say. Qaboos points to three ways in which he has delegated authority and allowed for democratic input. Firstly, there is an extensive delegation to ministers to get on with their departmental business under a cabinet which coordinates and supervises policy. Secondly, he has instituted an annual 'meet the people' tour which gives him grass-roots feedback; and, thirdly, the State Consultative Council (SCC) is a more formal mechanism for public participation in government.

Ministers in Oman undoubtedly have latitude in management. Qaboos takes the line that they should only refer back to him when they need to and, in this sense, he is an excellent delegator. The problem is, rather, the reverse. To refer back to a Sultan is not the same thing, in Oman at least, as it would be to refer back to a prime minister. As has been seen there has been no prime minister, except insofar as Qaboos himself is prime minister, since Tarik resigned in 1971 and Qaboos as prime minister is indistinguishable from Qaboos as Sultan. Of the three deputy prime ministers Sayyid Fahd, as deputy prime minister for legal affairs, chairs cabinet meetings (unless Qaboos attends), but there is no formal control mechanism, outside Qaboos himself, over the cabinet.

Although in theory a prime minister would assist the process of control and supervision it is less certain that in practice there would be any improvement. Most ministers have their own lines to the Sultan, either directly or indirectly, and it is arguable that to interpose a prime minister would simply create different, perhaps more, channels of patronage and influence. Depending upon the strength of personality of the incumbent there would be created either a greater concentration of alternative power to the Sultan or a weakening of an existing system that, within its limits, functions adequately well and is, of course, understood by those who work within it. It is anyway, as far as can be judged, an academic point since Qaboos long ago decided against a prime minister.

The weakness of the current system is not the absence of a prime minister but the degree of detachment of Qaboos from his ministers.[119] This works in two directions. Qaboos himself is unlikely to be sufficiently aware of the way in which a ministry is being managed;[120] his information is likely to be skewed in favour of third-party sources and away from direct ministry channels. The minister, on the other hand, becomes subject to increasingly infrequent, and therefore formal, meetings with the Sultan. The opportunity for open discussion and criticism is reduced. These dangers vary, of course, with the strength of character and influence of the individual minister but in a society, which is by nature and design autocratic, the autocrat is perceived as becoming more detached and less approachable.

Qaboos, therefore, while absolutely correct in his claim that he delegates responsibilities to his ministers, has not necessarily answered the implied criticism that he is himself remote from government.

The question of democratic input, or participation, in the affairs of Oman is a separate one. The 'meet the people' tour which takes place annually has inevitably developed from a genuinely informal trip into the interior to an altogether more formal and complex regal circuit. It has become a mini-presidential progress complete with motorcade, helicopters, security, tented camp, communications and attendant ministers, courtiers, soldiers, camp-followers and diverse hangers-on. The theory is that Qaboos gets a feel for what the people think and how they are reacting to government, development and social pressures. What tends to happen in practice is that, apart from cheering crowds of children and tribesmen, he is peppered with individual complaints about minor local problems. This is healthy enough and keeps ministers, to whom the complaints are immediately diverted, on their toes. It often leads to expensive promises from Qaboos which have to be honoured but may or may not coincide with government planning. It is easy for Westerners to be cynical about Qaboos meeting the people;[121] it is equally easy for Qaboos to imagine that by meeting a few of them once a year he is keeping in touch with his grass-roots constituents. Nevertheless the tour serves an important purpose. It is in the tradition of Omani, and Arab, culture. It is a means whereby a Sultan can be seen by his people. It is, in UK terms, a mixture of the State opening of Parliament by the Queen and a party conference in Blackpool; in US terms it is a sort of presidential nomination tour. It should be seen primarily as symbolic and, in those terms, is more potent than as a practical piece of democratic machinery. Moreover, the evidence is that Qaboos positively enjoys the annual experience.

The State Consultative Council (SCC) is an altogether more serious affair.[122] It was established[123] in November 1981 as part of a policy 'to prepare citizens for voicing an opinion as regards the Government's efforts to implement its plans enhancing the country's economic and social development' and to effect 'the steady increase of such participation through firm cooperation between the Government and National Sectors'.[124]

It developed from a Council for Agriculture, Fisheries and Industries set up in 1979[125] which then served as the committee that worked out the form of the SCC. It was originally established with 45 members,[126] inclusive of the Chairman, of whom 17 represented the Government sector, 11 the Private sector and 17 the Regions. Appointment to the SCC is by

Royal Decree, its object[127] 'shall be to voice an opinion in the fields of economic and social development for the country. The Chairman of the Council shall be responsible for submitting its recommendations to His Majesty the Sultan.'

Membership was increased to 55 in 1983, the Government sector receiving 18 and 8 being added to the regional representation. Of the government nominees 11 are members by right of their position, usually under-secretaries of the ministries most involved with the work of the SCC. Those representing the private sector are nominated by the Chamber of Commerce, those representing the regions are nominated by the Walis. Nominations are subject to confirmation by the Sultan. The SCC has been formalised with an Executive office, Committees, a General Secretariat and its own budget.[128] The Chairman is now of Ministerial rank. Under the original statute 'Council sessions shall not be open to the public and shall only be attended by Members of the Council, the Secretary General and Government officials to whom the Council has granted permission to attend.'[129] Now, some of the proceedings are televised and recommendations are made public once they have been accepted by the Sultan.[130]

The establishment of the SCC, although hardly definable as democratic, was a positive initiative by Qaboos in 1981 towards participative government.[131] It has had some effect upon ministers who must be prepared to defend themselves and their policies, but the effect has been limited as the novelty of the SCC has worn off and it has increasingly become part of the furniture of government. Formalities and the demands of bureaucracy have tended to suppress any latent urge for freedom of expression.

To imagine, however, that the SCC was ever designed as an open debating chamber is to misunderstand both its purpose and the nature of the Omani character. Primarily it was seen as a sounding board for ministers and the Sultan and as a support, or modifier, of policy proposals. It was never designed to be, or likely to turn out as, an initiator or critic to any appreciable extent. It was supposed, and indeed turned out, to be 'part of the process of government'.[132] The part in which it has, perhaps, been most effective is an area which has received little comment. One of the duties of the SCC through its committees is to consult with representatives of Omani society throughout the country. Its executive officers and members have, therefore, travelled widely for discussions with Walis and sheikhs and with local authorities on the ground in, for instance, education, health and housing. This has been a two-way operation in which the thinking of central government has, through the SCC, been transmitted to the regions and the thinking of the regions has been filtered back to Muscat. The SCC has, in this context, become a sort of Public Relations arm of government, carrying out on behalf of ministers and undersecretaries what they should be doing more of themselves. Omani bureaucrats are no better at leaving their ministry desks than bureaucrats the world over.

What the SCC now needs is a stimulus to prevent stagnation. This must come from Qaboos who is perceived by many as having become bored by his creation. He formally opens proceedings every two years when new members are appointed but otherwise has little visible involvement with it. Recommendations are, of course, passed to him because that is what is laid down by statute, but there is no feedback from him to members of the SCC. They are, therefore, largely working in a vacuum. Likewise, although SCC proceedings are now televised, their formality and caution hardly provide prime-time viewing.

The SCC needs a new and more exciting image in order to deflect criticism from, and galvanise interest in, its functions. It is to be hoped that this may come from the new Majlis al Shura (consultative assembly), the creation of which was announced by Qaboos during the 20th Anniversary celebrations in November 1990. 'All the wilayats of the Sultanate are to be represented,' he said. 'There will be no government membership of the Majlis.' [133] It is claimed, but there has been as yet no official statement, that the new Majlis is intended to replace the SCC, but in what practical manner the Majlis will operate differently from the SCC remains unclear.

There is one other organisation which assists the process of Omani participation in affairs of the state even though it has not been designed to do this. This is the Oman Chamber of Commerce and Industry (OCCI), whose main purpose is, of course, to protect and expand the role of the private sector in the Sultanate and to act as representative of the private sector in contact both with government and with foreign business. Its terms of reference and constitution give it, however, a specific and special role within the country as a non-governmental organisation with defined relations and links with government. In this respect it is not wholly dissimilar to the SCC.

The OCCI, however, goes far beyond the SCC in certain respects. To begin with, every registered company must join the OCCI. At the end of 1988 there were over 35 000 registered companies, even though 30 000 of them were capitalised at under RO 25 000. [134] Their subscriptions enable the OCCI to run a technical secretariat and head office in Ruwi and branches in Ibra, Ibri, Nizwa, Sur, Salala and Sohar. This in turn means that OCCI officers visit the regions and they hold annual open meetings in each region. They transmit information on government policy and obtain reaction from the regions as to past and future development planning and the problems of society outside Muscat. OCCI has an obligation to report to the Minister of Commerce and Industry on an annual basis but is in practice working in close cooperation with that and other ministries. OCCI, therefore, is a valuable channel of information and opinion in both directions, a far less formal organisation than SCC. In practice, OCCI works with SCC on many projects; for instance, it has been active in preparing proposals on and participating in discussion of Omanisation and the role of the private sector in job creation, a subject in which the SCC has also been heavily involved. Its contact with visiting delegations from abroad gives it special insight into the needs of potential trading partners and investors. It is a pity, given the experience and knowledge gained by OCCI, that Sultan Qaboos appears to have no contact with it and no apparent desire to use it as a means of widening participation in the processes of government.

Participation, therefore, in any Western sense is minimal in Oman. Oman, however, is in no way peculiar in this respect amongst its GCC partners nor indeed amongst most of its colleagues in the Arab League. The absolutism of Arab rulers is nearly universal, even if it covers a spectrum from the benevolence of Gulf sheikhs to the dictatorial regimes of, for instance, Iraq or Libya. One element, however, that generates political ferment and is common to most Arab countries is virtually absent in Oman; that is Arab nationalism. The main reason for this has been an early policy decision to control immigration or visitors to Oman by a visa control based on a 'no objection certificate' (NOC); without an NOC nobody was able to enter the country and still today the NOC is the basis of immigration control even though the rigid application of the system has been relaxed at the margin.

The justification for this control, which was inherited from Said bin Taimur, was in the early days of the Dhofar war a straightforward security matter. Oman was threatened by the PFLO which was in turn supported by various extreme nationalist regimes including Iraq, Libya and the PLO. It was not surprising that, although Oman needed thousands of expatriate workers, it was extremely careful about whom it let in. Iraqis and Palestinians were particularly suspect.

This caution has been continued. It is now possible[135] to obtain a business visa at short notice, and in certain circumstance without sponsorship, and, under GCC agreements, Oman is open to entry by other citizens of the GCC, but the well-established and alert security organisation[136] is ready to keep out (or expel) anyone who is suspected of subversive political opinions or intentions. The result is that the most common source of democratic demand in the Arab world, the Palestinian community in general and other Arab nationalist groups, is not present in Oman to stir up what the authorities would define as trouble. Something presumably simmers beneath the surface somewhere but it remains subterranean and voiceless.

Nor is there any chance that such thoughts might emerge in the media. Television, radio and newspapers are bland in the extreme and rigorously controlled by the Ministry of Information. No whiff of critical, or even non-establishment, opinion ever appears. The result is tedious and, presumably because of convoluted security rules that prevent announcement of events that are well-known to anybody who reads a foreign newspaper or listens to a foreign news programme, the effect is often unreal.[137] It is only fair to add that Oman is not peculiar within the Gulf for its cautious approach to information and journalism. This is not a region where news is published. It is, however, a region where everyone who is in the least interested does in fact know precisely what the news is[138] and discusses it with as much fervour as anyone in Washington, Cairo or Tokyo; and local news has no need of machinery to quicken its transmission.

The result of official suppression of information and opinion is that news, controversial or otherwise, is the subject of private discussion. In the context of Oman, or indeed other countries of the Gulf, this is traditional and normal. It is simply updating the concept of the tribal majlis where everything, important and trivial, was discussed. The majlis now takes place within the hospitality of modern houses, the difference residing only in the subject matter of discussion and in the decor and detail of hospitality within which conversations take place. While for the visitor or foreigner who has no access to the private Omani household Muscat may feel sterilised by the absence of debate, for the Omani there is no lack of opportunity for, and no abnormal constraint over, discussing anything he wants to.

Law

For a country emerging from the anachronisms of life and rule under Said bin Taimur a particular challenge has been to ease the changing society into appropriate legal systems. The first lawyer imported into Oman by Tarik in early 1971 was a Syrian, Yasser Idlibi, but the person who had most influence on internationalising law in Oman was Tom Hill,[139] who was brought in by Robert Anderson as Legal Adviser during 1972, and was actively engaged in the drafting of commercial law for several years.

The basis of Omani law is the Sharia and this remains preeminent for all matters of personal and family law. As Hill[140] writes:

Sharia courts usually resolve all nature of disputes in the outlying regions. Nearer to the capital, and in major cities, the Sharia Court's jurisdiction has not been restricted but parties have recourse to other forums which they may believe to be more convenient or technically suited for these purposes. Therefore, the Sharia courts in these areas tend to hear cases relating to family law and minor criminal and commercial cases; in practice the Sharia courts will also generally refuse to hear commercial cases. The Sharia is therefore evolving to integrate with the requirements of modern Oman.

And Alastair Hirst,[141] who practised in Oman, makes the same general point:

At the present day the vast bulk of the judicial business transacted in Oman passes through the Sharia Courts in the various wilayats up and down the country, and in the more recently established Magistrates Courts having competence primarily in penal matters. The handling of commercial disputes under separate jurisdictional arrangements forms merely a part, albeit rather a specialised one, of the machinery of justice operating in the country as a whole. The Sharia Courts also perform a notarial and authenticatory function which can be of importance in commercial matters.

Apart from the Sharia there is, as Hill puts it, a statutory system of law expressed in Royal Decrees and ministerial decisions published in the Official Gazette and there is a private international law applying to commercial and financial transactions.[142]

The main pieces of business law which have been enacted to guide the structure and direction of modern commercial and business practice are the Foreign Business and Investment Law, the Commercial Register Law, The Commercial Companies Law and the Commercial Agencies Law. In addition there are relevant laws defining general matters, such as the Income Tax Law, the Labour Law and the Land Law, and other more specific regulations covering, for instance, insurance. Hirst[143] sums it up:

With the promulgation of the business legislation of the mid-nineteen seventies and subsequently, Oman has associated itself firmly with the mainstream of modern Arab commercial law. This is, of course, an extremely generalised term, but it can be used to denote the corpus of modern laws evolved in the Arab countries of the Middle East from the nineteenth century onwards, in answer to the needs of modern commerce.

And Hill[144] concludes that, although there is still much to develop,

> This volume of legislation has proved to be of major importance in that it has facilitated development of the country, its economy, and its people by providing an intelligible and comprehensive legal structure by which the business community has been able to operate with ever increasing sophistication.

There is one other element of the legal system that should be mentioned, the Authority for Settlement of Commercial Disputes.[145] This has been a development that is a good example of Omani pragmatism. As early as 1971 it became apparent that some kind of commercial court was necessary to deflect the problem of default by merchants declining, or unable, to pay interest on outstanding loans to the banks and claiming the protection of Sharia Law. So, within the Ministry of Economy (as it then was), a commercial arbitration section was discreetly established and, with the help of Tom Hill, turned into a Committee for the Settlement of Commercial Disputes.[146] In 1982 the Authority was set up as a separate organisation with Ali Daoud, who had been in charge of it since its original inception, as President. Discussing the role of the Committee, Hill[147] writes that it

> was originally created to have jurisdiction to hear and decide disputes between merchants, companies, managers, auditors and liquidators, but this was subsequently expanded to cover commercial and company activities. The Committee is not, strictly speaking, a court of law . . . . Its jurisdiction incorporates the whole of Oman and the Committee is authorized to interpret and pronounce binding judgments on disputes in connection with commercial contracts, agency agreements, contracts of sale, leases and loans . . . Decisions are written and enforceable but there is no system of appeal or precedents. As the decisions are made on an ad hoc basis, it is difficult to establish a system of precedents that would serve to provide an element of predictability in matters of litigation.
>
> The Committee has shown a keen appreciation of a wide range of important legal issues. It has enforced mortgages and caused foreclosure sales in favor of foreign banks against defaulting Omanis and has strongly supported standard banking practices in connection with letters

of credit. In all, it has established a reputation as being a successful forum for the settlement of disputes.

The Authority now has an Appeal Court, added in 1987, in addition to the primary court. An appeal can be lodged in cases where the judgment is for amounts in excess of RO 10 000. In 1988 there were 38 cases brought to appeal.[148] What is still lacking is a Law of Implementation, although this has been drafted and is awaiting promulgation. In the meantime implementation of the Court's judgments are carried out in practice and where necessary by the Royal Oman Police, who are empowered to obtain financial information through the Central Bank and, if necessary, in cooperation with the Ministry of Commerce and Industry to close a business.

Environment and Heritage
An aspect of Omani society to which the government pays an attention that would be appreciated by many nations whose leaders are considered philistine by its citizens is the environment. That is, environment in the widest sense that includes culture and heritage as well as preservation of nature and control over pollution. Indeed, the situation in Oman is almost the exact opposite of that in many OECD countries. In Oman the government inspires and leads, with most of the public, inasmuch as the public's view can be assessed, either disinterested or in opposition; in OECD countries it is usually the government that is seen as trying to put brakes on the enthusiasm of sections of the public. It should be added that the main inspiration for preservation of the environmnent in Oman comes from Qaboos himself. It is not fortuitous, for instance, that he has personally added a foreword to books both on the Plants of Dhofar[149] and Birds of Oman[150] besides at least three more to special reports published in the *Journal of Oman Studies*.[151] He has taken a special interest in the Arabian Tahr project and was personally responsible for initiating the Arabian White Oryx project, Oman's best known environmental success story. Without the commitment of the Sultan it seems unlikely that the Diwan would have appointed Ralph Daly as Adviser for Conservation of the Environment or that the government would have ended up with a Minister of Environment.

The inspiration of Qaboos has been complemented by the inspiration, enthusiasm and application of Ralph Daly,[152] who was appointed in 1974. The first project was the Oman Flora and Fauna Survey carried out in the Northern Oman mountains; a second survey followed in 1977 in the mountains of Dhofar. The results of both were published in the Journal of Oman Studies. More significantly for future work, Daly went as Oman representative in 1975 to the 12th General Assembly of the International Union for Conservation of Nature and Natural Resources (IUCN) and Oman was subsequently elected a State member. IUCN has been a strong supporter of Oman projects since, often in conjunction with the World Wildlife Fund (WWF) whose chairman at that time, Peter Scott, also became a keen supporter of Omani environmental projects. The Arabian Tahr project, for instance, was a joint effort between the Oman government, IUCN and WWF, carried out between 1976–78. A second project on the marine turtles of Oman was also supported by the Oman government, IUCN and WWF and carried out between 1977–79.

The Sultan has also been institutionally involved, at least in titular fashion. In 1979 The Council of Conservation of the Environment and Prevention of Pollution was established under the chairmanship of Qaboos.[153] In 1982 a Law for the Protection of the Environment and the Prevention of Pollution[154] was enacted and in 1984 the Ministry of Environment[155] was set up to enforce and implement a national plan for conserving the environment. The Ministry is also responsible for issuing a 'No Environmental Objection' certificate for any industrial or other structural project in the Sultanate.

The project for which Oman is best known is the reintegration of the Arabian oryx into the wild, another effort of cooperation between Oman, IUCN and WWF. However, the project which is the most important potentially for the long term preservation of the environment is the National Conservation Strategy. This is intended as an overall plan for the Sultanate building on a number of existing studies undertaken with the IUCN on coastal ecology and on the creation of Nature Conservation Areas within what is intended to form a National Land Use plan. The report was completed and presented to the government in February 1987 but no action has yet been taken on it. It is much to be hoped that Qaboos will himself take a further initiative to get the Strategy accepted and implemented; without such effort it may well fall between the stools of inter-ministerial interests and rivalries.

There have been other notable environmental efforts in Oman. The most scientifically important have been a Southern Region workshop held in Dhofar which led to the establishment of a Planning Committee for Development and Environment in the Southern Region, and the Royal Geographical Society survey of the Wahiba sands in 1985–87. On a regional level Oman became a signatory in 1978 to the Kuwait Regional Cooperation agreement for the Protection and Development of the Marine Environment and Coastal Areas; and was a founder member of the Marine Mammals Protection Agency for the Indian Ocean. On a more popular level a number of books have been published in Arabic and English including booklets for schoolchildren; and in 1982 The Oman Natural History Museum was set up under the auspices of the Ministry of National Heritage and Culture.

The Ministry and Diwan have to keep their eyes open. Recently it was suspected that organised gangs of poachers were hunting gazelle and other protected wildlife in the Sultanate.[156] A warning was issued by the Diwan of the Royal Court as follows:[157]

In order to comply with the instructions of His Majesty the Sultan on the conservation of wildlife of Omani environment, the Diwan of Royal Court would like to announce to all Omanis and non-Omanis resident in Oman that the deers and the rare birds and other wild animals are considered as national wealth and their hunting is therefore strictly prohibited. Recently these animals faced an aggressive attempt which is considered as a violation of the restrictions, and in order to stop such destructive attempt of the environment a serious surveillance action is being taken in the concerned areas. The Royal Oman Police will keep an eye at the borders to stop the export and sale of these animals. Furthermore, anyone who will try to violate these restrictions will expose himself to serious legal punishment.

Oman has been an exemplary supporter of conservation and protector of nature. It has created the legal foundations to underpin this policy and has invested money, time and effort in carrying it out. It was, therefore, a fitting tribute to those involved – the Sultan himself, Ralph Daly and those who have been carrying out in practice the environmental programmes – that the United Nations Environment Programme (UNEP) should have singled out Oman to receive its most prestigious award. On 5 June 1990, World Environment Day, Sayyid Shabib bin Taimur, Minister for Environment, was elected to the Global 500 Roll of Honour.

In spite of the positive official attitude to environmental questions, public attitudes are often little different from those elsewhere. Environmental objections to investment or planning proposals are viewed, at the private interest level in particular, as unnecessary potential blockages to economic development or profit. The tussle between short-term and long-term interest is as great in Oman as anywhere else, so that the guardians of environmental policy and legislation will have to work hard to hold their corner. In the meantime it would be of great symbolic and practical assistance to them if the Global 500 Award could be celebrated in Oman by official and public adoption of the National Conservation Strategy.

The Ministry of National Heritage and Culture deals in a different piece of Oman's environment. As with so many of Oman's institutions, the Ministry graduated to an independent status through a series of previous subsidiary positions. Heritage activity first came under the Ministry of Information, but a Department for the Collection of Omani Heritage[158] was set up within the Ministry of Education and Tourism at end-1973; a year later the Ministry of Education and Tourism became the Ministry of Information and Culture[159] and in 1976 the Ministry of National Heritage[160] was established.

The first archaeological teams came to Oman in early 1973. A Danish team excavated in the Wadi Jizzi and at Bat, near Ibri, and a Harvard team studied flints in South Oman. The Bat beehive tombs of the 3rd millenium BC have subsequently been placed on the UNESCO list of World Heritage Sites. Bahla fort has recently been put on its list of World Heritage Monuments in Danger. Oman joined UNESCO in 1974 and there has been close contact since. The Omanis have taken a leading role in support of the UNESCO Silk Road project[161] for which three separate expeditions have been planned – the Steppe Route starting from the North coast of the Black Sea, the Desert Route from Turkey and the Maritime Route. The latter, the Voyage of Dialogue, is planned to start in Venice on 23 October 1990 and to terminate in Osaka three months later. One of its ports of call is to be Muscat and Qaboos has lent his royal yacht, Fulk al-Salamah, to the expedition. Its arrival in Muscat has been arranged for 17 November as part of the 20th anniversary celebrations of the Sultanate.[162]

Given the history of Oman, maritime research has been a natural subject of interest. Prior to the Silk Roads project Sultan Qaboos himself, and on his behalf the Ministry of National Heritage and Culture, supported the Sindbad Voyage,[163] a remarkable reconstruction by Tim Severin of the boat and route used in ancient times for trade between Arabia and China. The boat used, the *Sohar*, was for a time standing in front of the ministry building but has now been moved to a roundabout site facing the Bustan Hotel where it is permanently moored in symbolic anchorage.

An ongoing effort of the Ministry has been concentrated on the refurbishment and reconstruction of Omani forts. The forts are a quintessential part of the Omani scene, both on the coast and in the Interior, grey and looming over date groves and towns. They vary from the picturebook forts of Merani and Jalali guarding Muscat, to the battleship-like structure of Rustaq, to the huge circular tower of Nizwa, to the country-house atmosphere of Jibrin with its painted beams and ceilings. The restoration of Jibrin has been one of the Ministry's most successful projects, but all over the country work is under way to renovate these evocative castles.[164] In the days of Said bin Taimur and in the earlier days of Qaboos' reign they were often the offices, sometimes the homes, of Walis, but now they are more likely to be museums.

The latest museum to be set up is in Beit Fransa in Muscat, the house that used once to be the French Consulate.[165] During Sultan Qaboos' official visit to France in 1989 he donated the house to be a museum commemorating Omani/French relationships and it was officially opened in November 1990 as part of the 20th Anniversary celebrations.

Other heritage projects include the collection of historic manuscripts and documents, and the Sultan Qaboos Arab Names Project which will create something similar to a Dictionary of National Biography. Recently the Oman Centre for Traditional Music has published a Dictionary of Omani Music. The Ministry of National Heritage has been responsible for publishing the *Journal of Oman Studies* and has created the Oman Museum, the Islamic Library and the Natural History Museum. It is in charge of coordinating archaeological work in the Sultanate and has built a Cultural Centre in Salala. It has also arranged cultural exhibitions in UK, France, Spain, Germany and Austria.[166]

The commitment to preservation, and in many cases re-creation, of the cultural heritage of Oman has been consistent and practical. As with the natural environment, most of the inspiration has come from the Sultan himself and from the Minister, Sayyid Feisal bin Ali. There must be a question as to whether such an active Omani policy towards environmental and cultural matters will survive Qaboos; there is little evidence of public interest, even though that will be less important than the attitude of senior ministers. It would be an international loss if the momentum that has been generated were to be lost.

Women and Youth
The attention paid to women in Oman's modern society has already been stressed in a number of connections – the high percentage of women in education, for instance, and the concentration on the education of the mother in family health and childcare. This public acceptance of the woman's role in society has grown in the past 20 years all over the Moslem world. It has been particularly strong in Oman.

Once again the impetus for this must be attributed to the Sultan, for without that impetus it is hard to imagine that Oman would have taken the steps it has.[167] There has been one development which has, almost accidentally, speeded the process and, perhaps, made it easier for traditionalists to come to terms with it. This was the influx of East African Omanis back to Oman in the early 1970s. Many of them were married to women (whether of Omani families or not), and had daughters, who had been brought up and educated in the relatively tolerant British colonial atmosphere and had often taken up careers. When they returned to Oman they assumed that they would have similar jobs there. As a result the civil service obtained more than its expected share of competent female staff, Omanis became more accustomed to women in responsible jobs more quickly than might have been expected, and Omani women more quickly realised that careers were possible and acceptable.

To assist this process there is, within the Ministry of Social Affairs, a Directorate-General for Women's and Children's Affairs, set up in 1985, and, outside the educational system which provides vocational as well as professional training for women, a network of thirteen Women's Associations[168] have been set up. These are voluntary organisations that run courses, give training, administer child help and advice and in general work for the social development of women. The Association in Muscat is inevitably the most sophisticated and has the largest number of volunteers willing to help; its building near the Ministry of Foreign Affairs is elegant architecturally and busy with afternoon activity, including a clinic for handicapped children. The Women's Associations are backed by the Ministry who provide buildings.[169] They must first be supported by at least 30 signed-up volunteers and have the agreement of the Wali to their activity. Their main problem is operational finance and a consistent involvement by the volunteers who run them.

In Oman, therefore, women are treated as a national asset in a way that is immediately recognisable to European or other Western visitors.[170] So is the Youth[171] of the country, for whom, beyond education, the main concentration of effort is on the provision of sports facilities and the development of sport of all types at all levels, including for handicapped children. There are sports and youth centres all over the country, dominated by the huge complex opened in 1985 at Bowsher in the capital area, with a stadium that can seat 35 000 spectators.[172] There is a an Omani Olympic Association and Oman sent a team to the Seoul Olympics. In addition the scouting movement has been strongly supported since a Law for the Organisation of the Scout Movement[173] was introduced in 1975 and the sailing ship, *Shabab Oman*, is used for training purposes.

The Welfare State

What has happened in Oman is that the government has responded to the novelties and challenges of twentieth-century life in a remarkably generous manner. New ideas, new inventions, new opportunities, new ways of coping with the complexities of living are all viewed as desirable and achievable. This can be seen at all levels of activity. There is the sophistication of the centre for education technology at the University. At the Royal hospital they are planning for open heart surgery and have a kidney transplant team. Fibre optics are the basis of new communication systems. Paraplegic games are held. Social security systems are introduced. Research is carried out on honeybees and fish. Regulations cover hygiene in foodshops and restaurants and the practice of pharmacists. There are clinics and specialised centres for the deaf, blind and handicapped. And so on.

The universal excuse of governments that they cannot afford whatever they are being pressed to provide, usually dressed up as the need to give it further study, seems not to occur to Omanis. If there is a need it should be provided; this may be an exaggerated view of Omani government, but nevertheless it is the impression given by the extent of their participation in so much.

It does, however, raise the question, which will be dealt with in Part Three, of the psychological impact on Oman of what has become a pervasive welfare state and what that is going to mean for future demands on the government by the Omani people. Part of this question concerns also the ongoing cumulative cost of these multifarious government programmes.

A different question, which will also be dealt with in the final section of the book, arises not so much out of the willingness of the government to provide social needs but from the way in which the government goes about its perceived task. One of the main criticisms of Said bin Taimur was his paternal attitude to his country, the way in which he considered himself the arbiter of what was right and what was wrong for his people down to the last detail. The question is whether that attitude is not persisting – at a completely different level of generosity, of course. It is perhaps unfair to take a quotation from 1971, but Sultan Qaboos made a revealing reply to Eric Rouleau when asked about the publication of the budget. 'That's a technical question,' he said 'about which virtually none of our people understand anything at all. We take decisions which are in the interest of the country and it is better that they should not be debated by those who are ignorant of these matters.'[174]

These questions, however, are for the future. At the end of 20 years of what Oman calls, with some reason, its renaissance, its society seems well satisfied with all that has taken place. This is, if it is what it seems, a reasonable reaction. The story of the last pages is the evidence. Even to write 'seems' instead of 'is' may appear churlish. It is done only because the evidence is hearsay or personal experience and there is no scientific, or even the most pseudo-scientific, evidence to add to personal feelings.

This is primarily because there is no public or press reporting or discussion of events. Because newspapers, and other media, are government controlled and, for all practical purposes, censored there is no way in which any critical opinion about government policy can be expressed in public; nor would any event in Oman that was thought to be critical of, or express opposition to, government be reported. It would simply be confined to private gossip and not made public. This is not to suggest that there is any widespread dissatisfaction with what has happened in Oman, merely to make the point that the public expression of it is not possible.

This situation is not peculiar to Oman, but common to other GCC countries and to many of those in the Arab League and beyond. It is, however, oddly oppressive in the GCC countries where there has been so much social and economic success that more openness would seem affordable. Private grievance and grumbling is most often simply symptomatic of a relative downturn in the economy, reflecting not so much internal dissatisfaction as annoyance that external international developments have affected the ability to make money. Personal attitudes in Oman and other GCC countries are more often influenced by materialism than by politics or social conscience. Oman is a curious amalgam; on the one hand it is a highly materialistic society, built on deep loyalties to family and tribe, and based on free-market principles for trade and commerce; set against this are strongly statist principles for welfare provision and a binding commitment to the Islamic religion. The result is a society which, although on the surface is highly Westernised, below the surface is utterly different from Western societies. For example, the fact that newspapers are censored or devoid of what Western editors think of as news is not particularly worrying to Omanis and would not necessarily be put on the debit side of a 20-year balance sheet of Oman's achievements.

Indeed, the achievements have been so impressive, obvious and satisfactory that there is not much that Omanis would place on the debit side of the balance sheet. Most of it would concern cases of private business dissatisfaction – loss of opportunities, failure to gain a contract, the irritations of bureaucracy, envy. This does not imply that Oman is trouble-free. Success creates the problem of how to preserve that success. It is probably fair to say that for Oman the first 20 years have been the easiest. Twenty is a somewhat arbitrary number but it happens to coincide with the end of three 5-year plans, with a period of extensive development followed by several years of economic constraint, with the end of the Iran-Iraq war which consolidated Oman's international position. It is certainly seen by Sultan Qaboos as an appropriate milestone for celebration. More than all this, however, it has coincided, by some quirk of chance, with the crisis created for the Gulf and the Middle East by Saddam Hussein. That in itself has closed a chapter and created the need for fresh assessments of how the problems of the 1990s are going to be faced.

Oman, with 20 years of success behind it, was always going to have to face up to the problems lying in wait for it in the next ten, or twenty. Some of them have been created by the process that brought the achievements, others are independent of that process. The last section of this book will consider the main problems facing Oman as it looks towards 2000 and will try to determine how critical they might be for Oman's continuing success as a small country in a dangerously important part of the world.

Part Three
Towards 2000

Part Three
Towards 2000

INTRODUCTION

There is a general point to be made when looking to the future. Many of the problems that Oman has to contend with are similar to those faced by other countries of the GCC. They will be dealt with here, of course, in the particular context of Oman but they will often have a more general application. The searing effect of the Iraqi invasion and appropriation of Kuwait, followed by the horror of war, has accentuated the special characteristics and isolation of the Gulf area and has, in important respects, universalised the particular experiences and concerns of any one member of the GCC. Oman, still satisfactorily remote in geographical terms, has been yanked further towards centre stage than it had probably intended.

As Oman looks towards 2000 it will be concentrating on a number of different areas of concern. There is, first and foremost, a collection of concerns connected with the economy. These include the overall capacity of the economy to maintain and keep up to date the civil and military infrastructure of the state, the whole question of diversification and the ability to provide Omanis with jobs. There are other particular problems of which the water resources of the country may be the most crucial.

A second group of questions concern the governance of the country, the relationship between the Diwan, the military, the ministers and the people.

Thirdly, there is foreign affairs. There is the question of the role of the GCC and the status of Gulf countries in the aftermath of the 1990 crisis and the relationships that Oman will wish to develop regionally and internationally. Lastly, attention will continue to be focussed on the progress of the internal integration within the country, in particular the state of North/South unification which Sultan Qaboos put at the forefront of his first broadcast to the Omani people on 9 August 1970.

ECONOMY

Water[1]

It is hardly surprising that a country on the Arabian Peninsula should have a
problem with water. Oman, however, did not have an appreciable problem
before 1970. Its traditional water-channels, the falaj system, carried water
from springs and hill sources to villages, and the mountainous nature of
the country attracted an adequate rainfall in most years. The Batina coast
held in its gravel subsoil much of the water that might otherwise have gone
straight to the sea. Pre-1970 agriculture in Oman was, compared to much
of the Peninsula, widespread in a traditional form and Oman's reputation
was for agricultural resource rather than poverty.

The economic and social transformations that took place once Qaboos
became Sultan had a drastic effect upon water usage, particularly on the
Batina coast. There was no control over pumping, with the result that
subsurface water was quite unable to meet the new requirements of
modernised farm equipment, the vast increase in land under agriculture
and a population that used water ever more liberally for personal and
community purposes. For example, in the capital area alone consumption
increased from 9 million gallons in 1970 to 63 million a year later and 185
million by 1973.[2]

In his first broadcast to the Omani people, on 9 August 1970, Qaboos
had drawn attention to the problem of water resources. It has remained a
problem ever since, perhaps one of the least tractable and most ignored. In
1990 a Minister directly and solely responsible for Water Resources was,
for the first time appointed. The post was given to Khalfan bin Nasir who
began his ministerial career as Minister of Labour in 1972 and has since
been Chairman of the SCC and Minister of Electricity and Water.

Ever since 1970 the water problem has been bedevilled by opposing
interests. There has been the interest of the individual who has naturally
wanted to use water without limit, whether for his house, garden, swim-
ming pool or farm. There has been the interest of the community which
has enjoyed the beautification of the local environment and for whom
the sight and sound of water in a desert country is an emotional and
physical pleasure. There has been the interest of those who believe that
agricultural development has the top social priority in the country. Then
there are those who try to assess economic priorities and the allocation of
available resources to the different parts of the economy. In between there
are other shades of opinion and pressure groups. As Khalfan bin Nasir said
to me, 'water is politics'.

There are two fundamental problems about water in Oman. The first is, very simply, that there is not enough of it for what it is being asked to do. The second is that there is not enough knowledge about the reservoirs, their capacity, replenishment and wastage. In one important respect the years since 1970 have been wasted. If a National Water Master Plan had been initiated immediately in 1970 there would by now have been a greatly wider scientific base from which to plan and there might have been, given political will, more effective water management. As things stand there is insufficient knowledge; what there is tends to be concentrated in limited research areas which cannot with any certainty be generalised. Beyond that, there is no clear policy as to what part agriculture should play in Oman; the most pernicious statements come from those who suggest that Oman can, indeed will, be self-sufficient in providing its food. Finally, there is no water management; so that wastage is widespread.

Many useful projects have been carried out and research accomplished, but the effort has been too diffuse. Aid money has been provided, by the UN agencies, US government, UK government, and by Japan. There were early surveys by Gibb and Partners, later ones by Mott MacDonald and for a number of years Tetra Tech were responsible. In 1977 a Council on Water Resources was set up, in 1981 responsibility passed to a Ministry of Environment and Water Resources, in 1986 a Council for the Conservation of Environment and Water Resources was created, in 1989 a Public Authority for Water Resources took over and in 1990 the Ministry of Water Resources was finally established.

The continuing change in formal management of Water Resources did not necessarily mean lack of control. In practice, however, it indicated uncertainty as to how to handle water problems. Confusion was made worse by the role of the Ministry of Electricity and Water whose responsibility was to meet demand for water irrespective of resource capacity, and the Ministry of Agriculture which has been responsible, beyond its agricultural remit, for the recharge dam programme and aspects of well development. There has been only limited coordination between all these various bodies, nor have the aid agencies, willing though they have been to give technical help either for agriculture or for water, done anything to create an overall plan for both.

The result has been some useful research into some aspects of the water problem in some parts of the country but there has been no consistent or continuous study of the complete scene. There is a need for fundamental understanding of rainfall patterns, water flow, salinity, the recharging of aquifers and, in the Southern Region, assessment of fossil water reserves.

Only then can water usage, particularly for agricultural purposes, be rationally allocated from a scientifically established database.

In the meantime the new Ministry of Water Resources has the major immediate problem of trying to impose some rational management over water usage in an environment in which for 20 years there has been minimal control and in a society for whom the provision of water is seen almost as a symbol of virility. In a desert climate water has the moral equivalence to a virtue, god-given. The ministry is, therefore, faced by awesome difficulties.

These difficulties are, at least for the time being, increased by the proclaimed policy of food self-sufficiency. In the *Times of Oman* National Day Supplements for 1989 and 1990 headlines were 'On the road to food self-sufficiency' (1989) and 'Inputs boost in race for food self-sufficiency' (1990). The policy is nonsensical because it is unachievable and there is a real danger that Oman will follow, if at a lower degree of waste, the disastrous Saudi policy of subsidising wheat production. The grandiose policy headlines are distinct, of course, from the excellent research and extension work that goes on in the country to develop agricultural products on a sensible and manageable scale.

A particular aspect of this unreality towards agriculture is the question of recharge dams. These are a relatively cheap and simple (though not as cheap or simple as is sometimes claimed) method of holding back floodwaters so that, instead of rushing uselessly out to sea or desert, they can seep back into the gravelly subsoil and reinvigorate the water-table. The technique has been proved over many years in the United States and has been used elsewhere in the Arabian Peninsula but it is not a complete solution. Nor has the effect yet been properly evaluated on the Batina coast or in the Interior. When fully understood the system will undoubtedly help in the conservation of water in Oman, but it is not, and is never likely to be, a complete answer. One of the problems for the water authorities in Oman is that the recharge dam has, because of publicity and public announcement, been clothed in quasi-magical dress and people may persuade themselves that the problem of water has been solved.

As mentioned, the programme for building recharge dams has been in the hands of the Ministry of Agriculture. Logically it should be transferred to the Ministry of Water Resources and, until it is, there must be a question as to whether the water problem is being seriously addressed by the government. It may be an unexciting and semi-invisible problem but it is one that will undermine the capacity of the country to develop if it is not treated as a long-term subject of critical importance.

Diversification and Jobs

Oil provides in excess of 80 per cent of the government's total revenue. There are about 75 000 people employed in the Civil Service, of whom 40 per cent, or 30 000, are non-Omanis. Every year there are around 25 000 Omanis coming out of the primary/preparatory school system, more than 3000 from the secondary/technical system and close on 1000 university graduates. Those requiring employment will increase each year.[3]

The problem is well understood by the government. Diversification of the economy is one part of the hoped-for solution. This would help to reduce dependency on the single commodity of oil and would provide more jobs. The other is Omanisation of existing jobs. The dilemma posed by education versus jobs is no different in Oman than in many other countries of the world and its solution no easier.

The Omani market is small and unable, without uneconomic subsidies, to underpin local industry. The possibilities for export, apart from oil (a notably slender source of jobs), are extremely limited. The GCC provides a market ten times as large as that of Oman, but each country within the GCC is faced by most of the same problems as Oman. Whatever may have been formally agreed for the creation of a GCC common market has had little practical result. Dubai, in particular, although supposedly an integral part of the UAE, acts, as it always has, as an independent entrepreneurial entrepôt and takes a large proportion of the transit trade of the whole Gulf area. It is cheaper for Omanis to import from Dubai than through their own port of Mina Qaboos (and the same goes for at least the Eastern side of Saudi Arabia).

One reaction within Oman to this situation has been to propose the construction of a new, larger, more modern and more efficient port. It is an attractive solution for those whose companies might participate in the contracts surrounding such a huge investment project. It is, however, difficult to see what would be the economic justification for such expenditure unless it is simply in terms of filtering money into the economy, but that too could be done more fairly in other ways. The only possible real justification for a new port, and there is no reference to it or inclusion of it in the new 5-year plan, would be if it were an integral part of a defined long-term strategy for the country.

The need for a long-term strategy has been realised by some of those in government and, in particular, by the Minister of Planning himself, Mohammed Moosa. A study was commissioned in 1988 from Whitehead Middle East Ltd. and Birks Sinclair Ltd. under British Aid arrangements and this attempted, with some originality, to address the problem. Its solution explicitly turned away from trying to compete with Dubai as an entrepôt and towards turning Oman into the regional centre for international investment in and production of branded goods and the services, such as advertising and media expertise, that go with them. Whether this concept is feasible or acceptable within the Omani system is debatable; whether it is being debated is uncertain. There are two other studies in train which may lead to new thinking; one is a master plan for industrial development which is being prepared by UNIDO, the other an agricultural master plan being drawn up by the Japanese Agency for International Cooperation.[4]

The only reference to a Long Term Strategy in the documentation on the new 5-year plan is hidden under the heading of 'Targets and Basics'[5] where the final one (number 16) reads 'Upon the ratification of the Integrated General Strategy concerned agencies shall reassess the Plan, to the extent necessary for the present plan period.'

Whatever strategy Oman pursues, however, it seems essential that it should be aimed at the whole GCC market and should find a niche which has not already been filled and which can appropriately and efficiently be taken over by Oman rather than another member of the GCC. If there can also be a spin-off beyond the GCC into other neighbouring Gulf countries so much the better. Without some vision of this kind it is difficult to see how Oman can escape turning into an ever more pervasive social security system, although even that will depend on a continuously increasing level of oil revenue. Oman is caught in a circle from which most exits are culs de sac. This is not to suggest that the culs de sac should not be entered, but if the expectations and promises attached to them are pitched at unrealistic levels the difficulties in the future will be all the greater.

Fourth 5-Year Development Plan[6]

(a) Recurrent Expenditure
Omani statistics record public finance as divided, on the expenditure side, between 'Recurrent' and 'Investment'. 'Recurrent' is in turn subdivided under the main headings of 'Civil Ministries' (or 'civil recurrent') and 'Defence and Security'.

As a country becomes more sophisticated in its infrastructural development so the cost of maintaining the infrastructure grows greater. The annual cost of 'civil ministries', excluding the government share of PDO, rose from RO 272 million in 1981 to RO 535 million in 1988, an increase of nearly 100 per cent.[7] In the same period GDP has risen, in the non-petroleum sectors, by 70 per cent.[8] In the fourth 5-year plan 'civil ministries' expenditure is set at RO 622 million in 1991, rising to

RO 714 million in 1995, an increase of only 15 per cent over 5 years. As a percentage of total expenditure (including investment) the share represented by 'civil ministries' was 22 per cent in 1981, 34 per cent in 1988 and is planned to be 35 per cent both in 1995 and as a proportion of the whole 5-year plan expenditure.

To achieve this greatly reduced annual rate of increase and at the same time to freeze the proportion of expenditure attributable to the civil service the planners have heavily cut back on expenditure on Defence and National Security. They have, in effect, applied an Omani 'peace dividend' to the 5-year plan, given the military saving to civil development and at the same time restricted overall expenditure to an annual increase of only 3–4 per cent, more or less in line with expected revenues (corrected for transfer to the SGRF).

To what extent can this be considered realistic? The only statistical clue, and its value must be seriously in doubt, is the actual outcome of the third 5-year plan compared to its objective. For what is is worth, Table 9 shows that comparison together with the fourth 5-year plan figures.

Two main budgetary pressure points can be expected. The first is whether the government can hold the cost of the civil service to a 3–4 per cent annual increase. The objective is commendable but clearly its achievement is by no means certain. Far less likely of achievemnt is the security expenditure objective. There are two particular reasons for this.

The first is the attention that Sultan Qaboos himself pays to the military. His main interest and involvement is with the military, with geopolitics in general and with the role of Oman in regional and international strategy. It is difficult to imagine that the Iraq/Kuwait crisis will have reduced either Qaboos' interest in such matters or his perception of an Omani role.

The second reason is that the 1990s are seen by the armed forces as the decade of modernisation and re-equipping. The navy is to be re-equipped with a new and larger fleet of corvettes. The airforce is planning for a new generation of planes. Tornados were cancelled, but Hawks are on order and that is unlikely to be the only requirement. The army is certain to be close behind in wanting to upgrade its capability. It is hard to suppose that Qaboos will be inclined to oppose the wishes of his armed forces commanders.

Within the budget Defence and National Security expenditure has always been given as one lump sum figure, with no breakdown or detail. It is, therefore, impossible to assess how in the past military capital and current expenditure has been divided nor can past experience give any guidance as to the reality of current expenditure estimates. Nevertheless, given the importance of the military in Oman and the special position they hold

TABLE 8   *5-year plans: estimates, and actuals*

RO Millions	First 1976–80				Second 1981–85				Third 1986–90	
	Plan	%	Actual	%	Plan	%	Actual	%	Plan	%
Revenue Total	2797		3383		6947		7525		6490	
–Oil	2236	80	2850	84	6376	92	6649	88	5045	78
Expenditure Total	2509		3341		7368		7872		8164	
–Defence/Security	971	39	1449	43	2973	40	3247	41	2716	33
–Civil Recurrent	727	29	899	27	2165	29	2132	27	3339	41
–Development	811	32	904	27	2155	29	2161	27	2020	25
Development Total	935[1]		1204[1]		2155[2]		2165[2]		2050[2]	
Goods Producing	235	25	272	22.5	925	43	680	31	710	35
–Petroleum/Mining	154		248		676		561		670	
–Agriculture /Fisheries	41		18		82		43		28	
–Industry	40		1		166		82		22	
Services	193	21	200	16.5	516	24	549	25	468	23
–Trade/Tourism	12		18		70		124		87	
–Electricity/Water	123		131		186		234		71	
–Housing	29		30		134		99		87	
–PTT	12		16		67		93		141	
Infrastructure	507	54	732	61	715	33	936	43	972	47
–Roads	163		193		285		282		165	
–Education	26		27		65		164		111	
–Health	34		22		34		72		126	
–Airports/Ports	61		66		67		32		19	
–Town Planning/ Municipalities	na		39		26		111		113	

SOURCE: Column 1–1st 5-year plan, Tables 4, 9; Column 2–3rd 5-year plan, Tables 37, 38 and 2nd 5-year plan, Table 32; Column 3–2nd 5-year plan, Tables 26, 32; Column 4–3rd 5-year plan, Tables 12, 18; Column 5–3rd 5-year plan, Tables 36, 38, 41.

[1] Includes civil expenditure carried out under Defence allocation.
[2] Excludes civil expenditure carried out under Defence allocation.

for the Sultan, the objective of holding Defence and National Security expenditure at its proposed 1991 level for the succeeding four years will be difficult to achieve.

(b)   Development Expenditure
Civil Development expenditure, because of the oil price collapse after 1985, has been severely curtailed since that year. In 1988 less was spent than in 1981. In 1981 20 per cent of all expenditure was attributable to civil

development, by 1988 only 13 per cent.[9] This has since dropped further but in the new 5-year plan there is to be a partial recovery. The 1991 figure of RO 206 million is no higher than that of 1988, and represents less than 12 per cent of total expenditure, but this will rise to RO 300 million, or nearly 15 per cent, by 1995. It is to be supplemented by an additional allocation of RO 150 million over the period to cover 'specific additional demands which cannot be met from the present approved investments'.[10] The money for this will be taken from the Contingency Fund or from additional revenues if oil prices increase beyond the estimated level.

A list of the main projects foreseen to be undertaken during the five years is included in the budget documentation.[11] These are much as would be expected. A new port is not included although, more realistically, there is provision for three new fishing harbours. There are large projects for water and electricity in the Muscat area, the first part of the new hospital programme is included and the recharge dam programme is being maintained. Table 9 shows the main areas of development expenditure compared with previous expenditure under the same headings.

(c)   General Policy

The Deputy Prime Minister, Qais Zawawi, and the Development Council Secretary General, Mohammed Moosa, gave a press conference on 8 January 1991 to launch the fourth 5-year plan. Behind the figures they presented lay a number of principal objectives.

The first is the diversification of the sources of national income away from dependence on oil. The difficulty of doing this has already been discussed. The somewhat optimistic impression given by figures quoted at the press conference (38% increase over the third 5-year plan) is, in important respects, misleading since 'total non-oil revenues' include

TABLE 9   *Third 5-year plan (1986–90), expenditure objectives versus outcome and Fourth 5-year plan estimates*

RO millions	Third Plan		Fourth Plan
	Plan	*Actual*	*Estimate*
National Security and Defence	2716	3056	2904
Civil Ministries	2527	2772	3336
Civil Development	1314	1186	1279
Total Expenditure	8164	8577	9450

SOURCE: Third 5-year Plan, Table 36 and Fundamentals of Fourth 5-year Plan, Annex 2 (Ministry of Information Press Release, 8 January 1991).

revenues from gas, interest from investments and customs duties, none of which represent effective diversification.

Nevertheless, the plan grapples seriously with the problem and aims to 'intensify the private sector's role in all economic activities'.[12] It envisages private sector participation in areas that have so far been the preserve of the public sector, for instance in some gas developments, in toll-roads, sanitation and waste-water schemes. It also plans for the sale of some government assets to the private sector. Whether these ideas will lead to diversification of the economy or simply a re-allocation of resources remains to be seen.

A purposeful effort is also being directed towards the employment problem and Omanisation of jobs currently held by expatriates. Funds will be allocated for an Oman Business School, vocational and technical training and, in rather woolly terms, 'for the implementation of the Omanisation policies both in the public and private sectors'.[13] It is foreseen that the plan will provide 161 000 new employment opportunities and that the ratio of expatriates in the total labour force will fall from 61 per cent in 1990 to 55.4 per cent in 1995.[14] At this stage it is hard to judge whether these are realistic figures, but at least the intentions are rightly conceived.

The second main objective is the boosting of development in the regions 'through the use of 60% of new government investment funds for the development of areas outside Muscat by comparison with only 34% in the third 5-year plan'.[15] The third 5-year plan had in fact divided new government investment in the ratio of 30 to Muscat and 70 to the other regions, but there has now been a reallocation to each of the 7 regions with a large balance of non-regional projects (such as, for instance, Tourism, TV and Radio, the University and a population census). Table 11 shows how the division of investment has now been made. There is no question that a strong commitment to regional development is being fostered.

The third objective of the plan is to strengthen 'the state's financial standing through increasing the transfer rate to the SGRF from 5% to 15% of net oil revenues'.[16] In addition the deficit on current account is not to exceed 10 per cent and a Contingency Fund is to be established, over and above the SGRF, 'to receive 7.5 per cent of net oil revenue if oil prices range between $18–20 and 10 per cent if the price is $20–22'.[17] This second fund is designed 'to cope with any international or domestic variables that might emerge during the plan's implementation', which is based on an oil price of $20 during the five-year period.[18] This policy shows a typical Omani sense of budgetary caution and insurance against an unknown future.[19] A further important financial control is 'to maintain the external debt at the level prevailing at the end of the third 5-year plan',

TABLE 10   *Development expenditure allocation (%) shares*

	1976–88	Third 5-year Plan	Fourth 5-year Plan
Roads	20	6	4
Electricity/Water	16	15	18
Education	9.5	3	8[1]
Town planning/Municipalities	7	9[2]	8[2]
PTT	6.5	13[3]	7[3]
Health	6	3	6
Housing	6	5	3
Airports/Ports	4	1	2
Agriculture/Fisheries	3	7	9
Irrigation/Water Resources	2	0.5	3
Total Expenditure RO millions	2888	817	1375

SOURCE: Column 1–*SYB* 1986, Table 217 and *SYB* 1989, Table 224. Columns 2 and 3–Basic Components, Appendix 5, where figures are only broken down by Ministry and are not, therefore, exactly comparable with column 1.

[1]Includes new faculties at Qaboos University.
[2]Includes expenditure by the Diwan of Royal Court for Muscat Municipality and Sohar Development Office.
[3]Includes expenditure by GTO which is self-financed.

although there is a potential weakening of this firm principle when it is added that 'no additional net external borrowing will be permitted without a Council of Ministers sanction'.[20] Financing of the deficit implicit in the plan is to be arranged partly by withdrawals from the Contingency Fund and partly by issuing government bonds to be sold through the Muscat Securities Market in cooperation with the Central Bank.[21]

In spite of the doubts that can be legitimately expressed about certain elements of the 5-year plan it is, in overall terms, an encouragingly restrained and careful assessment of future economic activity and development. It is disappointing only in the context of what was perhaps an inflated expectation of change, in which the 5-year plan would be integrated into a Long Term Strategy and would be reviewed annually on a 5-year rolling basis. This may still happen. The Secretary General, Mohammed Moosa, has indicated that it will and that, in spite of documentation reference to a fifth 5-year plan,[22] this is the last plan of this type and formula; and the reference to an Integrated General Strategy also exists in the documentation.[23]

As it stands, however, the fourth 5-year plan looks much like its three predecessors. Those three have, nevertheless, generally created a sufficient framework from which to operate and there is no reason why this fourth plan should not do likewise. However, new visions are still required for the decade and it is to be hoped that they are being evolved within the Omani system. In the meantime a strong control over expenditure will, as always, be needed if it is to be kept within the limits ordained for it by the Council of Ministers.

GOVERNANCE

The question of governance[24] is of special importance to the social and political stability of the country. I have described the development of some of its aspects in earlier sections but a further more general discussion is necessary.

The point at issue, if indeed it is at issue, is democracy. I suggested earlier that the urge for democratic development in countries like Oman tends to be pushed by those outside the country rather than by those within, but admitted that this had to be a subjective view since there was no objective source of measurement – no newspaper or other media commentaries or discussion, no opinion polls.

Within the rest of the GCC, is there any evidence that there are internal democratic urgings which might be translatable to Oman? Well, yes, there were in Kuwait. Almost inevitably, however, it has to be added that Kuwait is different. This difference is two-fold. There is the differing status of citizenship given to people holding Kuwaiti nationality, and there is the strong influence of the Palestinians in Kuwait. Kuwait set up an Assembly, or Parliament, in 1963. Votes were given only to 'first-class' citizens, those who could prove that they were residents, or the descendants of such residents, before 1920. Many more citizens, whose antecedents were more recent, were disenfranchised (more correctly, never given the franchise) and an even larger number, who had lived and worked there for tens of years, were denied citizenship at all. Most of the latter were Palestinians who, by nature, upbringing and experience, were more politically aware and vocal than those brought up over several generations in Kuwait. Later, the Assembly was dissolved,[25] but inevitably this created greater subterranean political agitation and dissatisfaction amongst the activists. Added to this was the fact that the Kuwaiti press was relatively free to publish political and other criticisms of the regime. Other GCC states do not have grades of citizenship; nor do they have elected assemblies; and the press is under stronger control, even though it is not necessarily under government ownership as in Oman. The past experience of Kuwait has not

TABLE 11   *Regional Investment Split: Third and Fourth 5-year plans*

	Third five-year plan		Fourth five-year plan	
	RO million (%)		RO million (%)	
Muscat	195	27	236	18
Other Regions	241	34	745	58
Non-regional projects	277	39	304	24
Total Expenditure				
RO millions	713		1285 (excl. GTO)	

SOURCE: Basic Components, Table 8, page 20.

NOTE: In the original third five-year plan Table 45 gave the split as Muscat RO 200 million (29%) and Other Regions RO 493 million (71%).

provided convincing evidence for Oman or other GCC countries in the context of democracy. It is still too early to know how post-war Kuwait will evolve and what lessons it may then have for other GCC countries.[26]

There is another point. For countries of the Arab League, even those far from the specialist atmosphere of the Gulf, the exercise of basic democratic rights has not been widespread nor, with rare exceptions, satisfactory. Few Arab governments have been elected and elected assemblies have generally been controlled by the regime – and dissolved when they have become either critical or useless. Democracy, in the OECD sense, has hardly been part of Arab political baggage.

This does not, of course, mean that democracy should not take over. Trying to impose it from outside, however, is doomed to failure, and revolutions that have set out to provide democracy, however defined, have usually ended by simply transferring power to themselves. So, in the interests of a country like Oman, it is safer and kinder to let political development grow out of its own traditions at its own pace. If Omanis want to speed it up they can find the means to do this; if not, they will leave well alone.

This may seem a laissez-faire attitude to what no-one pretends is anything other than an autocracy, but as long as the autocracy satisfies the people, the case for external tampering with it is full of danger. In practice, it is inevitable that there will be efforts to induce change. The Gulf war is likely to intensify such efforts. Oman, in spite of its relative distance from events, is part of the GCC and will be included in whatever clamour for change develops. Demands are likely to come from the Arab world and from the OECD world, but for different reasons and with different objectives in view. Oman is about to join the mainstream of Arab and international politics in a manner and at a time that will not have been at its own choosing.

A more immediately pertinent question remains: in 1990, does the current exercise of autocracy in Oman satisfy Omanis? I have hinted at the areas in which I believe there may be degrees of dissatisfaction. The problem for Qaboos, as autocrat, is, firstly, to control and use his appointed advisers, and secondly, to be seen to do and have done this. He needs to use them to determine and carry out policies and to control the way in which the policies are carried out. If the ministers and other advisers do their job he will in practice have absorbed a range of advice and be confident of a broad base of support. If other parts of society are reasonably assured from their own experience that this is happening they will be adequately satisfied. If, however, this simple chain of confidence and communication breaks down mistrust and suspicion are likely to breed.

It would seem that Omanis, and Qaboos in particular, need to be increasingly aware of, and sensitive to, the danger of this sort of breakdown of confidence in the coming decade. Signal cones are beginning to be raised in two important areas. The first is the power of the Diwan in relation to the rest of government. This has a two-way connotation. On the one hand the Diwan, because of its direct link to the Sultan, may get things done in his name more quickly than other government departments which have budgets, systems and bureaucracies to work through. On the other hand, it is easier for the Diwan to distort or override policies and budgets that have been agreed. If the Diwan takes over too much business it depreciates the value of government departments and ministers. By 1988 it had in fact become responsible for 15 per cent of total non-military expenditure which, even taking into account that it included the Sohar Development Project, seemed a huge proportion for an office whose prime responsibility was the business of the Sultan himself.

The second area in which dangers are looming is the relationship between Ministers and civil servants and the merchant community.[27] In Oman government employees are permitted to carry on their own private business providing that it is exercised within the terms of the Conflict of Interest Law. What has happened is that the proportion of business belonging to government employees and, in particular, to Ministers has grown enormously over the past few years of low oil prices in which business in general has anyway slowed down. It is only necessary to look at the main contract work being carried out in Oman and the list of major importers to see that companies in which ministers, ex-ministers, under-secretaries and members of the Royal family – or their families – are owners or large shareholders are amongst the largest and most influential. Worse than that, it is frequently alleged, is the fact that government contracts for equipment, services and investments will, in spite of tenders, the Tender Board and the regulations laid down, end up with those same companies.

These matters are, of course, impossible to check. Equally, those who fail to get contracts will often have reason to construct excuses as to why they failed. However, in a society as small and as closed as Oman nothing much is unknown to Omanis and, even for non-Omanis, it is evident enough that many senior government officials are remarkably rich. Even for a society in which there is no puritanical constraint upon conspicuous consumption, examples abound of some massive individual expenditure. Many of these have, of course, been made by the very people who today are the critics of others.

Some of the criticism is well-founded and genuine. Some is self-serving and simply expresses the envy of someone who resents that he himself is not more successful. Much comes from Western visitors who wish to apply what they believe to be their own standards to their hosts but choose to ignore, or forget, what goes on back home. But, having said all this, there remains the core point that the opportunities for corruption exist, that the dangers were foreseen when the original laws – those that set up the Tender Board and which define Conflict of Interest – were introduced and that there is no obvious mechanism to ensure that the laws are in fact upheld. When, and if, laws are perceived to be broken by the people who created them and are supposed to foster them a breakdown of trust and confidence is likely to occur.

Another aspect of the autocracy question is the grey area of paternalism, that shadowy region that lies between freedom of choice and regulation. Said bin Taimur was both an autocrat and a paternalist. He knew, with an almost divine clarity, what was best for Oman and ensured that Omanis got it – or, more often, because of the economic state of the country, did not get it. Everything in the days before 1970 was on such a small scale that he could do this, taking the most detailed decisions himself even though he remained immured in Salala.

A benevolent autocrat is a paternalist, a malevolent one a dictator. Gulf states, and this includes Oman, have by now grown so relatively socially and economically adult that the paternalism of the ruler has been diluted. Ministers and civil servants take decisions and issue regulations. Social services are provided by the state rather than the ruler. Citizens do not necessarily equate government with the ruler himself, particularly when the economy is strong. There is, moreover, widespread freedom of choice in most of the areas in which democracies are accustomed to exercising such freedoms.

Nevertheless, the dangers exist. Any challenge that is issued, any complaint made, is an indirect criticism of the ruler and in that sense is to some degree treasonable. Within limits the system is usually, and certainly in Oman, flexible and resilient but, if ever it is driven beyond those limits, the autocrat is tempted towards dictatorship.

These threats to the position of the ruler are, in the nature of things, more acute in times of economic hardship than in a period of boom. For Oman the years from 1980–85 were a time of plenty; 1986–90 have been years of stringency, but have been successfully bridged. The 1990s look hopeful, but that should not prevent the Sultan from attending to the possible centres of discord in this part of the system. In particular, he will need to steer between two dangerous extremes. One is that he is seen as the author of decrees that are perceived as unjust or irrelevant (which is how his father was seen), the other is that he is seen to be detached from the initiation of such decrees. A further development of the consultative process is essential to maintain a course that avoids these hazards.

In the end it is likely to be the state of the economy that keeps people happy or that drives them to seek change. Oil price is outside the power of Oman to influence. It is all the more essential that it does use to its advantage the pieces of the jigsaw that are within its control. As mentioned earlier there is one piece that can be used more imaginatively and to better effect than it now is, the State Consultative Council (SCC) – or the Majlis al Shura if and when that replaces the SCC.[28] It is not a question of proposing that members be elected; that is unlikely to be acceptable to the Sultan and is not the main point at issue. What is wanted is a body which is able to provide a different feedback voice to Qaboos and to the Ministers, one that is heard and is clearly perceived by those who have an interest in such things to be part of the consultative process of the state. This needs to be a two-way exercise and effort. The Sultan will have to show his confidence in, and the importance he attributes to, a Majlis/SCC by responding to its proposals and comments; the response may be positive or negative, but needs to be the result of some exercise in dialogue. The Majlis/SCC will need to relax its formality and gain the confidence of those with which it confers, particularly people in the regions. The Chairman, with one or two other members, needs to have open access to Qaboos as well as to ministers, the military and independent advisers; and, in turn, they should use the Majlis/SCC as an independent source of opinion and information.

As with most things in the country, Omanis would quickly be aware of any alteration to the status or significance of the SCC. Since, as in other areas, reality is only effective if buttressed by the public perception of that reality, this immediacy of communication within Omani society is highly effective.

The relative isolation of Oman from external ideological influence has been accentuated by its immigration policy and the extreme youth of much of its population. Over the next decade this isolation may be diluted. Many of the students emerging from technical colleges and universities are already part of the Qaboos generation and soon they all will be. The family disciplines inherited from pre-Qaboos times are likely to weaken. Much will depend on the availability of jobs and whether the standard of living graduates achieve is thought by them to be satisfactory. If it is, the attraction of alternative policies and systems of government will be less alluring but, if not, whatever nationalist, or, perhaps, fundamentalist, concepts may be swirling around the Arab world at the time may seem tempting. By then, moreover, the promoters of such ideas may find it easier to get into Oman as activists. The regime of 'no objection certificates' is likely to be more difficult to sustain in the post-1990 era, particularly if there is pressure for Arab nationals to do more of the jobs that so far expatriates from the sub-continent have performed.

These are, for the time being, indistinct and indeterminate possibilities. Tourism is another. Many countries have found to their cost that the destabilising effect of tourism on their social traditions outweighs whatever economic advantage it was envisaged to bring. Oman has plans for tourism. The Ministry of Commerce and Industry has commissioned, through UNDP, a Tourism Master Plan from the World Tourism Organisation. It has been stressed that 'emphasis will be placed on the concept of controlled and limited, as opposed to mass, tourism and on maintenance and enhancement of the cultural values, historical heritage and environmental objectives of the country'.[29] This is encouraging and typical of Omani caution; it is also well-conceived, for it is difficult to think of many examples of cultural values being enhanced by tourism. As long as the right kind of tourists[30] come no harm will be done; if Oman were to copy the efforts of the UAE, for instance in Sharjah and Jebal Ali, the results could be counter-productive. It seems doubtful, moreover, that tourism is ever going to add greatly to the earning power of Oman, attractive though the country is.

There is, of course, the danger that without a sufficient injection of all these external ideas and inputs Oman may become disembodied, set in aspic. That would itself lead in time to upsets and turmoil. Somewhere there is a balance to be found. It is up to the Sultan and his advisers to find it; or, rather, since the country at the end of twenty years is in most respects finely in balance, to keep it there.

FOREIGN AFFAIRS

The Iraqi invasion of Kuwait and the Gulf war will, once the turmoil is over and order re-established, challenge all Arab states to reappraise their policies and attitudes. The challenge will be as acute for the Gulf states as for any of the others in the Arab League.

In the new maelstrom of Arab political development Oman will have certain potential advantages. There is, firstly, the consistent clarity of policy that Qaboos has been following during his reign; secondly, there is the independent line that he has pursued and, thirdly, the relative remoteness of Oman from the scenes of Arab turmoil. Qaboos' aim in the coming years will be to maintain these positive factors and prevent them from transmuting into disadvantages.

Oman's independent foreign policy principles have in practice merged into, or been part of, its consistency. Oman policy was not diverted by the Iraq-Iran war, but lines were carefully kept open to Teheran throughout. 'There is no alternative to peaceful coexistence between Arabs and Persians in the end' said Sultan Qaboos in 1985.[31] Oman was not seduced by the Arab Summits of 1978/79 into withdrawing support from Egypt. It went ahead with the Access Agreement with the US in spite of opposition from its GCC colleagues at the moment that the establishment of the GCC was being negotiated. It is this firmness of purpose that has given Sultan Qaboos a regional and international voice greatly stronger than the size of the country might have suggested. The fact that Oman is, as it were, at the end of the regional line and that a certain isolation has been encouraged – by, for instance, its immigration policy – has helped to keep Oman away from the spotlight at times when, if it had been closer, the glare might have been uncomfortable.

Is this satisfactory state of affairs likely to be upset when the dust of the Gulf war has settled? Or will Oman be dragged into situations which it will find destabilising? Those seem to be the fundamental foreign policy questions facing Qaboos during the 1990s.

At this stage there is no way of answering them because the dust has not settled. The atmosphere, moreover, is likely to remain hazy for a long time. Nevertheless, we can be reasonably certain that, if external developments permit it, Qaboos will remain constant in his attitudes and relationships.

The main threat to Oman's independence has historically been from Iran, Saudi Arabia or, in the days of colonial expansion, various European powers. In the more recent past, however, it is Saudi Arabian intentions that have provided a nagging concern to Oman even when the PFLO, aided and abetted by PDRY, Iraq , Libya and others, were a more direct and active threat. The creation of the GCC greatly alleviated this concern but it was more conclusively laid to rest by the recent border settlement signed by Sultan Qaboos and King Fahd in January 1990.[32]

There is a further distinction to be made, which is important in terms of modern Oman. Saudi pretensions in the past have been focused on Northern Oman – old Muscat and Oman – while the PFLO/PDRY war was directed primarily, and largely in tribal terms, on Dhofar. It is true that in ideological terms the PFLO objective was the whole of Oman and, indeed, in its first incarnation as PFLOAG, all Gulf states. It is also the case that Saudi Arabia has at times infiltrated into the South.[33] For Oman today, therefore, the unification of the country into the Sultanate of Oman has a distinctive foreign policy angle in that old claims on territory, whether based on real or imagined grounds, are diluted by a fundamental change in the nature of the territory itself. It remains true, of course, that, in spite of this, territorial claims, particularly in regions in which boundaries have been drawn by colonial or semi-colonial powers, always remain a potent cause of subsequent turmoil.

The point is that for Oman in the next decade there is no obvious foreign policy threat from Yemen. The interest of Yemen in the Southern Province of Dhofar is likely to be re-awakened, if at all, only by the internal dissolution of Oman itself. Nor now is there a threat from Saudi Arabia. What might recreate that threat, however, is not internal to Oman but the dissolution of the GCC or, worse, a change in Saudi Arabia.

It is precisely in this area that the Gulf war crisis is likely to cast its deepest shadows. The GCC, as has been seen, is at best a tender plant. Its roots are shallow. Iraq was able to tear away one of its branches. As an organisation it is little more than a club of rich autocrats of which Saudi Arabia is by far the most influential. While the club members were left alone by those who might have been inclined to interfere in their activities the GCC prospered in a relatively harmless and unexciting manner. It tried to create common rules for its members and in some, mostly unimportant, areas it had a degree of success. In others it failed completely, as, for instance, in its efforts to create a common set of import duties. Dubai, nominally part of the United Arab Emirates, carried on performing its immemorial functions as an entrepôt run by entrepreneurs which made nonsense of pompous pronouncements about unifying anything to do with trade/ and commerce.

In its internal tussles over defence policy the GCC was really doing no more than playing with theory, but was anyway overtaken by events. The Omani position, for what it was worth, proved to be the more realistic one, as was proved by developments during the Iran-Iraq war, but the Kuwait crisis finally showed GCC defence policy to be what it is. It has revealed the extent of GCC nakedness and the empty reality of its inordinate expenditure on the engines of war. Only the bases were of value, and they had to be filled by foreign defenders.

After 2 August 1990 the GCC countries quickly jumped from the safety of their fencetops to the US side of the ground below. Fortunately they found themselves joined by some valuable colleagues, the Egyptians and the Syrians, and supported by a number of UN resolutions. These are, however, short-term supports; longer-term, the battle-lines are likely to be drawn in a less comforting manner. The probability that they will be less comfortable also for the US and Egypt is of little reassurance to a country like Oman.

The Gulf states have been widely castigated for being reactionary and anachronistic. This relates exclusively to their autocratic non-democratic governmental system, for in other respects their citizens enjoy the most enlightened and generous social services. As discussed, it is likely that any attempt to impose democratic procedures by external persuasion or threat on a social structure that is unprepared, and probably unwilling, to receive them is more likely to produce instability or a new autocrat than democracy. Unfortunately, that does not mean that there are not those who will try, either from a desire to create mischief or because they want power for themselves.

As it happens, Oman is probably better placed to withstand or escape such external efforts than other GCC states, including Saudi Arabia. But, if any radical change were to occur in Saudi Arabia it is difficult to see how it would not ricochet down the Gulf and end in Oman. The GCC is clearly irrelevant in such circumstances. Indeed, the GCC is probably irrelevant already except for the institutional insurance that its members may think it provides to them.

The question is, therefore, as it has been for years: is Saudi Arabia at risk? This is, of course, far too complex a question to be dealt with in a book on Oman but it is a question that Sultan Qaboos must think about if only to determine whether, if it is, there is anything that he should be doing about it in the interests of his own country, Oman.

It is evident that the pressures on Saudi Arabia will, in the aftermath of the Kuwait crisis and Gulf war, be much greater than they have been so far. The Saudis have sat, precariously but safely, on an Arab fence ever since the creation of Israel. Their balancing pole has invariably been the main asset they have, money. The Iraqi invasion of Kuwait forced them from the relative comfort of the fence onto the more hostile ground beneath it. It confirmed their dependence upon the US, which was then reconfirmed in more conclusive and brutal fashion by war itself. Of course, it was already understood, but explicit admission is different from implicit understanding.

Precisely what this will mean in the coming years is unclear. It depends on the timing and content of whatever occurs. We can be sure, however, that one subject that will be in the forefront of future political wrangling will be the future of the Palestinians. The Arab world, at best an elusive (if it exists at all) entity, has been torn to shreds by the Iraqi takeover of Kuwait and the Gulf war. It coagulates only on the subject of Palestine and even on that the bonding is of variable strength. The countries which have depended on the US for their response to Iraq are destined to be ranged against the US in their support for the Palestinians. High on the list will be Saudi Arabia.

Prediction is futile, but what can be said is that the props of Saudi Arabian stability are at risk from many directions, of which the Palestine question and dependency on the US are likely to take priority. And it can be added that when and if the systems that hold Saudi society together are weakened the effect will, like an electric current, leap down the Gulf and round to Oman.

Another direction from which the seeds of change may come is Islam. Fundamentalism is a portmanteau word that carries much that is misunderstood by non-Moslems, but it contains genuine inspiration in the Moslem world. It is a word as emotive, and dangerous, as nationalism or Israel. It is a word, however, which is not going to disappear from our vocabulary. What its effect will be on the Gulf states is hard to judge. Ironically enough, they are states which, in one persona, are already fundamentalist, although in another they are as materialist as the most irreligious society in West or East. No more can be said about the practical influences of religion at this stage than can be said about Palestine. Both are pregnant with possible turmoil and the Gulf war has, in different ways, made the turmoil that they represent more rather than less likely, sooner than later.

These are matters that Omani foreign policy can hardly touch. Oman is too small and too remote from the mainstream of Arab politics to be able to exert much influence. In the past, theorists have suggested that a Greater Oman, grouping Oman and UAE together, would be a stronger, even a more natural, entity than two separate states. This is mere musing. It will not happen; nor, if it did, would a Greater Oman be any more competent to cope with the sweep of history than it would in its current component parts.

These threats are not, however, certain to evolve over any particular time span nor can we know whether they will necessarily turn out to be threatening. In the meantime, Omani foreign policy is likely to follow the natural inclinations of Sultan Qaboos which have so far served the country well and, if not overwhelmed by external factors, have every chance of continuing to be successful.

UNITY

It may seem perverse to bring up the question of unity when the Al Said dynasty has ruled Muscat and Oman since 1749 and has been in control of Dhofar at least from 1897.[34] For twenty years Sultan Qaboos has confirmed the country's unitary state by calling it the Sultanate of Oman.

Nevertheless, the unity of the country is now of far greater significance for Oman than it ever was in the past. The Southern region today contains a large proportion of the oil reserves, an appreciable part of the defence apparatus and a considerable infrastructural investment. If it was arguable in the days of Said bin Taimur that the excision of Dhofar from Muscat and Oman would have mattered little except to Said bin Taimur himself that proposition is assuredly indefensible today. Any threat to the unity of the Sultanate now and in the future would have drastic, if unknowable, consequences. If we look at the future, therefore, one of the more fundamental elements to be considered is the resilience of Oman as a unitary state.

Qaboos has been aware of this from the start of his reign and expressed this awareness by changing the name of the country to the Sultanate of Oman. In 1970 people's perceptions were distorted by the Dhofar war and unification was a remote and insubstantial concept. It became, nevertheless, a real one. The creation of the Dhofar Development Programme in October 1972 and the investments that were undertaken under its auspices were the practical expression of what might have otherwise seemed to have been no more than a good idea.

It was not only the Southern region, however, that Qaboos had to weld into a state. The regions of Northern Oman were also jealous of their own interest and individuality. It should be remembered that, back in 1970, Muscat was almost as detached from the Interior regions as from Dhofar, and even the Batina coast was remote.[35] The mechanisms that kept the country together were the army, the walis, and the tribal sheikhs. The country was essentially an interior tribal agglomeration superimposed on a coastal trading community and held in suspense by the mobility of the army and personality of the Sultan.

All this was, as we have seen, changed by money, communications and the removal of restrictions, and backed by a massive government investment programme. An important social result has been that regions have to an extent lost their individuality and the tribal role has been diminished. Government ministries, active all over the country even if concentrated in large buildings in the capital, dispose of money and services. Tribal sheikhs are paid a salary and have certain residual duties, but their influence has been eroded. This does not imply that they are useless or unregarded. Qaboos understands as well as any Arab ruler that tribal loyalties run deep and must be given attention. They will never wither away. Even when they appear desiccated they lie, like seeds in the desert, ready to flourish when the climate changes.

Nevertheless, regional bonding has taken place largely at the infrastructural level. Some of the ministers are now concentrating their efforts on regional rather than central organisation. Whether this will be effective, or simply lead to a more extensive bureaucracy, will only be determined in practice. If it is successful it will, perhaps, have an example to export, at least to many European countries in which the tussle between central control and regional devolution is never-ending and apparently unresolvable. Oman has the advantage, in theory, that the regional traditions and tribal groupings should make devolution both acceptable and easier to achieve.

Oman still, however, has the problem of the South. In general the Northern interior tribes, even when historically split,[36] are recognisably similar, for instance in their Ibadhi religion and in their life-style. The Southern tribes are different, fashioned by language, climate and an economy based on cattle. Said bin Taimur made no attempt whatsoever to integrate North with South, nor even to create links between them. Qaboos' intentions and practices have been novel.

Have they worked, and will they continue to work? There is little doubt that they have worked up to a point. Proof of this is the evident fact that the Sultanate is, and is seen to be, one. The degree of integration, however, is not as deep or complete as appears. Dhofar still thinks of itself as Dhofar,[37] Muscatis do not on the whole think of Dhofar at all. At a senior level there is considerable exchange and there is, of course, communication at the ministry level, but neither northerners nor southerners have much interest or pleasure in being posted away from their home base. In the case of the military there is normally one unit only posted to Dhofar from the North; this is partly because, when they get there, the Northern regiments do not understand the nature of the problems, or the character of the people, in the South and partly because they cannot easily get back to their homes for the weekend.[38] Precisely the same applies to Southerners who are transferred to the North. Within the Northern regions these problems are far less acute, although they exist, simply because the distances are more amenable to relatively quick movement and, as indicated, the people are far more similar in character and outlook.

Integration, therefore, is in part a function of infrastructure and investment. That is an essential and, hopefully, will be a sufficient part of the process. There is, however, another element in the growth of Oman's integration that has taken place. This is Sultan Qaboos himself; or, more precisely, Sultan Qaboos through his mother. Qaboos' mother comes from the Beit Maashani, a section of the important Qara tribe. Qaboos, therefore, is seen by Dhofaris to be Dhofari – or, at least, sufficiently Dhofari to be accepted as one. In a tribal society this is an incalculable asset. The fact that he often stays in Salala and is seen by the Dhofaris to be living there is a further advantage.

This means that Dhofar is loyal to Qaboos. So is Northern Oman. The loyalty of Northern Omanis to the Al Said family, however, is looser and less deeply personal than the link that Dhofaris feel towards Qaboos, a link and loyalty that derives from his mother rather than from his father and the Al Said dynasty. This has been of strong significance both to Qaboos and to Oman for the past 20 years, but what of the future?

In other societies down the centuries, and still today in many, the solution to this type of territorial problem has been marriage. In the Arabian peninsula, and most obviously in Saudi Arabia, marriage has been a constant mechanism by which tribal cohesion has been strengthened and alliances have been created. It would appear also to be an appropriate way in which to consolidate relationships in Oman and to prevent the risk of future fractures.

It has not happened. Qaboos himself is unmarried and has not, therefore, produced an heir.[39] This, in Arabian dynastic terms, is not necessarily a problem, for there is usually an extended family from which to pick a successor in the absence of direct male descent. This is the situation of the Al Said even though the family is not as numerous as many in the Arabian peninsula. But the family, or at least those with some clear claim to consideration for the succession, have not apparently given much thought to this situation. They have not, at any rate, entered into any dynastic Dhofari marriages. Nor have they, as far as can be judged, taken any interest in the circumstances of Dhofar or its people. It seems a pity, even if it turns out not to be of future significance, that a more overt interest in Dhofar has not been shown by the Royal family, and that none of them has apparently seen the value of an insurance investment in this direction.

It happens that in Oman the subject of succession is treated with great circumspection. In itself that is not significant, if only because Sultan Qaboos himself is only 50 years old and there is no immediate urgency to deal with it. What is less clear is whether, or to what extent, there is an Al Said strategy for the future. Outsiders cannot know whether or not there is one, but it would be reassuring to feel that the family has taken into considerataion the factors which might one day threaten the unity of the state.

A different direction from which unity of the state might be challenged is religion. The sect of Islam that is, and has been, pre-eminent in Oman is Ibadhism. Historically, its strength and influence has resided in the interior mountain districts. One of its characteristics is that it is led by an elected Imam.[40] The first two Al Said Sultans were also, as was then customary, Imam: temporal and religious power were united in one person. Said bin Sultan (1806–56), the architect of modern Oman, had no personal interest in the Imamate; nor, with the exception of Azzan bin Qais (1868–71) have any of his successors. Since 1810, Imams have been elected from other Interior families and the Imamate, representing the interior tribes, has frequently been at odds with the Sultanate, representing the coastal districts, trade and international relations. The most recent clash, politicised far beyond religious differences, took up most of the 1950s.

There is no clash today, but neither is there an Imam in Oman. Dealing with religious matters, or at least those that are the province of the Sharia courts is a Grand Mufti who, appointed by the Sultan, is in some sense the senior representative of Islam in Oman. Between him and the Sultan there is, with undefined authority in this area, Sayyid Fahd, the Deputy Prime Minister for Legal Affairs. To what extent Ibadhis recognise the religious authority exercised by either Sayyid Fahd or the Grand Mufti, both representing the Sultan, is unclear. In 1990 it is not a point at issue for it has not been challenged, but it may be a latent cause for future dissension.

No discussion of unity in a Middle Eastern state can ignore the role of the armed forces. In one of their functions they are the guarantor of the status quo. This role depends upon their reflecting the social structure of the country. If the armed forces are strongly skewed towards any particular region or stratum of society, that is a distortion which could, given the circumstances, be dangerous. This is not a danger for Oman in 1990, but the point should be kept in mind.

All these matters are only speculative. They may never become an issue for Oman, but they need to be rehearsed if only to ensure that they do not turn from passive possibilities to active threats. The most continuing and necessary task for Oman is to ensure that it keeps the unity that Qaboos has given it.

Epilogue: 20th Anniversary, November 1990

A million light bulbs fluttered like nocturnal butterflies. A million explosions turned night into pyrotechnical day. Bands thumped out their instructions to parades of soldiers and children. Speeches were made and banquets consumed. Transformations took place; bare rock became a roadside vision of living nature, an area of despondent mangroves in Qurm became a public garden. Oman knows how to put on a celebration and this was celebrating two decades of Oman's renaissance.

There were other more tangible expressions of public rejoicing. PDO built a technical library in the shape of its fossil logo and provided the first 10 000 volumes for it. The Sultan directed that 50 per cent of farmers' and fishermens' outstanding loans with the Oman Agricultural Bank should be cancelled. The Sultan Qaboos rose, a beautiful rich red floribunda specially developed in Holland under the auspices of the World Federation of Rose Societies, was formally presented to him.[1]

Concerns about the future were banished for a few days of thanksgiving and celebration; not that concerns about the future are as high on the normal Omani agenda as on that of non-Omani commentators. This particular set of celebrations,[2] however, held in November 1990, neatly symbolised aspects of Omani policy and character. They took place in the midst of the Gulf crisis at a time that many analysts had predicted as the most probable for an outbreak of actual war. Qaboos took the line early on that, in the interests of normality, he would not be deflected from what had been planned. Other Gulf states had cancelled their National Day celebrations in the belief that celebrations were out of order at a time when the political future of the Gulf seemed dangerously threatened and so much at risk. As so often, Oman took the long view of consistency rather than submit to arguments of short-term expediency. There were many who doubted the wisdom of the decision, but they were silenced or remained silent. In the event everything went like clockwork. The renaissance was properly observed.

Renaissance may sound somewhat pretentious as a description of Oman's last 20 years but the justification for it is visible all over the country. The renaissance has, in large part, now been completed. The next 20 years will be the years of consolidation or, perhaps, expansion. They may be less exciting year on year but there will be no lack of things to achieve.

In some respects visitors find Oman almost too good to be true. Compared to the rest of the Gulf it is better ordered, more polite, cleaner, more welcoming, more scenically attractive. Compared to the rest of the Middle East it is quiet, unexcitable, a bit unexciting, perhaps, but without that insistent stridency that can be so exhausting. It may be a bit dull for some, but for others it is an oasis of relaxation where, within defined limits, there is little of the hassle that fills so much of the world.

I have tried to show that this appearance of calm purpose and achievement is no less at risk than anywhere else, but that the sense of purpose and desire for achievement has been a continuous refrain. Oman has been lucky in many respects – geography, oil price, expatriates, external political developments – but all this could have been thrown away if different people had been managing the country and if there had been a managing director in charge other than Sultan Qaboos.

Appendix: Press Release, 26 July 1970

Press release from the authorities of the Sultanate of Muscat and Oman (26 July 1970): We have received the following statement from Sayid Qabus bin Said, Sultan of Muscat and Oman, to all people of his country.

Fellow countrymen. I speak to you as Sultan of Muscat and Oman having succeeded my father on the 24th of July 1970, 19 of Jamada al Uwla 1390. I have watched with growing dismay and increasing anger the inability of my father to use the new found wealth of this country for the needs of its people. That is why I have taken control. My family and my armed forces have pledged their loyalty to me. The ex Sultan has left the Sultanate.

I promise you all that my immediate task will be to set up as quickly as possible a forceful and modern government whose first aim must be to remove unnecessary restrictions under which you, my people, now suffer, and to produce as rapidly as possible a happier and more secure future for all of you.

I ask the help of each one of you in this task. In days gone by our country was great and powerful, and with God's help, if we work together to recreate our nation we shall once again take our rightful place in the Arab world.

I am taking the necessary constitutional steps to receive recognition from foreign countries with whom we have relations, and I look forward to the early establishment of friendly cooperation with all nations, notably with our neighbours, and to an era of active consultation with them on the future of the region.

My friends, I urge you all to continue with your normal lives, knowing that I will be coming to Muscat within a very short period, and that my major concern will be to tell you, Oh my people, what I and my new government plan to do to achieve our common aim. My friends, my brothers, yesterday was dark, but with God's help, tomorrow will dawn bright for Muscat and Oman and all its people.

May God's blessing be upon us and on our endeavours.

Notes

Preface

1. The dynasty has in the past usually been known as Al Bu Said, but under Sultan Qaboos it has changed to Al Said.
2. Ian Skeet, *Muscat and Oman: The end of an Era* (Faber & Faber, 1974); reissued in paperback as *Oman before 1970: The end of an Era* (Faber & Faber, 1985).
3. Under the 30-year rule British Government documents, from Foreign Office or other sources, will only be available in 2000 even for the year 1970. US documents are, in theory, more readily obtainable under the Freedom of Information Act, but there is no guarantee that they will be forthcoming and they may be heavily edited when produced.
4. I have also been fortunate to have had access to private papers which have provided a valuable record of some parts of the story.

Part One: Scenes – Oman 1990

1. The architect was Fitzroy Robinson and Partners who have cleverly used modernised forms of traditional design and decoration throughout the building.
2. In June 1990 the three services were given the Royal Title. Accordingly, what had been SAF (Sultan's Armed Forces) became the Royal Army of Oman (RAO), the Sultan of Oman's Navy (SON) became the Royal Navy of Oman (RNO) and the Sultan of Oman's Air Force (SOAF) became the Royal Air Force of Oman (RAFO). SAF remains a generic title for the Armed Forces as a whole. I shall use the old-style SAF and SOAF titles in cases in which they are more relevant to the period being described.
3. From 1806 'effectively', records John Wilkinson in *The Imamate Tradition of Oman* (Cambridge University Press, 1987), chart on page 14. It can be argued that 1807 is a more correct date.
4. Under RD 60/79 published in the Official Gazette of 19 November 1979. The development contract, in practice controlled directly by the Diwan, was given to Tetra Tech International, a subsidiary of Honeywell. Tetra Tech also provided technical advice to the Ministry of Oil and Minerals for a time (see *New York Times*, 25/26 March, 1985, articles written by Jeff Gerth and Judith Miller).
5. These facilities were in place when I was there in 1990.

6.   The main contractor was George Wimpey International and the architect was the Percy Thomas Partnership.
7.   The contractor was Cementation International and the architects and planners were YRM International.
8.   Sultan Qaboos has always taken a particular personal interest in the university project. A nice example was his insistence that the red sandstone used in the construction of the main buildings should be taken from the quarries used by Lutyens for imperial New Delhi.
9.   For this section see Article by Ralph Daly 'And what, said the Sultan, shall we do about the oryx?' read to 4th World Conference on Breeding Endangered Species, Holland, 1984, and Mark Stanley Price, *Animal Re-introductions: the Arabian Oryx in Oman* (Cambridge University Press, 1989).

Part Two: Behind the Scenes: The Creation of Oman, 1970–90

First Things First, 1970–75

1.   For a fuller discussion of all these matters see Skeet, *Muscat and Oman*.
2.   He first spent a week or two in hospital recovering from wounds he received during the coup.
3.   See *Declassified Documents* 1984, Vol. X, no. 2, item 000781 dated 19 May 1975. See also note 36 below.
4.   For details of developments in South Arabia see Fred Halliday, *Arabia without Sultans* (Penguin Books, 1974), an account which is written from a strong 'revolutionary' and anti-imperialist point of view. The DLF was formed in 1962 but only became militarily active in 1965.
5.   South Yemen gained its independence on 30 November 1967 and changed its name to People's Democratic Republic of Yemen (PDRY) on 30 November 1970.
6.   In a move that may have been guileful or unintentional, but certainly proved confusing, PFLOAG merged in 1971 with NDFLOAG to be reconstituted yet again as PFLOAG which now stood for Popular Front for the Liberation of Oman and the Arab Gulf. In May 1974 PFLOAG split, the Oman constituent being converted into PFLO, the Popular Front for the Liberation of Oman.
7.   Dickens papers (see note 16, below).
8.   Sir Stewart Crawford was Political Resident in the Gulf, based in Bahrain, at the time. It is a curious coincidence that the announcement of his replacement by Geoffrey Arthur was made on 27 July, one day after the public announcement of the coup in Salala.
9.   The house was built specially for him by his father. It took so long to complete that his return to Oman was delayed by months; when he finally got there he found that, Arab style (in those days), there was

no plumbing.

10. For the text of the announcement see the Appendix.
11. He told me when I met him that he had particularly looked forward to seeing the forts about which he had heard and read so much.
12. *The Times*, 1 August 1970
13. The link between Tarik and Muscat was Malcolm Dennison, the Director of Intelligence in SAF, and it was he who contacted Tarik after the coup to bring him back to Oman.
14. So described by Tarik in a conversation with a friend in 1970.
15. The post was upgraded to Ambassador in June 1971. Donald Hawley, appointed Consul General in April 1971, thus became Her Majesty's last Consul General and first Ambassador to the Sultanate.
16. I have been fortunate, thanks to the generosity of Mrs Mary Dickens, to have access to papers and notes collected by Captain Peter Dickens. These are now lodged at the Three Services Record Dept., Central Historical Section, Ministry of Defence, London and are held in the Historical Library dedicated to 22 SAS Regiment. Also, see Tony Jeapes, *SAS: Operation Oman* (William Kimber, 1980) and John Akehurst, *We won a War: the campaign in Oman 1965–75* (Michael Russell, 1982).
17. One exception to the general silence was a speech broadcast by Qaboos on 28 May 1972 when, out of the blue, he justified the bombing of Hawf, a PLA base over the border in PDRY. This was part of a concerted Omani effort to present the background and reason for the attack both in the Arab League and UN.
18. From the Arabic word for 'enemy'.
19. The operation was carried out down from the Nagd, not up from the Salala plain.
20. It is situated in the Maashani tribal area, the tribe of Qaboos' mother; it was, therefore, an act of particular meaning.
21. See McKeown, M.Phil. submission, Cambridge 1981 (Dickens papers).
22. By now Popular Front for the Liberation of Oman and the Arab Gulf.
23. Lecture given to the Staff College, 1980 (Dickens papers).
24. Ibid.
25. Subsequently, Colonel Dennison became Adviser on Security and Lt. Colonel Nightingale became Director of Intelligence. Both were members of the Council. The Wali of Dhofar was also added as a member later. The composition of the Defence Council recorded here is slightly different to that given in Townsend, p. 139.
26. The Shah's courtiers had first to establish that Landon was indeed a genuine emissary from the Sultan. At this time Oman's ambassador to Iran was the ex-wali of Muttrah, Ismail Rasasi, whose standing was unequal to the pomp and formality of the Iranian court and who would not anyway have been used on such a sensitive assignment.
27. Figures quoted by Jeapes in *SAS: Operation Oman*.
28. Dickens papers.

29. For instance, Creasey put it like this: 'He who controls Oman, and particularly the Musandam, controls the Gulf. He who controls the Gulf controls the Gulf oil supplies, and these are crucial to both the West and Russia. The fall of Dhofar would lead inevitably to the fall of Northern Oman and the Musandam, and thus of the Gulf – a classic example of the Domino theory' (Dickens papers). Maybe Creasey was *parti pris* and exaggerated the argument, but the principle would have been accepted by many analysts.

30. Six more were killed in the Jebal Akhdar campaign of 1958/59.

31. There is some evidence that these included the decision to retire the chief British advisers and the advice (if it were in fact needed) to call back and appoint Tarik as prime minister.

32. The core group seems to have been Hugh Oldman, who acted as Chairman, Brigadier John Graham (CSAF), Francis Hughes (General Manager of PDO) and Bill Heber-Percy (Secretary General of the Development Board); Sayyid Thwaini bin Shihab, who became Personal Adviser to Sultan Qaboos and who had lived in Muscat during all the later years of Said bin Taimur, was Omani representative on the Council. Other people who attended were Peter Mason (BBME) and Ali Sultan, a leading Omani merchant.

33. Leslie Chauncy was Personal Representative of the Sultan, Neil Pelly Secretary for Financial Affairs, Leslie Hirst Secretary for Petroleum Affairs, and John Shebbeare Secretary in Internal Affairs.

34. Figures quoted by John Peterson, *Oman in the 20th Century* (Croom Helm, 1978), p. 207.

35. Zanzibar obtained its independence on 9 December 1963. The government was overthrown on 12 January 1964 and union with Tanganyika was signed on 27 April 1964.

36. Articles entitled 'Oman ou la Révolution Refoulée' published in *Le Monde* on 26–30 May 1971. See also *Declassified Documents* 1984, vol. X, no. 000781 dated 19 May 1975, which refers to an interview in *The Sunday Times* of 12 November 1966 in which Tarik announced a political movement whose objective was to remove Said bin Taimur and create a constitutional monarchy.

37. *SYB* 1986, Tables 5 and 38.

38. The Question of Oman originated in 1957 when a request to consider 'The armed aggression by the United Kingdom of Great Britain and Northern Ireland against the independence, sovereignty and the territorial integrity of the Imamate of Oman' was put forward. In 1963 an ad hoc Committee was formed to investigate the situation of 'the Arabian territory of Oman'. A UN debate on the subject was an annual event until 1970. For further details see John Wilkinson, *The Imamate Tradition of Oman* (Cambridge University Press, 1987) pp. 325–6.

39. One of his nephews is today in a Government department in Muscat.

40. The circumstances of the appointment were an example of the underlying problem that Qaboos and Tarik had in communicating with each

other. Tarik felt unable to ask for the appointment, Qaboos implied, but was not explicit, that the appointment had been made. Third parties had to be called in to get matters formalised.

41. This quotation and the details about Shakir are taken from a CIA report of 4 March 1976 published in *Declassified Documents*, 1984, vol. X no. 1, item 000067.

42. Quoted in articles by Jeff Gerth and Judith Miller in *New York Times*, 25/26 March 1985. See also article by Joe Rigert in *Minneapolis Star and Tribune*, 5 July 1983.

43. *New York Times*, ibid.

44. *New York Times*, ibid.

45. The CIA report says: 'He [Shakir] and his Rome based Libyan partner, Yahya Omar, are generally considered to be the Sultan's most trusted advisers on both foreign relations and development contracts . . . in 1974 Shakir even shared in the military procurement function.'

46. For further details see John Townsend, *Oman: The Making of the Modern State* (Croom Helm, 1977) pp. 88–91. Also see *Financial Times*, 4 February 1972.

47. *New York Times*, ibid.

48. These were expressed to me by Sultan Qaboos in conversation with him.

49. Quoted in Townsend, *Oman* p. 127.

50. John Townsend, *Oman: The making of a Modern State* (Croom Helm, 1977).

51. Anderson only visited Oman once, in October 1971, and then only for a few hours. He used to meet Sultan Qaboos and, of course, Shakir and Omar in Europe.

52. Their IMF quota was $7m, their IBRD subscription $6m.

53. Their subscription for IFC was $36 000 and for IDA $311 000.

54. *SYB* 1986, Table 215.

55. See Townsend, *Oman* p. 150, and press reports of the time.

56. See, for instance, *Egyptian Gazette*, 21 June 1973.

57. There is now an airstrip there, and a memorial to an SAS paratrooper who was accidentally killed in the drop. There has been no offensive freefall drop since.

58. The naming of the new airport gave rise to a problem that was finally solved by the issue of a decree on 8 June 1972 which ordered 'the cancellation of our decree dated 8 May 1972 changing the name of Mazoon airport to Oman International Airport. Aviation experts have pointed out the possible ambiguity in naming the airport thus (it might be confused with Amman, Jordan) or in calling it Muscat airport (there might be confusion with Moscow). So we have, with regard to ensuring safety in air travel, decided to name the new airport Seeb International Airport. This should preclude any confusion'. Mazoon was, incidentally, the name of this area of the country when under Persian control in pre-Islamic times; the original proposal to use this

name must have been put forward by someone who had not checked his history.

59. RD 9/72; subsequently the *Gazette* was filled with lists of boycotted firms, a job first falling under the Ministry of Commerce and Industry and later, in July 1977, being transferred to the Royal Oman Police.
60. RD 35/73.
61. Later it became the Ministry of National Heritage.
62. In London, New York, Tunis, Cairo, Beirut, Delhi, Jeddah, Kuwait and Teheran.
63. RD dated 17/7/72 provided for Territorial Waters extending for 12 nautical miles and for Restricted Fishing Rights extending 38 nautical miles beyond. RD 44/77 dated 14/6/77 extended the Restricted Fishing Zone to 200 nautical miles from the coastal baseline and added median line provisions. RD 15/81 dated 10/2/81 brought in the concept of the Exclusive Economic Zone extending 200 nautical miles from the coastal baseline.
64. Later, in 1977, a Housing Bank would be established. This forerunner was set up by the Government (37.5%), BBME (37.5%) and public (25%).
65. *SYB* 1986, Table 169.
66. *SYB* 1986, Table 215.
67. It may be noted that these three were all in Salala at the time of the coup. Qaboos has always stood by and given his trust to those whom he knew before he came to power.
68. Before the arrival of Hill, Tarik had introduced a Syrian friend of his, Yasser Idlabi, into Oman as his own adviser on legal matters. His efforts to devise laws for Oman were not successful.
69. Dr Jamali was acting as Prime Minister for a few weeks, in name if not in formal rank. He was the person who delivered Tarik's letter of resignation to Qaboos, and he made the announcement of the new government on 1 January 1972.
70. Qais Zawawi has been Minister or Deputy Prime Minister for either Foreign Affairs or Finance and Economy ever since.
71. These details were given to me by Dr. Omer Zawawi.
72. Those who know anything of the Middle East will be aware that the women of a family may be as influential as the men.
73. There had previously been a Committee of Contracts but this decree formalised and publicised the system.

Second Thoughts, 1975–76

1. See Townsend, *Oman* p. 148.
2. By 1990 we have become, perhaps, more accustomed to cost overruns. This note is written as Eurotunnel are concluding their call for more than £2 billion extra funds to deal with increased costs of the Channel Tunnel.
3. Much of this section is based on these documents.

4.   Formed under RD 41/74 of 17/11/74 and published in *Official Gazette* dated 1/12/74. The ministers were Interior, Health, Commerce and Industry, Communications, and Agriculture, Fisheries, Petroleum and Minerals.

5.   Formed under RD 44/74 of 15/12/74. It was in fact described as the Board for Financial Affairs and the members were the 'economic advisers'.

6.   Here, and below, information and quotations are taken from the Report on the Economic and Financial Position of Oman, March 1975.

7.   When I spoke with the Sultan he also mentioned that a new contract with Shell at that time was to their advantage as well as to the advantage of Oman. The reference is almost certainly to the variations in royalty and tax which were being introduced into oil concessions as a result of the Opec meetings and agreements of 1974. On 1 July royalty was increased from 12.5 per cent to 14.5 per cent; on 1 October royalty was again increased, from 14.5 per cent to 16.67 per cent and the tax rate was increased from 55 per cent to 65.75 per cent. These changes, in the form of Opec resolutions, were automatically also given to Oman. A further Opec resolution increased royalty from 16.67 per cent to 20 per cent, and tax to 85 per cent with effect from 1 November. In this latter case PDO argued that because of the comparatively costly Omani operation a tax rate of 85 per cent would be punitive and counter-productive. They proposed 80 per cent. This was accepted by the Sultan. However, because it was thought that this might create adverse criticism against both Oman and the company if known, it was not made public. Indeed, it was only published on 1 April 1976 when a Decree was issued; and this was done only because by then, for tax reasons, it was necessary for Shell to have official evidence of the change.

8.   In the same conversation the Sultan claimed that he had never believed the crisis to have been as serious as was made out, and this seems to have been the opinion also of at least some American observers. The point is that the creation of the study team was itself the catalyst for change; by the time it reported attitudes had changed.

9.   Set up under RD 9/75 dated 1/2/75 and published in *Official Gazette* dated 15/3/75.

10. Set up under RD 26/75 published in *Official Gazette* dated 15/7/75.

11. This later became the Office of the Deputy Prime Minister for Legal Affairs.

12. Set up under RD 3/75 published in Official Gazette dated 1/2/75. A brief description of the development of these laws and the text of some of them may be found in 'The 5-Year Development Plan 1976–1980' published by the Development Council of the Sultanate of Oman.

13. Townsend, *Oman* p. 108.

14. Townsend, *Oman* p. 107.

15. The actual outcome, recorded in the second 5-year plan was 25 per

cent.

16. In 1990 it was about 100 000; in 1975 it was probably no more than 50 000, the figure given by Townsend, p. 107. The birthrate is estimated to be at least 5 per cent per annum.

17. RD 32/76 published in *Official Gazette* dated 1/9/76. See Table 8.

18. Although some percentages were close. The greatest variations resulted from the steep increase in oil prices in 1979/80 which provided more revenue and wider opportunity to spend.

19. RD 9/75 published in *Official Gazette* dated 15/3/75.

20. RD 3/75 published in *Official Gazette dated* 15/7/75. This law was complemented by the Law of Control and Censorship of Artistic and Literary Productions which was contained in RD 45/76 published in *Official Gazette* dated 15/1/76. It was amended in RD 49/84 published in *Official Gazette* dated 2/6/84, but the content was hardly changed in concept.

21. RD 40/75 published in *Official Gazette* dated 1/10/75.

22. RD 16/76 published in *Official Gazette* dated 1/6/76.

Growth, 1976–90

1. For a full discussion and background, see William Stivers, *America's Confrontation with Revolutionary Change in the Middle East 1948–83* (Macmillan Press, 1986) and Gary Sick, *Evolution of US Strategy toward the Indian Ocean and Persian Gulf Regions* in Alvin Z. Rubinstein (ed.), *The Great Game: Rivalry in the Persian Gulf and South Asia* (Praeger, 1983).

2. For instance, Admiral Johnson wrote 'as dismemberment of friendly colonial empires into neutralist nationalisms proceed the US would lose access to foreign bases and ports vital for sustained naval operations' (in *Long Range Objectives 1968–73*, 5/9/58, Command File, Serial 0055 P93, p. 30).

3. For instance, see 'The Indian Ocean: Political and Strategic future' 92nd Congress, 1st Session 1971 (Foreign Affairs Committee) in which R. I. Spiers, head of the Politico-Military Bureau makes the point that The Diego Garcia base is not a reactive response to USSR threats but 'the culmination of our efforts to meet a naval communications requirement dating back to the early '60s' (p. 165). He goes on to say that 'there are three policy dilemmas as we look to the future:
   (a) the response to the Soviet naval presence in the Indian Ocean
   (b) how to encourage economic development, political responsibilities and domestic political stability in the surrounding countries
   (c) how to ensure free transit through the key access points to Indian Ocean.'
   It is interesting to note that there is, in over 200 pages of this report, no reference to Oman.

4. BIOT remains (in 1990) a UK dependancy, Crown property, adminis-tered by a Commissioner resident in London. Its area is only 23 square

miles.
5. Sick, p. 64.
6. With W. A. Stoltzfus as non-resident ambassador based in Kuwait.
7. The activities of Robert Anderson were almost certainly self-generated, with only tangential attachments to the CIA. See above, pages 59–60.
8. David Rockefeller visited Sultan Qaboos in Muscat in 1973/74 and is believed to have added his influence in speeding-up the ambassadorial appointment.
9. John Peterson, *American Policy in the Gulf and the Sultanate of Oman* (American Arab Affairs, Spring 1984, no. 8).
10. See J. E. Peterson, *Defending Arabia* (Croom Helm, 1986) p. 25 and Calvin H. Allen Jr., *Oman, The Modernisation of the Sultanate* (Westview Press, 1987), pp. 110–111. Also R. J. Gavin, *Aden under British Rule 1834–1967* (C. Hurst, 1975) pp. 282–3.
11. For the text of the Agreement see British and Foreign State Papers 1947, Part 1, vol. 147, p. 928; also recorded in UN Treaty Series no. 412, vol. 27, p. 288).
12. See Gerrard Mansell, *Let Truth be Told* (Weidenfeld & Nicolson 1982) p. 243.
13. Except for the Relay Station. At end-1990 negotiations were in progress with Oman for a new and more powerful transmitter.
14. *Middle East Contemporary Survey* (MECS), vol. 1, p. 350.
15. Reference to this agreement can be found in a CIA report on Qais Zawawi (Declassified Documents, vol. X no. 2, item 000782, dated 6/9/77), in which it is stated that 'in the spring of 1977 Zawawi participated in talks with US officials concerning the use of Masira island (recently vacated by the British) for the maintenance and refuelling of US aircraft'.
16. The Wolfowitz Report, 'Capabilities for limited contingencies in the Persian Gulf', dated 15 June 1979, was prepared in the office of Assistant Secretary of Defence, Programme Analysis and Evaluation.
17. 'The objectives of the overall study on the Persian Gulf region are threefold' the Report says 'to assess the emerging threat to the environment, including the potential role of the Soviet Union; to analyse relevant capabilities of the US and its allies; and to identify useful changes in the Defense Program'. Elsewhere it says 'Options should be developed for pre-positioning equipment and supplies so that the US could more rapidly build up ground forces and tacair (sic) in response to [security deletion] crisis.' And ' . . . and also the fact that we cannot even predict who will be the enemy of whom five years hence in the Middle East it follows that our contingency force should be diverse and flexible.' The last excerpt, quoted by Stivers, is an attractively realistic comment.
18. The Chief Representative of the company was Jim Critchfield; his involvement in this contract added to the suspicions of those who saw the hand of the CIA behind US interest in Oman.

19. See report in *New York Times* of 12 February 1980. Also *The Times* and *Daily Telegraph* of 13 February 1980. For April meetings see *New York Times* of 9 February 1980.
20. Sick, p. 76.
21. Quoted by Sick, p. 76.
22. In the Senate Armed Services committee, Frank Carlucci as Deputy Secretary of Defence said, when putting forward expenditure authorisations for 1982 'The fact is that for the most effective deterrent we need both sea based and land based forces' and 'once our determination becomes clear to our friends and allies in the Middle East, they will become more forthcoming on the kinds of access we need' (quoted in Stivers, p. 99).
23. To be found in US Treaties and other International Agreements, 32 UST 1636.
24. The text can be found in Treaties and Other International Acts series, TIAS 10189
25. An unspecific reference to the undertaking can be found in US Security Interests in the Gulf, Report of a Staff Study Mission to the Persian Gulf, Middle East, and Horn of Africa, October 21–November 13, 1980 to the Committee on Foreign Affairs, US House of Representatives, March 16, 1981. There is a somewhat clearer reference in the Hearings of 66th Congress, 2nd Session where the following exchange took place: 'Is there a Presidential letter relating to the agreement? I don't know anything about the contents of that letter.' 'I will have to check on that.' A footnote adds: 'The subcommittee pursued the matter privately with the executive branch.' Both these documents are quoted in Liesl Graz, *The Omanis, Sentinels of the Gulf* (Longmans, 1982).
26. This said: 'I wish to renew to Your Majesty the assurances which have been made to you several times in the past, that the United States is interested in the preservation of the independence and territorial integrity of Saudi Arabia. No threat to your Kingdom could occur which would not be a matter of immediate concern to the United States.' Quoted by Daniel Yergin in *The Prize, the Epic Quest for Oil, Money and Power* (Simon & Shuster 1991).
27. *American Foreign Policy*, Current Documents, 1983 Document 276, 2/3/83.
28. Ibid., 1985 Document 199, 19/2/85.
29. Ibid., 1986 Document 172, 19/2/86.
30. Ibid., 1985 Document 244, 21/3/85.
31. In the six years 1981–86 the total military appropriations were $268m and for economic aid were $105m.
32. Ibid., 1984 Document 214, 19/5/84.
33. The quotations are taken from the records of the House Committee on Budget, 'Military Readiness and the Rapid Deployment Joint Task Force', US Government Publications, February 1981. They have a certain heightened interest in the context of the 1990 Gulf crisis.

General Kelley was the first in a line of Task Force commanders of whom General Schwarzkopf is (1991) the latest.

34. Diplomats may report each hearsay but this is generally unavailable under confidentiality and/or release rules. Even when available, however, these reports are subject to the usual concern about the degree of reliability that can be attached to them.

35. Although the terms had already been agreed in principle.

36. See in particular Oman's Perspectives by Hermann Frederick Eilts in *Cross currents in the Gulf*, ed. H Richard Sindelaar and J. E. Peterson (Routledge, 1988).

37. *New York Times*, March 25/26, 1985, articles written by Jeff Gerth and Judith Miller.

38. Back again in Oman, this time as Chief of Staff. He was in Oman as a Major in 1959, as a Lieutenant Colonel in 1970, as Major General in 1979 and as Lieutenant General in 1984. He became Sir John Watts in 1988.

39. Eilts, p. 34.

40. The 1990 Gulf crisis has changed things again.

41. Technically it is an Executive Agreement, not a Treaty, and is, therefore, sent to Congress for information rather than approval.

42. What is proposed by the Administration and accepted by Congress is not necessarily the same, a point that ESF recipients sometimes find it difficult to comprehend or accept.

43. See *Times of Oman*, 3 May 1990. A discussion on TV by satellite between the two capitals was a novel way of marking the anniversary.

44. *Times of Oman*, 28 December 1989.

45. *Times of Oman*, 29 March 1990, quotes the communique issued at the end of the visit. Ratification took place in May 1991 (see *MEES*, 27 May 1991).

46. Nadav Safran, *Saudi Arabia, The Ceaseless Quest for Security* (The Belknap Press of Harvard University Press 1985) p. 265.

47. For details of these meetings and visits see Safran, pp. 266–70.

48. Quoted in *Middle East Contemporary Survey* (MECS), vol. 1, p. 330.

49. Some remained until after the Shah had left Iran in early 1979. The Shah visited Qaboos in Muscat, his only visit, in December 1977.

50. Nor the last; these words are being written in August 1990.

51. It was on 4 October 1978 that Iraq expelled Khomeini, at that stage signalling that it preferred to maintain the status quo in Iran under the Shah.

52. *Middle East Contemporary Survey* (MECS), vol. IV, p. 201.

53. Safran, pp. 364–75.

54. Its full official title is Cooperation Council for the Arab States of the Gulf.

55. See John Christie, in *The Gulf Cooperation Council: Moderation and Stability in an Interdependent World*, ed. John A. Sandwick (Westview Press for Arab Arrairs Council, 1987).

56. *Middle East Contemporary Survey* (MECS), volume V, pp. 458–464.
57. See Armed Forces, July 1985. It seems, however, that only minor payments, if any at all, have ever been made under this arrangement.
58. Since Iraq invaded Kuwait attitudes have, of course, been quite different.
59. The only other countries of the Arab League to absent themselves and, in practice, abstain from condemning Egypt were Sudan, Somalia and Djibouti.
60. This does not mean, however, that the border is settled. In 1987, and again in 1989, incursions from PDRY took place.
61. See John Duke Antony in *Oman: Economic, Social and Strategic Developments*, ed. B. R. Pridham (Croom Helm, 1987). In his article he discusses the benefits gained by Oman from its membership of the GCC.
62. For details see *The Military Balance*, (Brasseys for IISS, 1990–91).
63. Iran played a part in assisting Qaboos in this matter.
64. Qaboos received the credentials of the first USSR ambassador on 7 July 1986.
65. See Oman 1990.
66. Shareholding is currently Oman Government 60%, Shell 34%, Total CFP 4%, Partex 2%.
67. Apart from PDO there is some minor production from concessions operated by Elf, Occidental and Japex.
68. see PDO annual reports for details.
69. Said Shanfari was appointed Minister in 1974. He was one of the first Dhofaris to be appointed and was a confidant of the Sultan from early days in Salala.
70. *Times of Oman*, 3 May 1990.
71. *Shell World*, January 1990; and PDO Annual Report 1988.
72. Although there is no published inflation figure for Oman its effect can be approximately assessed from the Unit Value Index of Imports published in the *Statistical Year Book*, since virtually everything consumed in Oman is imported. On this basis the Omani riyal lost approximately one-third of its purchasing power between 1980 and 1988.
73. Table 8 contains a digest of the 5-year plans and their outcome.
74. This represented 15 per cent of total development and civil recurrent expenditure, and 9 per cent of all expenditure including Defence and National Security.
75. It was nearly RO 3500 million in 1985 and, in 1988, it dropped slightly to RO 2919 million. See *SYB* 1986, Table 221 and *SYB* 1989, Table 229.
76. *UN World Development Report* 1989.
77. First 5-year plan, 1976–80, p. 13.
78. *SYB* 1989, Tables 222 and 223.
79. *SYB* 1989, Tables 183 and 185.

80. *SYB* 1989, Tables 156 and 157.
81. See also *Ministry of Petroleum and Minerals book*, published November 1985.
82. 5-year plan 1981–85, Table 32, and 5-year plan 1986–90, Table 41.
83. Set up under RD 51/77.
84. Set up under RD 50/81, operational from 1982.
85. Set up under RD 31/76, formed in 1978 and operational from 1979.
86. See *Annual Report of the Oman Development Bank 1988*.
87. See *Annual Report of the Bank for Agriculture and Fisheries 1988*.
88. See 5-year plan 1981–85, Appendix A, Table 13 and 5-year plan 1986–90, Appendix A, Table 14.
89. See Fourth 5-year plan, Basic Components and Main Indicators, Appendix 6.
90. It was set up under RD Decree 97/81.
91. *SYB* 1986, Table 218, and Third 5-year plan, Appendix A, Table 30.
92. That is what I was told when I visited it.
93. *SYB* 1989, Table 196.
94. As published in *Oman Daily Observer*. According to the Director General the volume had increased to a daily figure of RO 142563 by end-1990 (*Times of Oman*, 16 January 1991.
95. The text of the decree is quoted in the Second 5-year plan, as Appendix D.
96. *SYB* 1989, Table 222.
97. It would if one had not looked at pre-1988 *SYB*s.
98. An IMF unpublished report of 1988 does, however, confirm the belief. SGRF foreign assets are reported as in excess of RO 1 billion in 1986/87 and investment income as around RO 80 million per annum.
99. Third 5-year plan, table 37.
100. *SYB* 1989, Table 222.
101. See MEES of 11 September 1989, quoting OECD 'Financing and External Debt of Developing Countries, 1988 Survey'. See also *Military Balance 1989–90* (IISS, published by Brassey's).
102. *SYB* 1989, Table 62.
103. *SYB* 1989, Table 66.
104. *The Times of Oman* reported that at the end of the 1989/90 academic year 18070 teachers and their families were being flown out of Oman, of whom about two-thirds would be on 61 chartered flights.
105. *SYB* 1986, Table 63 and *SYB* 1989, Table 69.
106. *SYB* 1989, Table 70.
107. *SYB* 1986, Table 68 and *SYB* 1989, Table 73.
108. *SYB* 1989, Table 115, 116.
109. *SYB* 1989, p. 3.
110. Note that a population of 1.4 million which grows at a rate of 4 per cent per annum will reach 2 million after 10 years and 3 million after 20 years.
111. Third 5-year plan, Table 45. This included, however, 'non-regional'

projects which in the fourth 5-year plan have been split out (see Table 11).

112. It had originally been intended, in fact, that the university should be sited in Nizwa, but the lack of water resources prevented this taking place.

113. Mohammed Moosa has been in charge of Oman's planning, either in the Ministry of Finance or the Development Secretariat, since the early 1970s.

114. *SYB* 1989, Table 8.

115. He took part in the Musandam landing in 1970 (see above, page 66), and was later in Dhofar during the war.

116. The *SYB* duly records the number of immunisations etc. carried out annually; see, for instance, *SYB* 1989, Table 48.

117. Set up under RD Decree 43/80 in May 1980.

118. Third 5-year plan, Tables 15, 43 and p. 63.

119. None of the ministers I met admitted to audiences with the Sultan more than a few times a year. His appearance at cabinet meetings is also limited to a few formal occasions. One of these took place on 10 September 1990 and was reported on the front page of the *Times of Oman* (13/9/90) with a large photograph showing the ministers sitting at attention with arms folded on their knees, each in front of a blotter with a memo pad dead centre, along a long curving board room table with Sultan Qaboos framed at the far end. Twelve lines of subtitle ended: 'Concluding the meeting, he (His Majesty) issued directives to Ministers to provide a suitable atmosphere for the participation of citizens in the country's development.'

120. There are some people who believe that he knows everything that is going on.

121. For instance, here is a quotation from the Oman Daily Observer from November 1989. 'In Ibra, the citizens used the occasion to express their warm love and absolute loyalty to their leader. His Majesty's meetings with his people were marked by modesty and openness. As a manifestation of their affection for their ruler, they lifted and carried his vehicle across a wadi.'

122. For a full discussion of the background and mechanisms of the SCC see J. E. Peterson, *The Arab Gulf States: Steps towards Political Participation* (Praeger, 1988, for CSIS).

123. In RD 84/81 and RD 86/81, published in the *Official Gazette* 228, dated 1/11/81.

124. Preamble to 84/81.

125. In RD 19/79 which was specifically cancelled in 84/81.

126. Article 2, 84/81.

127. Article 6, 84/81.

128. About RO 1 million per annum, see *SYB* 1989, table 226.

129. Article 27, 86/81.

130. See *Oman 1989*, p. 26.

131. The first Chairman of the SCC was Khalfan bin Nasr, who has been a minister since 1972 and is currently (1990) Minister of Water Resources.
132. As it was described to me by someone who had himself been a member.
133. See *Times of Oman*, 22 November 1990.
134. *SYB* 1989, Table 156.
135. Since 15 January 1990, see *Times of Oman*, 28 December 1989. A friend of mine told me he had tested the new regulation and it worked.
136. The Internal Security Service (ISS), inevitably a secretive organisation, has its headquarters on a hill near Medinat Qaboos.
137. For instance, there was still no media mention on 14 March 1990 that four days later the first GCC-EEC meeting at ministerial level would be taking place in Muscat. In its way this was a historic occasion and a coup for Oman that the meeting should be in Muscat. The foreign press had been covering the subject for weeks.
138. And will own the most advanced technical equipment to ensure he does.
139. See in particular his article (Thomas W. Hill Jr.) on 'The commercial legal system of the Sultanate of Oman', published in *International Lawyer*, vol. XV11, no. 3, Summer 1983. See also a paper by Alastair Hirst, a partner of Fox and Gibbons and Co. (unpublished), and the section entitled 'Doing Business in Oman' in *Oman*, a MEED practical guide, 2nd edn, 1984. See also a paper by John McLees, a partner of Sidley and Austin, given at a Conference on Business in Saudi Arabia and the Gulf: Settlement of Disputes, held in London 22–23 November 1982 and organised by MEED.
140. Hill, p. 511.
141. Hirst, p. 2.
142. Hill, p. 507
143. Hirst, p. 3.
144. Hill, p. 510.
145. Established by RD 79/81, published in *Official Gazette* of 1/10/81.
146. RD 54/75, published in *Official Gazette* of 1/1/76.
147. Hill, p. 519.
148. In the first six months of 1988, 497 cases were heard in the Primary Court.
149. *Plants of Dhofar, the Southern Region of Oman; Traditional Economic and Medicinal Uses*, by Tony Miller and Dr Miranda Morris.
150. *Birds of Oman*, by Michael Gallagher and Martin Woodcock (Quartet Books, 1980).
151. *Journal of Oman Studies*, Special Report 1, Oman Flora and Fauna Survey, 1975; Special Report 2, Oman Flora and Fauna Survey, Dhofar, 1977 published June 1980; Special Report 3, Scientific Results of the RGS Oman Wahiba Sands Project 1985–87 published July 1988.

152. He had spent several years with PDO in Oman after leaving Aden. For this section see, in particular, his lecture given to the Zoological Society of London, Scientific Meeting, 9 June 1987.
153. It had started a few months earlier as the 'General Authority'.
154. Under RD 10/82.
155. In 1985 Water Resources was added to the remit of the Ministry but removed again in 1989. There is now, since October 1989, a Ministry of Water Resources.
156. See *Oman Daily Observer*, 21 February 1990. Practically all wild life species are legally protected in Oman. Hunting is forbidden, as is speargun fishing.
157. See *Oman Daily Observer*, 14 February 1990.
158. RD 44/73 published in *Official Gazette*, 1/12/73.
159. RD 49/74, published in *Official Gazette*, 15/12/74.
160. RD 14/76, published in *Official Gazette*, 1/5/76.
161. Project for the Integral Study of the Silk Roads, 'The Roads of Dialogue Project', first conceived in 1983. Oman is Deputy Chairman of the Advisory Council.
162. See article in *Times of Oman*, 13 September 1990. It duly arrived on 17 November.
163. See Tim Severin, *The Sindbad Voyage* (Hutchinson, 1982).
164. Oman has an agreement with Morocco to assist in this work.
165. It is the house in which I and my family lived from 1966–68, see Skeet, *Muscat and Oman*.
166. See *Oman 1989*.
167. When I spoke with him he made the point specifically that the future of the country resided in the education of both boys and girls.
168. There were thirteen at end-1989, with several more waiting for approval and registration.
169. The new buildings will have multipurpose halls, a theatre, a kindergarten, play grounds for children and other facilities – as reported in the *Times of Oman*, 20 April 1990.
170. Although they might be surprised by a rule, imposed in 1986 (RD 5/86), which forbids Omanis to marry non-Omanis.
171. It is no accident that in 1986 the Ministry of Education was renamed the Ministry of Education and Youth.
172. It cost RO 31 million up to 1985, with a further RO 7 million to be spent in 1986–87 (see third 5-year plan, Table 14 and Appendix A, Table 7).
173. Under RD 10/75, published in *Official Gazette* dated 15/3/75.
174. Quoted in his article in *Le Monde*, 30/31 May 1971. Since 1976 and the First 5-year plan budgets have, of course, been published. The Decree (RD 5/86) that, in apparently Draconian fashion, forbade marriages between Omanis and other nationalities is another example of what might be thought of as paternalism, although, as is so often the case, there are understandable reasons for it.

Part Three: Towards 2000

1. This section is concerned only with natural water. Desalination plants are an important addition to the water supply but are limited by cost, geography and a sufficient population concentration.
2. *SYB* 1986, Table 99.
3. This figure of 25–30 000 is approximately calculated from current student numbers; a large proportion are female, many of whom will not enter the job market. Whitehead/Birks Sinclair (see below) give a figure of 13 000 in 1989 rising to 27 000 in 1995 who will be seeking jobs.
4. Speech by Mohammed Moosa to the Anglo-Omani Society, London, 25 January 1990. The text was issued by the Oman Embassy on 24 January.
5. See Basic Components and Main Indicators of the Fourth 5-Year Development Plan (1991–1995), p. 4.
6. For this section the following documents are relevant: Press Conference given by Qais Zawawi and Mohammed Moosa, and outline documents on the plan attached to the press release covering the conference, dated 8/1/91, issued by the Ministry of Information. Also Basic Components and Main Indicators of the Fourth 5-Year Development Plan (1991–1995) published by the Technical Secretariat of the Development Council, January 1991.
7. *SYB* 1989, Table 222.
8. *SYB* 1989, Table 229.
9. *SYB* 1989, Table 222.
10. *Basic Components*, p. 21.
11. *Basic Components*, p. 33, Appendix 6.
12. *Basic Components*, p. 21.
13. *Basic Components*, p. 23.
14. *Basic Components*, p. 24.
15. Press Conference, 8/1/91.
16. Press Conference, 8/1/91. See also *Basic Components*, page 3, item 7. Note that the calculation for transfer to SGRF and Contingency Fund is made, in rather complicated fashion, on the basis of net, not gross, oil revenue.
17. *Basic Components*, p. 3, item 8.
18. *Basic Components*, p. 3, item 6.
19. The 1990 oil price for budgetary purposes was set at $15. The outcome was in practice in excess of $20.
20. *Basic Components*, p. 4, item 12.
21. *Basic Components*, p. 13 and Press Conference.
22. *Basic Components*, p. 21.
23. *Basic Components*, p. 4, item 16.
24. The 'manner' as opposed to 'system' of governing.
25. First in 1976 and then again, after being revived in 1981, in July

1986. For further discussion of the Kuwaiti experience see *Persian Gulf States, Country studies*, ed. Richard F Nyrop (US Govt., 1984) – *Kuwait* (Darrell R. Eglin and James D. Rudolph). Also J. E. Peterson, *Arab Gulf States, Steps towards Political Participation* (Praeger, with CSIS, 1988).

26. As this is being written, March 1991.

27. This now includes the military, who, after 20 or more years of service, are beginning to retire and do not want miss commercial opportunities.

28. How the newly announced Majlis Al Shura will affect the SCC is still not clear (June 1990). It does not, indeed, matter whether the SCC or Majlis acts in the capacity described provided that one of them does.

29. Quoted from an undated briefing note from the Minister's office given me in March 1990. Tourism investment has only an allocation of RO 6 million in the new 5-year plan, a sum that does not seem excessive (*Basic Components*, Appendix 5).

30. Described to me as middle-class, middle-aged Swiss.

31. *Al Musawwar*, April 1985. Perhaps more adventurously, Youssef al Alawi, the Minister of State for Foreign Affairs, said ' . . . in the end there will be direct negotiations between the Palestinians and Israelis . . . the Palestinian people have rights and Israel's people have rights' (*Al Anba*, 28 September 1985). Both statements are quoted in *Middle East Contemporary Survey* (MECS), vol. IX, pp. 411–415.

32. It is significant that, in his 20th anniversary speech on 18 November 1990, Qaboos went out of his way to give his support to King Fahd personally, and to Saudi Arabia in general, for their reaction to and policy on the Kuwait crisis.

33. There was the peculiar incident in May 1971 when a so-called Colonel Karama appeared in Dhofar from across the Saudi border with a group that described itself as the Mahra Liberation Army; and in 1986 a Saudi armed detachment arrived in Mughsin, whence they were quietly and diplomatically removed before any embarrassing incident could develop.

34. From 1829–97 there was a strong Omani claim over Dhofar, but control was interrupted by a number of local uprisings and lack of interest.

35. For those whose experience goes back far enough they will remember the Ruwi customs post. See Skeet, *Muscat and Oman*.

36. For instance, into Hinawi and Ghafiri.

37. Dhofari members of the Chamber of Commerce, for instance, have from time to time suggested that they should be separate from the Muscat, or Oman, one.

38. The two-day weekend, introduced in July 1989, has had a disturbing effect on work since every Omani now considers it his right to return to his home, wherever in the country, every weekend. This applies as much to military personnel as to civilian.

39. In passing, it may be noticed that a number of the Al Saids have ousted their predecessors, starting with Ahmed bin Said himself.
40. The office can remain vacant if there is no suitable candidate.

Epilogue

1. It won prizes at the International Garden and Greenery Exposition in Osaka in 1990 and was also shown at the Chelsea Flower Show. It will be blooming in many European gardens (including mine, I hope) as well as in the new Qurm public garden in Muscat.
2. The first National Day was held on 23 July 1971, the anniversary of Qaboos' accession, but since then National Day has been transferred to his birthday, 18 November. As much as anything this was to permit the celebrations to take place in a tolerable temperature.

Bibliography

Documents and References

United States
American Foreign Policy, Current Documents 1977–80, 1981 to 1987.
Declassified Documents, Retrospective Catalogue and Quarterly Catalogue, 1975 onwards.

US Congressional Papers (US Government Publications)
1971 – The Indian Ocean: Political and Strategic future (92nd Congress, 1st session, 1971).
1972 – US interest in and Policy towards the Persian Gulf (92nd Congress, 2nd session, 1972).
1973 – The Persian Gulf 1974: Money, Politics, Arms and Power (93rd Congress, 2nd session, 1973).
1979 – Capabilities for limited contingencies in the Persian Gulf, the Wolfowitz Report, 14 June 1979.
1980 – US Interests in, and policies towards, the Persian Gulf, 1980 (96th Congress, 2nd session, 1980).
1980 – Military Readiness and the Rapid Deployment Joint Task Force (96th Congress, 2nd session, 1980.

Treaties and other International Acts (TIAS).
US Treaties and other International Agreements.

Oman
First 5-Year Plan, 1976–80 (Development Council, Muscat, 1976).
Second 5-Year Plan, 1981–85 (Development Council, Muscat, March 1981).
Third 5-Year Plan, 1986–90 (Development Council, Muscat, June 1987).
Fourth 5-Year Plan, 1991–95, Basic Components and Main Indicators (Development Council, Muscat, January 1991).
Petroleum Development Oman *Annual Reports, 1969–90.*
Royal Decrees/*Official Gazettes.*
Oman 1990 (annual publication of Ministry of Information).
A short history of Bait al Falaj Fort, Muscat 1985.
Statistical Year Books 1986 and 1989, Development Council, Muscat.

Other
Chatham House Press Library, London.
British Library, Press Section, London.
Middle East Contemporary Survey (MECS), ed. Colin Legum (Holmes and

Meier Publishers Inc.; later volumes published by Dayan Centre for Middle
East and African Studies, distributed by Westview Press).
Dickens Papers, Historical Library, Central Historical Section, Ministry of
Defence, London.
Middle East Economic Survey, (MEES) Cyprus.
Oman, a MEED practical guide, London (2nd edition, 1984).
The Military Balance, London: IISS.

Books

John Akehurst, *We Won a War: the Campaign in Oman 1965–75* (Michael
Russell, 1982).
Calvin H. Allen, *Oman, the Modernisation of the Sultanate* (Croom Helm,
1987).
John Duke Antony, *Historical and Cultural Dictionary of the Sultanate of
Oman and the Emirates of Eastern Arabia* (Scarecrow Press, 1976).
Glen Balfour-Paul *The end of empire in the Middle East* (Cambridge Univer-
sity Press, 1991).
Frank Clements, *Oman, the Reborn Land* (Longman, 1980).
Philipp Darby, *British Defence Policy East of Suez 1946–68* (Oxford Univer-
sity Press, 1973).
Ranulph Fiennes, *Where Soldiers fear to Tread* (Hodder & Stoughton, 1975).
R. J. Gavin, *Aden under British Rule 1834–1967* (C. Hurst, 1975).
Liesl Graz, *The Omanis, Sentinels of the Gulf* (Longman, 1982).
Fred Halliday, *Arabia without Sultans* (Penguin Books, 1974).
Donald Hawley, *Oman and its Renaissance* (Stacey International, 1987).
Tony Jeapes, *SAS: Operation Oman* (William Kimber, 1980).
Mark Katz, *Russia and Arabia* (Johns Hopkins University Press, 1986).
Gerrard Mansell, *Let Truth be Told* (Weidenfeld & Nicolson, 1982).
Richard F. Nyrop (ed.), *Persian Gulf States, Country Studies* (US Govern-
ment, 1984).
J. E. Peterson, *The Arab Gulf States: Steps towards Political Participation*
(Praeger for CSIS, 1988).
J. E. Peterson, *Defending Arabia* (Croom Helm, 1986).
J. E. Peterson, *Oman in the 20th Century* (Croom Helm, 1986).
Andrew J. Pierre, *The Global Politics of Arms Sales* (Princeton University
Press, 1982).
Mark R. Stanley Price, *Animal Reintroductions: the Arabian Oryx in Oman*
(Cambridge University Press, 1989).
Brian Pridham (ed.), *Oman: Economic, Social and Strategic Developments*
(Croom Helm, 1987).
R. K. Ramazani, *The Gulf Cooperation Council: Record and Analysis* (Uni-
versity Press of Virginia, 1988).
Alvin Z. Rubinstein (ed.), *The Great Game: Rivalry in the Persian Gulf and
South Asia* (Praeger, 1983).

Nadav Safran, *Saudi Arabia; the Ceaseless Quest for Security* (Belknap Press of Harvard University Press, 1985).

John A. Sandwick (ed.), *The Gulf Cooperation Council: Moderation and Stability in an Interdependent World* (Westview Press for Arab Affairs Council, 1987).

Tim Severin, *The Sindbad Voyage* (Hutchinson, 1982).

Ian Skeet, *Muscat and Oman, the End of an Era* (Faber & Faber, 1974).

William Stivers, *America's Confrontation with Revolutionary Change in the Middle East, 1948–83* (Macmillan Press, 1986).

John Townsend, *Oman, the Making of the Modern State* (Croom Helm, 1977).

John Wilkinson, *The Imamate Tradition of Oman* (Cambridge University Press, 1987).

Articles

Helena Cobban, Arabian Peninsula (*Christian Science Monitor*, 1–4 September, 1981).

Ralph Daly, Conservation in Oman and its role in Development, Lecture given to Zoological Society of London, 9 June, 1987.

Dale Eickelman, Kings and People: Oman's State Consultative Council (*Middle East Journal* 38, no. 1, winter 1984).

Jeff Gerth and Judith Miller, Articles in *New York Times*, 25–26 March, 1985.

Thomas W. Hill Jr., The Commercial Legal System of the Sultanate of Oman (*International Lawyer*, Summer 1983, vol. XV11, no. 3).

Jim Hoagland, The Arab Money Man (*Washington Post*, 14–19 September, 1975).

Ken Perkins, Oman 1975: the Year of Decision (*Journal of RUSI*, 124, March 1979).

J. E. Peterson, American Policy in the Gulf and Oman (*American Arab Affairs*, Summer 1984, no. 8).

J. E. Peterson, Tribes and Politics in Eastern Arabia (*Middle East Journal*, 31, Summer 1977).

J. E. Peterson, Legitimacy and Political Change in Yemen and Oman (*Orbis* 27, no. 4, Winter 1984).

J. E. Peterson, Britain and the Oman War (*Asian Affairs* October 1976).

J. E. Peterson, The Rebellion in Dhofar (*World Affairs 139*, Spring 1977).

Joe Rigert, Article in *Minneapolis Star* and *Tribune*, 5 July 1983.

Eric Rouleau, Oman ou la Révolution Refoulée (articles in *Le Monde*, 26–30 May, 1971).

William Stivers, Doves, Hawks and Détente (*Foreign Policy* 45, Winter 1981–82).

Index